FLIGHT OF YOUR LIFE

Confessions of a 1970s Air Hostess

Natasha J. Rosewood

Queries regarding rights and permission should be addressed to:

Natasha J. Rosewood
PO Box 22080, RPO Capri Center, Kelowna, BC. Canada V1Y 9N9

Website: www. natasharosewood.com
Cover design: Prominence Publishing
Typesetting: Prominence Publishing
Substantive Editing: Betty Keller
Copy editing/proofreading: Betty Keller/ Natasha Rosewood
Book concept and design: Natasha J. Rosewood
Photograph: Meredith Rose Photography

Note for librarians: a cataloguing record for this book that includes Dewey classification and US library of Congress numbers is available from the National Library of Canada. The complete catalogue record can be obtained from the national libraries online database at: www.nlc.bnc.ca/amicus/index-e.html

ISBN: 978-0-9734711-3-7

Printed in Canada

FLIGHT OF YOUR LIFE

Confessions of a 1970s Air Hostess

In *Flight of Your Life*, Natasha, a multilingual British air hostess recounts her uproarious adventures in the 70s flying short haul all over Europe for a notoriously unsafe airline while dealing with the idiosyncrasies of numerous nationalities–and survives to tell the tales. Not only do drunken exit-removing Scottish football supporters, naughty captains, haunted aircraft and flying on old, defective planes threaten her safety, she must also navigate the eccentricities of outrageous passengers and crew. Even on the ground, friends' "emergencies" and her own romantic escapades threaten to derail her. But through it all, Natasha shows us the best, the worst and the funniest sides of humanity and how imperfect and lovable we all are!

Table of Contents

WHY I WROTE THE BOOK

Writing a book for any writer is not an easy undertaking so writers often have at least one motivation. They want to share. I wanted to share, too—but there was more. Friends and family who have listened to me regale my adventures often *begged* me to write this book. Recounting my flying adventures and recalling the memories of the amazingly brave, funny characters I flew with was a wonderful flight over memory lane.

Despite the rumor that stewardesses were on board just to serve tea and coffee—and to look good—we were actually only there—and still are—to ensure the onboard safety of passengers. Our intensive emergency training prepared us, as well as for many other situations, to evacuate people out of a crashed aircraft within 90 seconds.

From a historical perspective, the first passenger flight took off in July 1949. But twenty-five years later in 1974, when I began my fun flying career, aviation was still evolving—and was often precarious. Unbeknownst to the general public at that time, the young "girls" who I flew with were often faced with great responsibilities and potentially dangerous situations, while having to remain calm and keep a smile on their faces. They also had to gracefully tolerate the male chauvinistic attitudes of the era. So I wanted to pay tribute to all the women who flew then and offer a "good luck" wish for all the men and women who fly today, albeit in safer aircraft but perhaps with a different breed of passenger.

In these interesting times in which we live, people seem to have forgotten their sense of humor and are taking themselves so-o-o-o-o seriously! Perhaps for us "hosties," who sometimes faced potential death, we decided that if time was going to be short-lived, then we may as well make it fun. And maybe it was suppressed hysteria? You will find in this book how we laughed at everything and everybody without judgement including people of all nationalities, sizes, shapes and skin colors, but we especially laughed at ourselves.

From working with the public, I learned that none of us are perfect, thank heavens, and it is our imperfections that make us the most interesting and lovable. Through these outrageous tales and irreverent humor, I hope you will see that underneath our idiosyncratic fears and egocentric behaviors, that we are funny, loveable, vulnerable beings just doing everything—like children—for the first time.

As the song goes, "We are only human after all." In this age of divisiveness, and distrust of each other, I also wanted to nudge readers to remember that our collective humanity is beautiful and, if we let go of judgment, together we humans can achieve anything.

Finally, I hope the stories will entertain, make you smile, and help you love yourself more just for being human after all.

Note From the Author

While the stories are based in my reality, I have—in some rare instances —employed creative fiction to complete the story and written what probably would have happened in those circumstances. According to my pilot friends, the aviation details are accurate.

While all of these characters existed, I have changed the names for their privacy and protection (with the exception of Gary Owen who I hope will be happy with my favorable portrayal of his big and fun personality.) All the characters in this book are remembered with great love and respect.

PROLOGUE

March 1974

Seven seconds! That's how long it takes employers to decide if they want to hire you. After the eighth—and to my great surprise—I was still sitting there in front of the panel of senior Dan Air stewardesses.

"What would you say to a passenger who is afraid of flying and wants to get off?" the red-headed deputy chief stewardess, Jane Philoughby, asked.

I'd say, 'I'll get off with you!' I thought. My own fear of flying made me tremble. What was I even doing here? "Er… er… well… I would probably remind him that flight crew are—unlike drivers of cars—highly trained, and that's why more people die in car accidents."

My interviewer suppressed a scoff, smiled, nodded and made a note.

The dumpy brunette to her left was studying me intently. "People applying for this job," she said, "think that they will travel and see the world. You'll see mainly airports. How do you feel about that?"

I shrugged, thinking of the monotonous two years I had just put in as a London secretarial temp. "I'd rather see airports than the inside of an office."

They all looked at me with. . . what? Approval? Curiosity? Disdain?

Jane Philoughby, who was sitting in the middle, leaned forward. "How will you feel if the aircraft is late inbound and you miss a date with your boyfriend?"

"That would only be tragic if I *had* a boyfriend. But I don't." I grinned, hoping they had a sense of humour.

"Yes." "Mmm." "Ah." They all nodded in commiseration, apparently all single.

Were they trying to put me off the job or hire me?

"What about working on Christmas and other holidays?" another questioned.

Since the ties between the members of my large family had disintergrated five years earlier, I hated Christmases. "I'll probably volunteer to work," I told the surprised panel.

"So? Do you think you'd like to fly?" Jane Philoughby finally asked.

"I'd love it!" I beamed. With no deadly dull office routines to endure, wearing a smart blue uniform, being able to make use of my three languages, meeting new people and flying to all kinds of new destinations in Europe and, after a year, flying long haul to other parts of the world, what was there not to like? But the actual flying? That was the only thing that might be a drawback. Going down in a ball of fire happened to be my absolutely worst fear. Oh well.

"We'll be in touch," the expressionless redhead said, dismissing me.

With emotions vacillating between excitement and dread, I waited an excruciatingly long week. Then—just in case the airline's letter had got lost in the post—I called them.

"Oh, yes," the friendly voice on the other end chirped. "We're behind in sending the letters out... let's see..." The interminable shuffling of papers on the other end made me nervous. "Yes, Natasha Rosewood," she affirmed when she finally came back on the line. "You're in. Your four-week training begins on the 5th of May."

Oh my God, I'm going to be an air hostess! I gulped. "Er... thank you."

And the rest, as they say, is what was to come.

1

TAKE-OFF

May 1974

"Jump! Just jump!" Val, the blonde trainer was urging Helga who was standing at the edge of the twenty-foot-high door sill of a mock DC10 fuselage just staring at the yellow thirty-foot-long nylon slide stretching out before her. She was the sole German in our group of twenty-eight trainee air hostesses and her eyes were wide with terror.

It was the second week of our emergency training, and we were practicing how to evacuate 119 passengers—in the event of a crashing on land or ditching on water—from an aircraft in ninety seconds by jumping down these slides. Most of us had gleefully leapt onto the slippery surface and landed unceremoniously on the mat at the bottom. Now we were waiting, amassed at the base of the chute, looking up at poor petrified-of-heights Helga.

The training stewardesses, Val and Jennifer, stood on either side of her, clutching her by the arms, edging her toward the sill. The closer Helga got to the edge, the bigger her eyes grew. Were they going to push her?

"*Nein! Ich kann nicht*"*!* she whimpered. "*Ich kann nicht!*"

"If you can't jump, Helga," explained Jennifer, the more sympathetic of the two trainers, gently but firmly, "you won't qualify to fly."

"I can't," Helga repeated, sobbing. I felt for her. But was she going to allow her fear of heights to deny her the chance to fly?

Val and Jennifer edged her forward a few more inches and waited. Helga's eyes went even wider, her tall, slim body weight sagged backwards. She pushed her feet against the floor as if they were magnets that would keep her rooted to the sill. Frustrated, Val said definitively, "If you don't jump in two minutes, we'll have to fail you."

"I can't do it," Helga moaned, letting her body slump to the floor.

Fear had won.

Sadly resigned to having to fail her, the two trainers relinquished their grip. Helga buried her face in her hands. Dejected and humiliated, the German girl turned back into the mock plane, ran to the rear and sobbing descended the wooden steps.

And then there were twenty-seven.

We all looked at each other and gulped. The four-week training in and around Gatwick Airport was intense and passing all the tests wasn't as easy as we had first thought.

During the first week I sat with the other trainees in a classroom learning all things aeronautical. Then at night while Grandie, my beloved grandmother with whom I was temporarily living, had giggled at *The Two Ronnies* on television and inhaled her nightly Snickers bar, I snacked on grapes and pored over the thick training manuals to absorb aviation abbreviations, alphabets, numbers and terms. We were expected to make better than an eighty-percent pass in the test to be given the following day. It was already evident to me that my mother's condescending comments about air crew being nothing more than glorified waitresses were all wrong. Although we did have to memorize cocktail recipes and know how to do inflight catering, most of the information in those tomes detailed types and numbers of oxygen bottles, fire and survival equipment operation, drills for crashing and ditching in emergencies, duty free customs and excise regulations, first aid procedures and currencies.

In the second week our physical emergency training had begun. After the leaping-down-the-chute exercise, we boarded a large bus and were driven to a field just outside the main airport. Anyone who had flown into Gatwick would have already seen the crashed, burned-out plane lying in that field, the fuselage broken in two, but none of us trainees asked—or wanted to know—if the plane had already crashed at Gatwick or had just been brought there for training purposes. Whatever the case, the sight of the torn, jagged metal and spindly wiring splaying out like frozen spider's legs made me shiver. The four firemen standing outside the fuselage, as if waiting for an accident to happen, were also a tad sobering. But the worst was yet to come.

In the morning sunshine, we all gathered around another trainer, Mr. Wilson, a short, stocky man in a grey suit that matched his grey hair.

"See this?" he said, holding up something that Darth Vader might wear. "You are all going to don one of these on-demand oxygen masks and find your way through that smoke-filled fuselage." Some of us turned and surveyed the inert metal tube beside us. I gulped. A knowing smile from one of the ever-so handsome firemen made me feel better.

"This plane has been set up to simulate a possible crash situation," Mr. Wilson continued in his emotionless tone. "The seats have been knocked off their struts and are all over the place. Just like in a real crash, there is debris in the aisle and wires hanging everywhere. Your job, without any lighting and in the smoke, is to navigate your way from the front to the rear and back, while wearing your mask and find the pretend dead body. The smoke is real, so you are not to remove the mask."

We all watched with dread as Mr. Wilson showed us how to don the contraption and tighten the straps at the back. With the mask covering most of his head, he now looked like a dwarfed version of Darth Vader. It took him a whole five minutes to remove the thing. Oh God!

"Once you put it on," our instructor added, as if we weren't already nervous enough, "the oxygen can take a while to flow. But don't panic. If you do get into distress, the fireman will be in the cabin with you to make sure you are safe."

Paula and I turned and fluttered our eyelashes at the four hunky men in their yellow and orange dungarees. They grinned, enjoying our apprehension and their role as our heroes.

"Any questions?" Mr. Wilson asked.

"Yes," the irrepressible Paula asked, grinning. "Do we *have* to do it?"

Mr. Wilson was not amused. "If you don't, you won't be able to fly," he responded drily. "Some girls can't handle the claustrophobia, but just remember—the idea is that in a real situation, you would need to wear this mask to assist passengers. Now who wants to go first?"

We all stood like frozen soldiers.

He sighed impatiently and pointed a finger straight at me. "You. Natasha, is it? Step over there and the fireman will help you put it on."

Why me first? Oh well. Get it over and done with, I thought. Admiring the twinkly blue eyes and very white teeth of the young, muscular fireman standing by the front entrance was a welcome distraction while I stood and allowed him to place the mask over my whole face, then contend with my thick hair as he tightened the straps at the back of my head. With the black contraption now squeezing my brains tight, the smell of musty rubber assaulted my nostrils.

"Okay?" Mr. Hunky mouthed at me through the thick plastic eye lenses as he gave me a cheery thumbs up.

Inside the mask, I couldn't hear anything but the sound of my own fear. I looked at his fuzzy image, nodded and said, "Yes," which sounded more like a donkey's *ee-aw* than a word. I took a deep breath ...and another ...and another ...and felt the warmth of my own breath in the mask. *Oh, no!* The oxygen wasn't coming through! How long would it take? Maybe I had a non-functioning mask? *Don't panic*, I told myself. But I *was* panicking, my breaths becoming shorter and shallower.

I was just about to grab the fireman by his bulging biceps and get him to rip the mask off when I suddenly heard a monster-like noise coming from ...me! The oxygen was finally flowing. But Darth Vader had nothing on my nasally breathing.

Inside the shadowy, smoky fuselage, the reality of what a crashed plane could look like hit me. Even the firemen posted at the front, centre and aft looked like ghosts. After swiping at dangling wires, stepping over god-knows-what in the aisle and around the chaotically arranged airline seats, I located the "dead body" on the floor toward the rear. Then I turned and groped my way back to the front and out into the sunshine. Once the mask was removed, and my brains could breathe again, I gulped in large intakes of fresh Sussex air laced with aircraft fumes.

"Good, Natasha." Mr. Wilson smiled unexpectedly, baring a row of yellowed teeth. I had apparently passed the find-the-dead-passengers-in-the-smoke test. *I hope I never have to wear that thing ever again,* I thought as I watched the others go through the same torture.

The following day we were all bussed out to the apron where a newish, empty BAC 1-11 awaited us. As we seated ourselves throughout the cabin, the man standing at the front introduced himself as Robert, our trainer for the afternoon. "Today," the slim, forty-something dark-haired man began, "we're going to talk about what to do in the event of..." He held up two fingers of each hand to punctuate the words, "an incident on the flight deck."

I leaned out of my aisle seat to get a better view of him.

Robert continued, "The captain or the co-pilot might become incapacitated, and you could be called to the flight deck to pull an unconscious pilot off the controls."

Great. We were going to be like Karen Black in the movie *Airport,* landing a passenger jet with the help of instructions from air traffic control.

Someone at the front must have asked him what kind of incident.

"Heart attack, food poisoning, nervous breakdown," he responded. "One time, there was a pilot in the US who suddenly thought he was back in World War II. He took the plane out of autopilot and into a steep dive while muttering about the Japs giving him hell."

Someone snickered while the rest of us sat in shocked silence.

"The co-pilot had to knock him out," Robert continued, "and the cabin crew had to pull him off the controls, sedate him and help the co-pilot land the aircraft." He glanced at our pale faces and grinned as he said, "So-o-o, I'm going to pretend to be a dead-captain today, and each of you will come up to the flight deck, one by one, and haul me off the controls."

When it was my turn, Robert instructed me, as he slumped forward, that the easiest way to lift him was to sling my arm across his chest. On my first attempt in the cramped space, not only was he impossible to lift, but I nearly strangled the poor man. Inert bodies are so heavy! If I couldn't do this on the level ground at Gatwick, how would I manage to heave a really-dead-man off the controls, back into his seat and fasten his harness while the plane was in a steep dive with possible G-forces at work? I could only hope that the fear of imminent death and seeing the ground coming up at me at 500 mph would create enough adrenalin for me to become wonder-woman.

"Try again," Robert said, "but stand here," he added pointing to a spot to the right of the seat. "That will give you some leverage."

Finally, I was able to pull him back, do up his full harness and pass the test. I returned to my seat, relieved.

The next lesson was evacuating the aircraft through the overwing exits. It was okay for Robert to casually order us to "jettison the windows" because gripping the handle at the top of the exit and pulling them inwards was easy. But when we had to lift them and push them outside onto the wing out of the way of evacuating and potentially panicking passengers, we found out how heavy they were. We were all reminded that if we couldn't do it, we failed the course. I didn't want to be number two to be sent home, and I discovered that, when one is truly motivated, a superhuman strength can suddenly materialize.

Our final cheery exercise for the day was learning about rapid decompressions. It was this mock rapid descent that brought home the reality of the career I had chosen. In the event of loss of cabin pressure, the flight deck crew would have to put the plane into a steep dive and descend within four minutes from 35,000 feet to 14,000 or 10,000 feet so that the plane would not implode and passengers and crew could breathe. "Oxygen masks will fall from the overhead panel," Robert said, pointing to the underside of the hat rack. "You, the crew must don oxygen masks first before the passengers."

"Isn't that a bit selfish?" I asked, surprised.

"If you are lying unconscious on the floor," he responded crisply, "you won't be able to help passengers and that's your job."

"Oh, yes. Of course," I said, feeling a little stupid, but then my mother had always instilled in me a duty to take care of others first, well her anyway. It was ingrained.

"Now I want you to sit and experience what four minutes of silence feels like during a rapid decompression. No talking."

While Robert stood at the front, with us sitting quietly and obediently in our seats, he started his clock watch. In the stillness of the cabin, the pretend four-minute fall-from-the-sky felt like an eternity. I knew that in a real-life decompression, the poor passengers and crew would not know if they were going to level out, or meet their maker. When the four minutes was up, Robert finally spoke. "Once the pilot gets to 10,000 feet, hopefully he would be able to level out. Also in a real event, the cabin would fill with a blue mist, and there would be a lot of noise— the hissing of oxygen masks, people screaming, farting, unsecured stuff falling." Noticing our ashen faces, he added, "Fortunately, rapid decompressions rarely happen."

Once back in the training building, and during our First Aid instruction class we had to give CPR and mouth-to-mouth to "Fred," a life-sized, blue-eyed, blond, plastic male dummy. If poor Fred had been made of flesh and blood and in cardiac arrest, he would probably have been very bruised—and dead. God help our passengers, I thought.

As a relief from the emergency exercises, we were finally introduced to the fun part of the job and we boarded an empty Comet to do a mock in-flight service. We learned how to make cocktails, do a catering service, sell duty frees and accept and calculate various currencies. Before disembarking, we also had to familiarize ourselves with customs and excise documentation.

In the next to final week, and as part of our First Aid training, we were told that watching a childbirth was on the agenda. As a reluctant spectator, I took my seat at the back of the Nissen hut. As the lights dimmed and the film began to roll, I could only see the black profiles of the other girls' heads before me and beside me. From the grainy quality of the movie I knew it was old, but it was still clear enough to see a vividly bloody and gory childbirth. The mother's screams were enough to put me off reproducing for life, but for some of my classmates, it was worse. One by one, the profiled heads in front of me fell right and left. I heard *thud, thud, thud, thud* as four of them fell to the floor in a dead faint.

In our last week for "the unlikely event of the plane crashing on water," we had to learn how to survive a ditching and save pretend-drowning passengers. "Ditching in the ocean," Robert informed us, "would probably cause the plane to break up, and it would be very unlikely that anyone would survive the impact, let alone live afterwards." When we groaned, he added cheerfully, "But I was in a ditching taking off from Hong Kong when the plane overshot the runway, and as you can see, I survived. We were able to wade ashore." Great, I thought. Very comforting.

Maybe it was a hysterical release from the intensity of the preceding weeks and the potential emergencies that we had been trained to handle, but when we were bussed to the local swimming pool to do our ditching training, we were like a bunch of children who had been let loose. As we inflated the emergency raft, familiarized ourselves with flares, saved the lives of drowning "passengers" and learned how to survive for ten days on the open ocean with powdered food and desalinated sea water, we goofed around while our trainers smiled indulgently.

At the end of the four weeks I had learned everything—or so I thought—about the old-but-graceful four-engined de Havilland Comets, the first jet-liners, and the newer two-engined British Aircraft Corporations (BAC) 1-11s. Except for Helga, my colleagues and I had passed all the tests with flying colors.

Once we were fitted out for our blue tunics, jackets, hats and coats and the white blouses which comprised our air hostess uniforms, we attended a formal ceremony where we were presented with a half-wing to be worn on our uniform jackets. We also each received an official certificate declaring that we were now fully and legally trained to fly on two types of aircraft. As well as the thrill of becoming a bona fide air hostess, I had made some new, fun and lifelong friends. My life was about to take off.

On the last day of training, we waited with great anticipation to receive our first two-week flight rosters—a one-by nine-inch strip of white paper with airport codes, departure times, day and night standbys and days off. As our training stewardess handed them out, she gave us one final warning. "Senior girls don't relish flying with new girls, and some might play a new girl trick on you. Don't take it personally. For the first month you might need a thick skin."

What "new girl trick" would they play on me? I wondered but quickly forgot about it in the excitement of seeing that my first flight was just two days away—MXP on the 1-11, an evening flight to Milano.

The day of my first duty, I double-checked my uniform, my 1-11 emergency drills, my crew bag, and then fretted. Did I have everything? Will I fit in? Will I make a fool of myself? More importantly, will we crash? As I entered the crew room that night, I braced for my crew's disdain for being "the new girl" …and emanated naked fear.

"Passenger load is light," Ken Stone, our young and very handsome captain announced to the three of us as we readied the cabin for passengers. "We'll need extra ballast up front for take-off." He grinned at me. "As it's your first flight, Natasha, would you like to sit on the flight deck for take-off?"

Hmmm? Should I be flattered or insulted? Ballast, after all, is another word for weight. And although I had shed ten pounds during training, I knew that with my hourglass figure I would never be classed as "skinny."

"Er …yes …okay."

After the pre-flight ritual was done and sixty-five nervous, crucifix-clutching Italians were fastened into their seats for take-off, I entered the darkened flight deck. The aircraft was already taxiing. In the shadowy cockpit, yellow and green lights flashed on the panels above the captain's and first officer's heads. With headsets on, they were busy talking to ground control and to each other while twiddling knobs and switches, listing aloud instructions from a pre-take-off check list and hopefully, not paying much attention to my awkward presence.

The flight deck jump seat for extra crew was a vertical slab and, when not in use, was stowed upright against the rear bulkhead of the flight deck behind the captain's seat. As it was usually difficult to extricate, I prayed it would cooperate and I could sit down before take-off. I gave it several strong tugs before it slid out and snapped into position behind and between the pilots' seats. *Phew!* I sat down, slipped into my safety harness, fastened it with a click and took the headset from the hook on the port bulkhead, placing it over my ears. So far so good.

The captain turned to check on me. "Ready for take-off?" I saw him mouthing at the same time as I heard his words through the headset.

"Yes," I muttered, giving him a "thumbs up," the secure sign, just in case he couldn't hear me.

"Dan Air 5428. Cleared for take-off." As the words came from the tower and into my headset, the plane began lurching—along with my stomach—down the dark runway with just the rapidly blurring yellow centre line for guidance.

"V1," the captain announced, "Rotate." Then as the plane lifted off the ground, and we went higher, "V2."

I watched, fascinated, as both men played with the dials and, in the muted light, reeled off yet another check list. There was a thud as, beneath us, the undercarriage retracted.

We were still climbing in a steep ascent when the captain suddenly started looking around him. He removed his headset and turned to me. "Can you smell smoke?" he asked urgently.

Wha-a-a-at? No-o-o! Am I going to die on my first flight?

I sniffed. Nothing. But I hadn't been blessed, or cursed, with a great sense of smell. "N-no, I can't smell anything." *Except my fear!*

Even more agitated, Captain Stone undid his seat harness, stood up and started poking around the nooks and crannies on his side of the flight deck.

"Bob, can *you* smell smoke?" He addressed the first officer who shook his head, more intent on the lighted panel in front of him.

"Get up!" he instructed me. "We have to investigate. I'm sure I can smell smoke."

"Maybe it's just people lighting up their cigarettes in the cabin?" I offered feebly.

"No." The captain pointed at the overhead panels. "The *No Smoking* sign is still on."

He turned and looked at me. Did he expect *me* to find the source of the smoke? Then I realized with me in his way, he couldn't get out of the flight deck. I removed the headset, undid my harness and twisted the seat handle. As the captain stood impatiently waiting to get past me, the seat snapped violently back into its vertical position. I shoved the device back against the bulkhead.

Captain Stone brushed past me in the tight space.

Stay calm, I told myself. And even though panic was rising in my chest, I stifled the scream. *Please don't tell me this is the end of my life before it's even begun.*

Envisioning the rear of the cabin ablaze, I followed the captain into the brightly lit galley. Coming from the darkness into the light, all I could see was yellow. But there was no sign of fire. Maybe someone hadn't been able to wait for a smoke and had gone down to the loo, thrown the butt into the chemical toilet, not realizing it could explode.

Through the open galley curtain, I saw passengers snoozing, reading and staring blankly out of cabin windows into the night. Colleen, the number one, was helping the galley girl, Annie, load up the drinks cart. The captain leaned against the passenger door.

They all studied my frantic expression.

"I don't see any smoke," I said, peering down the cabin.

"Better check the cabin and the two toilets, Natasha." The captain nodded toward the rear. "Maybe someone threw a cigarette down the loo. And don't forget to flap the toilet seat up and down about ten times. It helps get rid of the oxygen in the system, especially right after take-off."

I didn't remember anything about that *in training.*

The other two girls, heads down, returned to loading the cart.

"Okay," I said, hesitantly stepping into the cabin under the watchful eyes of some of the passengers.

As I went down the aisle, I checked to see that no one had lit up. I peered below and around the seats. Many of the passengers glanced up, frowning, vague concern in their eyes.

The two toilets at the rear of the plane were both empty with not a whiff of smoke. I did as the captain ordered and flapped the toilet seats up and down, counting aloud, "One, two, three…" first in the starboard and then in the port toilet, ten times each. When I looked up the cabin, I saw that he and the other two girls were watching me go from toilet to toilet.

I returned to the galley.

"Good job on de toilet flappin'," Colleen commented and then the two girls burst into giggles.

"Yes," I said, with a concerned face, "but it didn't get rid of the smoke in the starboard toilet."

The captain blanched and stood straight. "Smoke?"

"Oh my God, Ken! Do yer want me to check or will you?" Colleen yanked the curtain back and peered down toward the rear, then let it fall back into place.

"No, I'll go," he said, appearing worried.

I watched as he strode into the cabin, but I didn't let him go too far. "Gottcha!" I called after him.

He stopped, turned and frowned. "You mean…?"

"There's no smoke on this aircraft, just a lot of hot air..." I gave the other two girls a knowing look, "that needed to be deflated but I think the flapping of toilet seats took care of that."

The captain's shoulders sagged in relief, and he reentered the galley.

"Well, there's no flies on you, Natasha!" Annie laughed and shook her head.

Before the captain stepped back into the flight deck, he patted me on the shoulder. "Touché, Natasha. Well played."

"To be sure, Natasha," Colleen added, "With Dan Air, you'll need to be on de ball, and have a great sense of humour. And I'm tinkin' you've got both."

Yes, I thought, as Colleen and I took the drinks cart into the cabin to begin the service. My life is about to become exciting.

2

SCARED STIFF

June 1974

When I checked in for my Malaga flight that Tuesday, as routine demanded, I went straight to the beaten-up table in the center of the crew room, adorned with several full ashtrays and peered at the large white sheets of paper with their well-thumbed corners. Each twenty-four-hour period of flight destinations, flight numbers, flight deck and cabin crew names were detailed on these pages.

As it was only my second week and ninth flight—and still feeling vulnerable to tricks—my first concern on every duty was who was my number one? Then I saw her name. *Oh no!* Sheila Higginbottom was on the list for Malaga, DA 5622 on the Comet. My flight! Her reputation for striking fear into the hearts, livers and kidneys of all new girls preceded her.

She had played a particularly nasty new trick on my friend, Pauline. On that flight, while the aircraft taxied, Pauline had stood in the cabin demonstrating the life jacket. She saw that passengers were paying uncharacteristically close attention to her, appearing mesmerized by something on her life jacket. Anxious to keep up with Sheila's PA and her difficult-to-understand-cockney-accented instructions, Pauline went to pretend-pull the red toggle to inflate the vest. But instead of red plastic, she realized she was tugging on something soft and fuzzy. When she looked down, she realized why passengers were snickering. She was yanking on a large white Tampax. Red-faced, Pauline had rushed back to the galley and hidden behind the curtain, definitely *not* amused.

Better watch out for stray tampons, I thought. Or maybe Sheila would come up with something even worse?

Amanda Spencer and Felicity Farmsworth were the other two names of the cabin crew. Thank heavens! Felicity was one of my friends from training. I didn't know Amanda.

There was just one other girl in the crew room, sitting on a cracked plastic chair against the yellow-brick wall. With delicate features set into a pale freckled face, her body language reminded me of a trapped butterfly, as if she wanted to fly away, but not to Malaga with Sheila Higginbottom.

"You're on the Malaga?" I asked. "You must be Amanda?"

"Yes," she said, nodding. The poor girl looked terrified.

"Is this your first flight?"

"Oh?" She smiled. "Oh, no. This is my fourth," she added proudly, her face lighting up. "How long have you been flying?"

I sat down next to her. "Two weeks. This is my ninth."

"Do you like it?" Amanda asked, releasing the tight clutch on her crew bag and relaxing her shoulders slightly.

"I love it!"

"Do you really?" She looked away as if she had bitten on something and it had left a sour taste in her mouth.

"Yes. It's funny. I fell into it by accident," I told her. "Someone who didn't know me very well pushed me to apply. And she was right. It suits me."

"Oh. Not me." Amanda huffed. "I was the opposite. Since I was a little girl, I always wanted to be an air hostess. I dreamed about wearing an elegant uniform, travelling to exotic places, meeting handsome pilots and interesting passengers." She sighed, wistful.

It was my turn to say "Oh." The reality of flying for Dan Air was somewhat different.

"This ...," she said waving a vague hand in the air at nothing, "is more physically strenuous than working on a construction site!"

"Oh, I kno-o-o-w," I droned empathically and grinning, trying to lighten the mood.

"And some passengers are so rude. I really wanted to travel, but so far all I've seen are the airport buildings. We don't even get off the plane!"

"Didn't they tell you that at the interview?"

"Well, yes but ...I thought those were just scare tactics."

"I think if they wanted to scare us, they would have told us the whole truth," I said.

But the delicate Amanda would not be mollified. "And once the passengers have disembarked...," she blathered on as if I was an uninformed passenger, and not crew, "we have to prepare the aircraft for the return sector. We're lucky if we get to sit down for five minutes. On my first flight, I broke two fingernails!"

Oh, God. This wasn't going to be a fun flight. "Give it time. Maybe you'll come to love it."

The door to the crew room burst open and a short, stocky, bleached blonde stomped in, barely casting a glance at the two of us. She made her way to the centre table, glanced at the flight sheet, grunted, then strode over to the black ops phone in the corner and picked it up.

Then Felicity entered and approached our seats, her tall frame looming over us. "'Allo, darlin!'" She grinned at me. "Didn't know you were on the Malaga!" Barely acknowledging Amanda with a nod, she whispered, "Is Sheila our number one?"

"'Fraid so."

"Crikey!" Felicity pulled a face.

Amanda gulped.

"Roight then." Sheila stood at the table, reading the flight sheet again and glaring at the three of us. "Are you all bleedin' new girls?"

The three of us muttered something in the affirmative.

"Bloody 'ell!"

Yes, this was definitely not going to be a fun flight.

She addressed the timid Amanda. "'Ow long you been flyin' then?"

"Er…this is my fourth flight."

"And you two?" she snapped, waving a stubby finger at Felicity and me.

"Two weeks," we replied in unison.

"Stone the bleedin' crows!" Sheila shook her head. "Let's 'ope we don't 'ave a bleedin' emergency." She surveyed us, obviously debating something. "You," she said finally pointing to the almost paralyzed Amanda, "can do the galley. Natasha number three and Felicity, number four in the cabin."

"But I …" Amanda's mouth was open, but nothing was coming out.

Sheila stood, a hand on her hip, glaring at her. "You'll do what you're bleedin' told. All roight?"

Amanda stared at Sheila, maybe thinking my thoughts. How did a too-short, bleached blonde, crude cockney toughie qualify as an air stewardess?

"Com' on, darlin'." Felicity pulled the trembling Amanda up from her seat. "You'll be fine. We'll help you."

"Transport's 'ere." Sheila yelled, and like a family of ducks we followed our leader single file out of the crew room and onto the bus.

Inside the dark galley, Amanda clutched my arm and hissed, "What do I do first?"

I felt sorry for her. Perhaps relying too much on our common sense, training in galley procedures had been minimal. Usually, new girls would have to fly at least a month before taking on the responsibility of running the galley, feeding the flight deck, managing the catering and preparing for each service. Why had Sheila chosen the virginal and fragile Amanda for number two?

"Start with tearing the tops off the mineral boxes and slice some lemons," I suggested as I removed my hat and gloves, having observed how other girls set up the galley for flights. "Just prepare as much as you can for each service."

Once I had finished cabin duties—checking that the emergency equipment was present and correct and that the seat pockets in the forward part of the cabin had been replenished—I helped Amanda rip the tops off coffee packets and put ice in the coffee pots which doubled as ice buckets.

Amanda wasn't like other stewardesses. There was something about the more seasoned girls I had flown with, a je-ne-sais-quoi quality that seemed inherent, a kind of tough practicality. Whatever it was, Amanda didn't have it. This flying life was no place for princesses. As she cowered in the galley, she reminded me of a rabbit hiding from predators in her warren. It was only a matter of time before someone would smell out her fear and take advantage.

"Have they played a new girl trick on you yet, Amanda?" I asked, as I stowed ice-filled coffee pots in one of the galley cupboards.

Her eyes went wide. "I ...I don't think so ...although the captain on my first flight did ask me to take a bag of oxygen out of the flight deck. Do you think that was a trick?"

What? "And did you?"

"Yes. Well, he handed me a huge garbage bag full of air and told me it can be dangerous if it builds up."

"Amanda!" I shook my head.

"Oh." Even in the shadows of the Comet galley, I could see her blush.

I doubted if she would last long in the flying world. The tragedy was that what she had dreamed of for so long did not exist, not with this airline anyway.

"'Ere! You lot." Sheila had plonked herself down in the front row of passenger seats, her manila envelope full of flight paperwork on her lap. "Come 'ere."

Felicity walked down the aisle from the overwing, clutching duty free brochures. Amanda and I emerged from the galley and stood to attention in front of her.

"Floight time is about one hour forty-five so the service will be drinks, snacks, two teas and coffees an' duty frees. Got it?" she snapped. "Full load both ways. And," Sheila added, a wry grin on her face, "we're pickin' up a stiff in Malaga."

"A stiff?" Amanda blanched, making her freckles more noticeable. "Do you mean...?"

"Yeah. A dead body. Poor old bugger snuffed it over 'is scampi and chips on 'is first day on hols."

"Wh-where will they put him?" Amanda asked, her eyes wide, perhaps envisioning a dead man propped up like Lurch in a passenger seat.

Just then the flight engineer appeared and stood behind us. "Gooday, girls. Everything dinky die?"

"'ello Joe." Sheila looked up at the Australian and grinned as she took the paperwork out of her envelope. "Just lettin' these new girls know that we 'ave a stiff on board inbound. Amanda 'ere is new and is worryin' about where we're goin' to put the poor sod."

"Well, I think where we always put 'em." He smiled at Sheila. "In the hold under the galley. Isn't that right?"

Sheila nodded. "Yeah, ...that's roight. The electrical 'old."

Amanda's eyes grew even wider. "O-o-h."

"Don't worry, luv. 'e'll be in a pine box," Sheila added distractedly, completing details on her flight report. "They'll load 'im from below so you won't even see 'im—unless 'e decides to get out of 'is coffin and come upstairs for a drink." She cackled. "Now, get back to work."

The normally outgoing Felicity returned quietly to the rear of the plane to finish dressing both toilets while Amanda and I stepped back into the shadowy galley.

Amanda stared at the floor. "Is that where they'll put him?" she asked, pointing. Below the ovens on the left, a square metal rim was inset into the black rubber matting. We both knew this was the cover of the electrical hold beneath. That's where the flight engineer went to do his pre-flight checks. And that's where, apparently, the dead, cold, stiff body of the old man would be resting on the return sector.

"I'm terrified of death," she whispered.

This girl was definitely in the wrong career. Rehearsing how *not* to die in our emergency drills was part of our daily routine. "Don't think about that now," I reminded her. She was already nervous enough without thinking about working with a corpse beneath her feet. "Just focus on the service."

In the cabin, Sheila and Joe were in deep conversation and laughing. I thought I heard Sheila say something about "as much bloody use as tits on a bull." Was she referring to the hapless Amanda?

Hearing their laughter, Amanda muttered, "How could they be so callous? A man has died."

I shrugged. "Maybe you get hardened to it after a while."

Throughout the outbound flight, Amanda's uneasiness did not abate. "You're doin' all roight," Sheila commented. "Why are you so bleedin' jumpy?"

"Oh ...nothing," Amanda responded. Sheila was probably the last person she would confide in about her disappointment in her flying career ...and her horror of anything dead.

On the turnaround at Malaga Aeropuerto, and after in-flight catering had been loaded into the galley, Amanda, afraid to hear the sounds of a coffin being installed into the hold, went to sit in the cabin's front row. She picked delicately at the cheese sandwich she had hastily made from the meagre offerings in the hostie pack.

Felicity and I worked our way around the chatty Spanish cleaners as we replenished seat pockets containing tattered in-flight magazines, duty-free brochures, sick bags and emergency cards as well as browned apple cores, used Kleenex and other unsanitary debris. Even from the rear of the cabin, we could hear Sheila's coarse cackle from inside the flight deck where she chatted with the men. The next moment we saw her short and stubby profile standing in the galley opening. "Punters!" she yelled, warning us of impending passengers.

Felicity and I peered through the aircraft windows and saw a herd of people, some clutching fuzzy pink toy donkeys, surging across the tarmac. Amanda quickly emerged from the rear loo, her hair and make-up once again pristine, and hurried toward the front.

Amanda and I stood in the galley, wearing the mandatory hats and gloves, and intoning "Good afternoon" to returning, tanned and shorts-clad holidaymakers. After the last passenger was on board and I had closed the galley door, I reminded my ashen colleague, "He won't bite, you know" I said, referring to the corpse below our feet, "unless he's a vampire, of course."

She wasn't amused.

One hour into the return flight, Felicity and I were at the rear of the plane just finishing first teas and coffees when Sheila strode down the cabin toward us. "Oy, girls. When you're done, go and wait for me in the floight deck. All roight?"

Felicity and I both looked at her alarmed. *Was there an emergency?*

Seeing our expressions, she laughed. "Don't get yer knickers in a knot. We just need you on the floight deck for a few."

What trick did Sheila have up her cockney sleeve?

When we arrived at the front, Amanda was standing in the dimly lit galley alone filling more pots with tea and coffee for the second beverage service. She still seemed edgy, casting nervy glances down at the hold, eerily aware of what lay beneath.

Normally Felicity and I would immediately take the hot beverages and begin serving in the cabin, but when we explained to Amanda that Sheila had ordered us onto the flight deck, she looked alarmed. "I think Sheila might be playing a trick on us," I whispered.

"Oh," she responded, relieved.

Sheila blew into the galley, closing the curtain behind her, "Amanda, you start with coffees, will yer? Felicity and Natasha need to come up to the flight deck for a sec. Then they'll be roight wiv yer."

This was highly unusual. The number two rarely left the galley and Amanda knew it. "Oh? Okay," she mumbled picking up a steaming coffee pot and disappearing into the cabin.

"All clear?" The engineer was peaking out from behind the curtain and addressing Sheila.

"Yeah, you can go to the *loo* now," she grinned at him and snorted.

The engineer stepped into the galley.

"Go on then, you two." Sheila almost pushed Felicity and me through the entrance into the flight deck, making sure the thick curtain that separated the galley from the cockpit was pulled closed behind all three of us.

The four-seater flight deck was cluttered with large black flight manuals. Meal trays sat on the floor behind the captain and the first officer's seat, the food picked over. The two pilots, barely cognizant of our presence, were talking to air traffic control and to each other. Felicity and I exchanged glances. *What was going on?*

"Just wanted to make sure you two knew about 'ow to serve flight deck meals." Sheila grinned, the gaps in her poorly maintained teeth showing.

Felicity frowned.

"Never give them the same meal in case of food poisoning?" I obediently repeated the line from training.

A metal scraping noise came from somewhere behind me, but I couldn't place the sound. Felicity's eyes darted around the flight deck as if waiting for something to leap out at her.

"Yeah," Sheila nodded, distracted, "that's it." She turned and peeked through the curtain into the galley. What *was* she up to?

"All roight, you two." She opened the flight deck curtain a few inches wider and hissed at us, "Watch this."

At first, there was nothing to see, but then Amanda came back into the galley, empty coffee pot in hand. She glanced in the direction of the flight deck and frowned. Sheila quickly let the curtain fall back into place. She waited a few minutes then carefully grabbed a handful of fabric again and lifted it. We stood behind her short frame and watched.

With her back to us, Amanda was just about to refill a metal pot with boiling hot water when we heard her gasp. She stepped back from the urns, the empty vessel dangling from her right hand, staring down at the floor and fixated on the electrical hold cover. She stood frozen, almost over the top of the hold clutching the pot to her chest as if it might protect her, or come in handy as a weapon.

We heard a small noise and saw the square cover move, ever so slightly. "*Ohmigod. The dead man!*" I hissed. Felicity and I both covered our mouths. Sheila smiled wickedly and signalled us to "shoosh."

Amanda stood paralyzed. The cover moved again, making an even harsher scraping noise, then lifted slightly and shifted sideways. As if engaged in a game of cat and mouse, Amanda stood almost over the cover, as if ready to pounce on it and stop whatever was down there from coming up, or hit it over the head with the coffee pot.

Then the cover *lifted* and hovered in mid-air!

A deep moan came out of the black void below. Amanda whimpered and took a step back, then another, the coffee pot hanging from her now limp hand. Thick, bloodied men's fingers gripped the edge of the hold.

Amanda was out of our sight now. *She must have backed up against the passenger door,* I thought. There was nowhere else to go in that cramped space. All we could hear was a faint whimpering. The gory hand, attached to a man's arm in a white, bloodied, shirt sleeve, crept onto the galley floor. Out of the black abyss came another deep mournful moan. The hand flailed, reaching in Amanda's direction, fingers grasping at thin air, inching ever closer toward her. We heard Amanda whimper again. The dead man was coming ...for her.

"*Aaaagh!*" We heard her scream followed by a soft thud.

"Oh gawd," Sheila's voice broke the spell. She snatched the flight deck curtain back and stepped into the galley. "She's bleedin' passed out!" The hold cover quickly rose another two feet. Felicity and I gasped as a chalky white face, cheeks smeared with red gashes appeared.

"Bollocks!" the flight engineer cursed, as he pulled himself up onto the sill of the hold and then climbed into the galley, one shirt sleeve of his uniform covered in gooey red stuff. "I didn't think she'd take it *seriously!*"

Felicity and I stayed out of the way just inside the flight deck, but with the curtain wide so we could see what was happening. The tough-as-nails Sheila was now gently talking to the half-conscious Amanda crumpled in a heap on the dirty floor. "It's all roight, luv. We was just jokin'. It was just a joke."

Amanda must have opened her eyes as Sheila pulled her into a sitting position. Through her blur, the frightened girl stared at the engineer standing, leaning against the metal galley counter, his chalky white face smeared with red streaks and his left shirt sleeve and hand covered in red goo. He surveyed his victim, concern in his eyes.

Sheila helped Amanda up onto the jump seat and stood over her. Still stunned, Amanda peered around the galley as if to say, *Where am I? Oh yes. On the Comet. The hand. The dead man.* "I must have fainted," she said, embarrassed.

"Natasha, pass me a brandy miniature and put it in a cup o' black coffee, will yer?" Sheila snapped. "Felicity, you carry on with coffees."

Disappointed at missing the aftermath, Felicity disappeared into the cabin clutching a pot and a small tray. While I wrapped a napkin around the plastic cup and poured the coffee, the engineer slid the square hold cover firmly back into place and flush with the galley floor. He leaned back against the galley surface again, looking remorseful.

"I'm sorry, Amanda. I fink we took it a bit far," Sheila said sincerely. "'Ere, drink this." She offered Amanda the steaming brown liquid I had concocted.

"What is it?" Amanda wrinkled her nose, still shaking.

"Just coffee with a small shot of brandy," I reassured her.

She pushed it away. "No thanks."

"Look, Amanda." The tough Sheila was being uncharacteristically tender now. "We thought you would realize it was Joe down there. We fought it was funny. We didn't mean to ...scare you stiff."

"Funny?" Amanda snapped. "I was terrified."

"Amanda," Sheila began, "a new girl trick is just a way of initiatin' you. Everyone gets a trick. You need a bloody sense o' humour on this job, let me tell yer."

"I know," Amanda nodded and peered out of the portal window in the Comet door where there was just blue sky. She sighed. "I don't think I'm really cut out for flying." She turned back to Sheila and smiled weakly. "To hell with it, maybe I will have that brandy," she said reaching out for the cup, "and then I quit."

"Why quit?" Sheila handed the glass to Amanda. "You were doin' all roight." Sheila glanced at the engineer, nervously. "You know, the chief stewardess is goin' to give me a royal rollickin' for scaring a new girl away."

Amanda shrugged. "I was going to quit anyway. You just helped me make up my mind." She took another sip before asking, "But I have to know—was there really a dead body?"

"Oh yiss," the engineer affirmed. "The old boy's in the rear hold on top of the suitcases where we put a lot of the stiffs."

Amanda took another sip of the brandied coffee.

We all fell silent.

"Geez, I'm sorry, Amanda," Joe sounded sheepish. "I didn't mean to freak you out that badly. I thought you'd recognize my ugly mug. I guess the make-up was just too good."

"What?" Amanda peered up at Joe, grinning, her complexion a little pinker now, "You were wearing make up?"

"Ah, good one." He laughed. "So, you're saying it was my ugly mug that made you pass out!"

"If the shoe fits...?" Amanda raised her eyebrows in a question.

We all laughed then.

"But you've given me an idea," she sat up, excited. "I love doing make-up. Maybe I could become a make-up artist."

"That's great!" Sheila stood, reassured now that Amanda was going to be okay. The girl even had a sense of humour. "So the next time we need to scare the bejabbers out of someone, we can 'ire you to do a *real* make-up job."

A red light appeared on the panel in the galley, signalling a passenger call button.

"Oh, bluddy 'ell," Sheila moaned. "Back to work, girls."

3

MANURE OR ROSES?

July 1974

"Ee bah gum!" Julia exclaimed as she climbed the forward steps of the BAC 1-11 with me right behind her.

"What is it?" I asked.

"Look. Our Pauline's on this flight," she said, tossing the words to me over her shoulder.

As soon as we arrived at the top of the stairs, we could see our good friend standing in the vestibule of the plane, a fake smile plastered on her face as she greeted passengers. After only two months of flying, Pauline had already acquired an irreverent attitude.

The plane had been sitting, somewhat delayed, on the hot tarmac in Palma, Majorca, waiting for 87 "tacky tourists," on their inbound flight back to Gatwick. Julia and I were also flying as passengers, "positioning" in uniform, returning to home base. Earlier that same morning, we had operated a "fam" flight, bringing a mob of travel agents to Palma for a familiarization tour. While our lucky number one stewardess and two pilots had been flown home first class on British Airways, Julia and I, the juniors, were left behind to travel on our own airline.

"Oh, my God!" Pauline beamed as she saw Julia and I enter the galley. "What are you two doing here?"

"Eee lass, we got up at crack o' dawn, we did, to cum 'ere." Julia grimaced. "But now we can put our feet up and you can wait on us 'and and foot."

Alicia, our other friend, and Pauline's quiet, shy partner-in-crime poked her head out from behind the curtain shutting off the other side of the galley. "'Ello, 'ello," she said, mimicking a bobby and smiling her enigmatic smile.

"Did they actually let you two fly together?" I asked.

"It's not us you need to worry about," Pauline whispered. "Louise Levers is our number one."

"Oo-ooh. You poor th—."

Before Julia could finish, Louise's rough voice came from the front of the cabin. We turned to see her standing like a bulldog ready to pounce. "Get a move on, you two," she bellowed. "This isn't a bloody party!" Couth obviously wasn't Louise's strong point.

Julia and I exchanged a subtle roll of the eyes with our friends as we moved into the cabin.

"You two sit at the emergency exit," Louise snapped. "A and B."

We nodded and moved around her, waiting patiently in the aisle while passengers stuffed their large pink plush donkeys, the usual Majorcan souvenirs, into the overhead hat rack.

"Oooh, that Louise Levers's a right one, in't she?" Julia whispered as we settled into our seats. "Knowin' 'er, she'll probably make *us* work while she puts *her* bloody feet up."

"Have you flown with her?'

"Aye. She's a right bully. I don't want to be mean, but one of these days I 'ope she gets a right come-uppance."

In-flight, despite dirty looks from Louise, Julia and I sat back and enjoyed being passengers for a change. Then just before the duty-free sales service should have begun, Louise's voice came over the PA.

"Ladies and gentlemen, on today's flight home, as well as offering you a duty-free service, we are going to do something fun." And as if speaking to children, she added, "We are going to have a raffle where you can win some lov-er-ly prizes."

A buzz of approval sounded all around us. Julia and I exchanged frowns. "What's the prize?" I wondered out loud. "A night out with the lascivious Louise Levers?"

"Tickets are five pounds each and you can win an elegant man's watch, a litre of Johnny Walker, a carton of cigarettes of your choice or ...a bottle of Yves St. Laurent Rive Gauche."

Julia gasped. "But that's ..."

"Illegal?" I offered. "And those watches only cost ten pounds!" I had to admire Louise's gall.

"Pauline and Alicia, your lovely cabin crew, will be coming around to sell you tickets so please have your money ready. And this is your lucky day. If you buy five, you pay just twenty pounds and get a free ticket. There are four prizes, so you all stand a great chance of winning. What do you say?"

A cheer went up in the cabin.

"Be it on 'er own 'ead," Julia muttered.

A loud chatter began in the cabin as passengers excitedly talked among themselves and reached for their money. Moments later Alicia and then Pauline emerged from the galley, each clutching a roll of tickets and one of the wicker baskets—normally reserved for extra sugars and creamers. Alicia started down the aisle heading for the rear of the cabin, her cheeks pink with embarrassment. She stopped by our row and bent over. "Are we allowed to do this?" she whispered.

"No, of course not," Julia hissed.

"Pauline told her she had the cramps," Alicia said, "but Louise threatened to give her a bad report if she didn't do it. And we all know what *that* means."

As new girls hoping for a permanent contract at the end of our six months' probation, we were all dependent on the senior's glowing assessments. The number one's words could mean the difference between an exciting flying career or being jobless at the end of the summer.

Pauline had started at the front of the cabin, her cringing body language giving the impression that if one of the hold doors beneath the aisle carpet should suddenly open and swallow her up, she would be eternally grateful.

At the front, Louise snapped the galley curtain back and peered down the cabin. Alicia, still hovering around our seats, noticed my eyes widen in warning of something behind her. Sensing Louise's eyes boring into her back, she moved on down the aisle. At the front, Pauline continued to offer tickets, droning, "Sir, Madam, would you like to buy a raffle ticket?"

Louise marched down to our row and leaned in. "You have to buy tickets, too, you know."

"Wha-a-at?" It was my turn to be shocked. "But we're in uniform!"

She leaned in, baring her not-so-white teeth, her pocked-marked complexion even uglier up close. "Exactly," she sneered. "Show some team spirit. Or do you want me to write a report on you two being disruptive passengers while positioning?" She had us over a barrel, and she knew it.

Julia and I stared at her and nodded, probably with the same thought in our head. *Bitch!*

When Pauline arrived at our seat, and we proffered our five-pound notes, Julia asked, "Are the passengers goin' for it?"

"Oh, they love it ...oh ...but you don't have to...," Pauline waved our money away.

Louise suddenly loomed behind her, peering over her shoulder at the basket and then at us.

"Er ...yes, we do," we said in unison, depositing our fivers into a basket already floating with notes.

As Louise turned and went back to the front, Pauline tore off our two tickets. "Sorry," she mumbled.

Soon Louise's voice came over the PA again. "*Ladies and gentlemen, thank you all for participating. Now here are the winners ...*"

A delighted yelp came from the rear of the cabin. Alicia was sent to present the woman with a man's watch. An old man three rows behind us pressed his call button and was given a litre of Johnny Walker.

Another passenger received a carton of Dunhill cigarettes. Then beside me, Julia exclaimed, "Oh, bluddy 'ell!"

"What is it?"

She was staring at her ticket. "I've bluddy won."

Pauline soon appeared in front us and proffered the Yves St. Laurent perfume. "Sorry!" she said again while handing it to Julia.

As if she was reaching for an unexploded bomb, Julia accepted the blue, silver and black metal container. "I'll give it to me sister," she said as if that would make it all right.

"Promise me you won't tell anyone about this," Pauline whispered.

"Don't you worry, chuck. It'll be our secret," Julia responded, as she tucked the perfume into her handbag and avoided the elderly woman passenger across the aisle who was beaming a congratulatory smile at us.

"I hope Louise is going to at least share her ill-gotten gains with you?" I whispered to Pauline.

"I hope she *doesn't*," she huffed as she turned and went back to the galley.

That evening, after picking up a few groceries at Horsham Tesco's, I was just stepping across the threshold of my house when—as if waiting for the moment of my return—the phone rang.

"We have to meet," Pauline hissed, no trace of the usual mirth in her voice and sounding as if an MI5 agent was standing right behind her. "Can you be at the Six Bells by eight?"

"Yes, but ...what's happened?" I asked.

"Didn't you get the call?"

"What call? No, I ..."

"I'll tell you when I see you," she whispered.

As I drove the narrow winding country roads to the pub, I thought about Pauline. Some wise person wrote that our character determines our fate, but if that were true, how come Pauline's character, which was in constant trouble, always resurfaced after each escapade ever more victorious? She could land in manure but always come up smelling of roses. And Louise, the bully, also seemed to be impervious to the bad karma she deserved. "The call" must have been from the airline and involved us all. What was my karma account looking like?

Inside the Tudor pub with its white-washed walls and oak-beamed lounge, Pauline and Alicia were already sitting at one of the old, knotted oak tables clutching their habitual Carlsbergs. Their expressions were uncharacteristically glum.

"Did someone die?" I asked as I joined them.

"Get a drink and we'll tell you," Pauline muttered, nervously glancing at the scattering of other patrons.

"Who's that for?" I asked, noticing another Carlsberg sitting alone on the table.

"Julia. She's in the loo," Alicia supplied.

As I waited at the bar to receive my glass of locally made blackberry wine, I thought, *this must be serious.* By the time I returned to the table, our Yorkshire lass, Julia, her thick blonde hair now cascading over her shoulders, had joined the other two. I slid onto the wooden bench next to her facing Alicia and Pauline.

"You start." The glum Alicia nodded at Pauline.

"We've been called up to the office. Tomorrow." Pauline's voice trembled. "We're probably going to get fired. Perhaps you, too, Natasha. They still haven't rung you?"

I shook my head.

"Ba gum, they called *me*," Julia moaned, taking a large slug of her beer. "Could I 'elp it if I won a bluddy prize?"

"Maybe they'll call me in the morning." I gazed sullenly into my drink. It would be so unfair if my new friends and I lost our jobs. I didn't even want to contemplate that scenario.

"How did Jane Philoughby find out so quickly?" I enquired, referring to our intrepid chief stewardess.

Alicia groaned. "One of the stupid punters called in ecstatic about the "Raffle Flight.' They wanted to know why Dan Air doesn't do raffles on *all* their flights."

"*Wh-a-a-at*?" Julia exclaimed. "A passenger complimented us?"

Ignoring her stab at humour, Alicia moaned, "We might even get arrested ...for being complicit."

"Hang on a sec," Julia said, inspiration dawning. "Did everyone buy a ticket?"

"Well ...not everyone..." Pauline sat up. "But some pax bought two or three."

"So 'ow much did she make on the raffle?" Julia persisted.

"Louise counted the money so we're not sure." Alicia frowned. "Why?"

"Oo-o-o-h, I bet she did count it, that little minx," Julia exclaimed. "Let's just say at least eighty tickets were sold. Multiply that by five which is ...four 'undred pounds! 'Ow much did she give you two?"

"Sixty." Pauline grimaced. "I didn't want to take it but she–"

"She would have had to pay the bar for the prizes," Alicia pointed out.

"Sixty!" Julia slammed down her glass on the table. "Eee, that Louise Levers. She's a right one." She shook her shoulders in her Hilda Baker imitation.

"You're right!" Pauline's already big eyes grew to saucer-size. "That means ...she took at least two hundred and fifty!"

I leaned forward. "But you do realize that's a good thing, don't you?"

Pauline and Alicia stared at me, mystified. "Why?"

"Well, if you can prove that Louise was conning *you,* as well as the passengers, it proves that you were *not* complicit."

"*And* that tart will 'ave to produce those raffle tickets to prove how much money was illegally collected!" Julia added, nodding in a told-you-so gesture, her arms still across her chest.

Relief flooded my friends' faces. I took a long sip of wine.

"That *bitch*..." Alicia muttered so softly it sounded almost sweet. "I really love flying. It wouldn't be fair if we lost our jobs."

"Eee, it won't come to that, chuck." Julia leaned back and glanced around the pub. "You two are the innocents. It's that bluddy Louise that deserves to get the chop."

Pauline nodded. "Yes. We *are* the innocents."

"Well ...this time." I smiled. "Don't get *too* carried away."

Julia stood up. "Eee, I'm glad we've got that sorted. I think this deserves another round, don't you girls?"

"Not for me," I told her. "I've got to go soon. I'm meeting Julian."

After Julia returned with three more beers, Pauline raised her full Carlsberg and happily clinked her glass on ours. "Cheers, ladies," she said, back to her cheery self. Then something across the other side of the room caught her attention. "Oh, bloody hell," she muttered.

I turned, following the direction of her gaze. Three jean-clad men sat on the far side of the lounge by the unlit fireplace, talking. The long, dark-haired handsome one was staring at our table.

"Do you know him?" I asked Pauline.

"It's John." She lifted her glass in a half-hearted greeting to him. "He sold me my MGB."

"And," Julia leaned in conspiratorially, "'e's got a thing for you, doesn't 'e?" She pulled her you-can't-fool-me face. "'E sold that car to you for dirt cheap. Poor bugger. 'E's besotted."

"Oh no!" Pauline hunched over her drink. "He's coming over. Alicia, do something."

The corners of Alicia's mouth curled up in her Mona Lisa smile. John approached and stood behind me.

"Hello, John," Alicia cooed.

I turned to look at him. He was handsome in a rough Mr. Marlborough-Man Australian kind of a way.

"'Ello, ladies."

"Bluddy cheek." Julia grinned up at him. "Who are *you* callin' a lady?"

He smiled down at her, grateful for her teasing welcome. "Me and the boys are goin' to a great party tonight. Do you wanna come?" The invitation was thrown out to all of us, but his eyes rested longingly on Pauline.

She smiled up at him. "Oh, what the hell. Yes, we need to have some fun. Why not?" she added, seeking agreement from Alicia. "Where is it?"

"Three Bridges. Five Cherry Tree Lane," he told her. "See ya later then?"

Once he was out of earshot, Julia whispered, "'Ee, you've got no 'eart, Pauline. Now you've got 'im all excited."

"Are you sure you're fit to drive?" I addressed Pauline.

"I'm fine," she said with a slur at the edge of her words. "But maybe we'll go the back way, you know, to avoid other cars."

And the police, I thought. "I'll follow you, until my turn off," I said.

As we stepped outside into the warm, clear and now dark night, I watched as the three girls, giggling, squeezed into Pauline's blue MGB. The roof was up, so Julia had to reach inside and grab the supporting roll bar and squeeze herself onto the parcel shelf which constituted a back seat while Pauline and Alicia got in the front.

Even when sober, Pauline was not the smoothest driver, erratically braking and accelerating, so I knew as I followed that I should keep my distance. As she roared off toward the back road, the only illumination in the dark countryside were the yellow cats' eyes delineating the winding narrow lanes. Despite her consumption of Carlsbergs, Pauline stayed within the tight curves.

We had only travelled five miles when, as we approached a very sharp left bend, it happened.

The MGB suddenly veered to the right across the center of the road. I watched in horror as her sports car headed straight for a thick hedge with God knows what on the other side, the boot of the car disappearing through the shrubbery, already precariously tipping to the left.

"Oh God. Oh God. Oh God," I cried as I tried to stay focused on the sharp bend in front of me. Immediately the road straightened, and a farm driveway appeared on the right. I pulled in, leapt out of my mini and ran back around the bend. I peeked through the hole in the hedge and in the moonlight, I saw something spinning.

Oh no! The wheels. The car must have flipped. I clambered through the hedge into the field and cursing my high-heeled boots, I stumbled across the clumpy ground, the pungent smell of manure already invading my nostrils. As I got closer, I heard ...could it be? ...giggling ...coming from the car?

A light in the farmhouse to the left went on. Now twenty feet in front of me I could clearly see all four MGB's wheels spinning in the air. The car must have landed on its roof! Would the roll bar have offered enough protection to prevent injury?

"Oh God!" *And what if the car burst into flames? My friends would be barbecued alive.*

"Pauline!" I yelled, terrified. As I approached the driver's side, I saw in the shadows my friend's head, then shoulders emerge out of the open car door. All three women were still laughing!

"For God's sake, get out of there! "I screamed.

I looped my arms under Pauline's armpits and dragged her away from the car. Julia followed crawling on all fours, muttering something about rabbits. Then I rushed to the other side where Alicia was sitting upright on the grass, stunned and cursing "bloody cows!" She had just plonked herself down in the middle of a cow pat. Despite the stench and my revulsion for manure, I helped her up.

"The car might blow," I urged, imagining in the darkness a large prang on the rear end near the petrol tank. "We have to get away!" But as we gathered on the driver's side, all three women were still laughing, obviously not feeling any pain. Or were they in shock?

"C'mo-o-o-n," I yelled at them, fearing the worst. Finally, leaning on each other, we stumbled over the lumpy grass and through more cow pats toward the hedge.

"What the hell do they put in those Carlsbergs, anyway?" I wondered out loud as I nudged Alicia through the wide hole in the hedge the MGB had created and onto the road.

"It was all the rabbit's fault," Julia complained. "He shouldn't 'ave run in't front of us like that."

Had a rabbit really run in front of them or was it just a figment of Julia's drunken imagination? "What shall we do about your car, Pauline?" I asked as we staggered along the road to my mini.

"Jush leave it." She waved a dismissive hand in the dark and I got a powerful whiff of manure. "I'll ashk John to come and get it tomorrow."

"Well, let's get you all home," I said as we clambered into my little car, "so you can have a nice hot bath."

"No-o-o," Pauline cried. "We want to go to the party, don't we?"

"You still want to go?" I asked, somewhat incredulous. "You're a bit stinky!" *Would anything stop Pauline from having a good time?*

"Oh, we can wasssh it off," Pauline insisted. "And I *haff* to shee John," she responded, as if it was a date with the queen, "about the car."

"What's that schmell?" Julia demanded from the back seat.

"You all landed in cow shit, Julia." I informed her. "But knowing Pauline, you will all probably come up smelling of roses."

The harsh ringing of the phone woke me up from a dream of spinning rabbits on a barbecue. Daylight was bursting through my window. I quickly reviewed the events of the day and night before.

"Miss Rosewood?" The female voice on the other end sounded officious.

"Yes?"

"Miss Philoughby has requested that you come into the office at 10.30 this morning."

"I'll be there," I said, gulping at the possibility of landing in manure and *not* coming up smelling of roses. Despite Julian's heroic attempts at cleaning my car seats the night before, I noticed as I drove to Gatwick that the inside of my car still needed more sweet-smelling fragrance.

When I arrived on the third floor, Julia was already sitting in the outer office. As usual, she appeared pristine, the quintessential hostess in her uniform, but there was something fragile and scared in her aura. When she turned toward me and removed her Jackie O sunglasses, I saw a slight discoloration on her neck that apparently the layers of *Sheer Genius* foundation had failed to hide. She must have stayed with her boyfriend, Adrian the night before, I surmised. A make-up called *Bloody Miracle* should be invented for such occasions.

"How are you feeling?" I asked as I sat down in the other chair.

"Oo-oo-oh, not so good, chuck." She donned her sunglasses again to shield her eyes from the sunshine pouring through the large office windows. "Ba gum, I don't know whether it's a hangover or the crash, but I feel like someone's beaten me to death with a cow pat."

"You're lucky to be alive."

"Aye, I know. Thank God you were there."

"I don't think I had anything to do with your survival. Thank Pauline and her charmed karma."

"Eee, well. We'll see about that today, won't we?"

Just then the door opened, and Miss Philoughby's assistant beckoned us into the inner sanctum. Julia and I exchanged looks of *good luck* and went in. On the left side of the office, the dreaded Louise Levers, looking pale, was staring out of the window at the plane-cluttered tarmac below. I was shocked to see that her cheeks were wet. Had she been crying? Alicia and Pauline sat frozen in their seats on the right side of Julia's massive desk.

The chief hostess pointed to the chairs in the middle of the room, and we sank down onto them.

Jane Philoughby, her delicate frame belying her position of authority, shuffled papers and then glanced up. When she spoke, I was transfixed by her bright pink lipstick which only accentuated her ghostly pallor.

"Well, Julia and Natasha, I've heard the accounts of what transpired yesterday." She looked at us with a what-were-you-thinking expression. Julia and I stole a quick glance at Pauline and Alicia who still sat woodenly, fixated on Miss Philoughby's desk.

"Now these girls have agreed to return the money collected. Julia, I would appreciate you returning the perfume and we will refund you the monies that you both paid."

"Of course," Julia answered as if she had expected this. She reached into her handbag and passed the contaminated Yves St. Laurent to Miss Philoughby.

"You must understand," Julia went on, "that this situation could have endangered the airline's license, and everyone's job. As such, Louise has now been demoted to a junior which, under the circumstances, is very lenient."

Pauline and I exchanged gloomy glances. Flying with Louise as a demoted angry, humiliated and ex-senior hostie might be even more awkward than working with her in her current senior position.

Louise sat up in her chair, suddenly present again. "Miss Philoughby?"

"Yes?"

"I think I should resign." For the first time, I thought I saw humility in Louise's features.

Julia sighed. "Well ...if you...,"

"It's better this way," Louise snapped, her voice breaking. She stood up and left the room.

When the door closed behind her, I wondered if Miss Philoughby could feel the huge collective sigh of relief that we all exhaled. If it had been any stronger, the force might have blown our frail boss against her office wall. "If this ever happens again," our boss continued, visibly shaken by Louise's sudden departure, "you are the ones to report any wrongdoing by *any* member of the crew, whoever they are. Don't leave it to the passengers to inform me of what happens on flights. I don't like surprises. Do you understand?"

"Yes, Miss Philoughby," we all chimed in unison.

"Good," she said, suppressing a smile. "Now go and enjoy the rest of your days off. And Julia," she said, her eyes still focused on papers on her desk, "I don't know what you've been up to, but you need more make-up to cover up those bruises on your neck."

The four of us waited until we were in the lift before we yelped with relief and delight. Not only were we all alive, and we still had our jobs, but Louise Levers had also got her just desserts. The bully was gone.

Halfway to the car park, I remembered something and stopped. "My God, Pauline, what about your car?"

"Oh, that. John picked it up this morning." She grinned mischievously. "He's offered to fix it for free. But he wants me to sell it. Thinks it's too dangerous ...or I'm too dangerous. And you'll never guess what?"

"What?"

"He's already got a buyer who's willing to pay another hundred pounds more than I paid for it in the first place."

I stared at Pauline and shook my head. Then I stepped closer to her and began sniffing.

"What? Why are you sniffing me? I don't smell of manure anymore."

"No, I know." I responded. "But you do smell of roses."

4

TRICKY DICKY

July 1974

"Och, I heard all about yooo two with Tricky Dicky in Glasgee." Janet, the Glaswegian approached us in the crew room as Felicity and I were sitting waiting for transport to our aircraft. Janet was shaking her head and giggling.

Uh-oh, I thought, glancing at my partner-in-crime for her reaction.

"What exactly did you hear?" Felicity asked, obviously dreading what version of the now infamous "ice cube incident" had spread around the airline.

The real story would take too long. Did I even want to repeat it?

"Transport!" our number one yelled giving us our cue to leave.

"So whawt re-e-elly happened?" Janet persisted, "Did a nude Tricky Dicky rre-e-e-eelly chase you up and doon the corridor?"

As Felicity and I got up to move toward the airside door, I teased her in her own brogue, "Och, Janet, let's just say it was a very tricky situation ...and it's prawbably best if I never tell."

The "Ice Cube" incident had happened in football season when it was our lovely duty to fly eighty-nine mostly male football supporters from Gatwick and deposit them drunk-as-skunks at Munich Airport. For the return, we collected another already inebriated mob of Scottish football fanatics and flew them into their home base, Glasgow, where we would night-stop. There we always enjoyed a fun evening at the Novotel with several other crews who were doing the same route. The following day we would repeat the flight, taking another load of Glaswegians to

Munich, collect more English hooligans and return them to Gatwick. On landing at our home base, it wasn't unusual for a passenger, roused out of his drunken stupor, to ask, "Where am I?" When he was told, "Gatwick Airport," he would frown and say, "But I drove to Munich!"

On this particular inbound Munich to Glasgow sector—just a one and half-hour flight—the rollicking supporters had already made the cabin look as if Hurricane MacTavish had blown through, leaving a tidal wave of food and beer can debris over and under seats.

During the drinks service, the question, "What would you like to drink, sir?" was met with either a "Gimme a beer an' a whisky chaser, eh?" or what sounded like "ahuh, ahah ahug ahau ahuh, eh?" So, we gave up asking and simply handed over a lager and a miniature Johnny Walker. The passengers either nodded and made a strange grunting noise of approval or got really excited and began gesticulating at the drinks cart, speaking other unintelligible words.

We were in the middle of the cabin and Felicity was working the forward end of the cart when one young man, a mop of curly black hair topping his tall, lean frame loomed behind her. His black leather jacket sleeves were pulled up revealing ominous tattoos, his blue jeans were smeared with paint. Apparently, he needed to get to the rear loo, but quickly. No doubt the copious beers and whiskies were having their effect.

"Ahuh aher ahuh ahoo," he grunted at Felicity.

She turned to stare at him, a blank expression on her face and a hint of disgust in her body language.

He waved his hairy, red and black marked arm at her, gesticulating towards the rear.

"Yes," she responded impatiently, "I know you want to get through, but can you please just wait a few minutes, sir? We just need to..." I'm sure Felicity was going to say, "...finish serving this row," but he didn't want to wait.

"Ahu ahoo ahuh aha fuckin' way!"

His last two words, of course, didn't require translation.

"*Wh-wh-what* did you say?" Felicity's already shrill voice rose in pitch. Fortunately, she was tall and could almost look him in the eye, but Glasgow was the crime city of the UK and some Glaswegians were famous for—if you didn't agree with them—slashing your cheek or cracking a broken bottle over your "heed."

"It's okay," I began, afraid for her safety and pulling the cart farther down the aisle to let him through.

But Felicity, who was now red in the face, was not going to let him off.

"*Wh-wh-what* did you say?" she asked again. Normally she had a great sense of humour, but not today. Not with this man. "Did you just tell me to get out of the fucking way?" she asked, adopting her haughtiest-do-you-know-I've-got-a-cousin-who-goes-hunting-with-Prince-Charles voice.

"Ahee ahu," he answered, nodding. For a moment, his face was so close to hers I thought he might give her a head butt.

"Well, *you* can just fuck awff then, cahn't you? And now," she said, "you'll have to wait twice as long. How do you like that, sonny Jim?" She swivelled around, leaned over and asked the passenger in the next row in her very Oxford-English voice, "Would you like something to drink, sir?"

I waited anxiously to see what potential-head-butter would do. To my surprise, his face suddenly broke into a huge grin and he burst out laughing.

"Ach, you're a wee spitfire, aren't' yer? Mebbe you should marry me, hen?"

So, he *could* speak English after all! Or a version of it anyway.

"Not if you were the last man on God's earth," Felicity told him dismissively. But she smiled then and signalled for me to pull the trolley out of the way.

While he was squeezing his hips between seats and drinks cart, he responded "Ach, hen, aher aha her." Although he had reverted to his

Scottish dialect, I translated his response to mean, "You don't know what you're missing." Felicity and I exchanged a rolling-of-the-eyes look.

"God, I can't wait till this flight is over," I said, believing that our challenges would be done for the day. But as the night unfolded, we would find out I was oh-so-wrong.

Once we arrived at our hotel and had changed into our civvies, it was dinner time. Too exhausted to go out of the hotel for our meal, the five crew members—Dick Roberts, Christopher Wolsesley, Marion Albright, Felicity and I—agreed that we would eat at the hotel restaurant. Afterwards Captain Roberts invited us all to his room 323 for drinks.

"Two more of our crews are coming in tonight," Felicity told me as we set off to collect some ice. "Janet Pearson and her *secret* boyfriend are on one of them."

"Do you think she knows that absolutely everybody knows about their *secret* affair?" I wondered aloud.

Felicity shrugged.

As we stepped into the lift descending to the second floor and the ice machine, I sighed. "God, I hope Christopher doesn't come on to me again," I said, referring to our first officer. "He was grabbing at me in the galley again today, offering to show me his knobs and switches."

"But I don't understand why you're not attracted to him, darlin'?" Felicity tittered into her hand. "He's *so* sexy in his Hawaiian shirt, safari shorts and sandals. And he simply *can't* resist *you*. You're just a little *femme fattle*, aren't you?"

I smiled at Felicity's Franglais version of *femme fatale*. "Oh, he's after everyone."

She nodded. "But he does crack me up when he makes his PAs." She adopted Christopher's deep voice, "'Ladies and Gentlemen ...er ...good ...er ...morning. We are now flying over ...er ...er ...oh yes, the Alps ...at a height of ...er ...er...'"

I laughed. Normally passengers just ignored flight deck PAs, but when Christopher did his, nervous passengers began peering out of the windows and praying.

"He's a knob," she said as the lift doors opened, "and you turn him on, but I think he's harmless."

"I wish I could switch *him* off. But you're right. He's too ridiculous to be dangerous." I followed her down the corridor. "But what about Dick Roberts? There's something I don't trust about him, and I can't put my finger on it."

"Tricky Dicky? Not sure." Felicity shrugged as ice tumbled noisily from the machine into our plastic bucket. "He's good-looking in a moody kind of way. I know he likes his drink."

By the time we returned to Dick's room, both men were seated like kings in the armchairs while Marion had found a stool to sit on. Felicity and I poured drinks into our plastic tooth mugs and plonked ourselves on the edge of the double bed positioned against the wall.

Once we had got the latest airline rumours and stories out of the way, Marion got up. "Sorry, everyone. I'm really tired," she said and downed the rest of her cocktail. "I'm going to me bed."

"Oh, just stay for one more," I urged, sensing something ominous might happen if our very grounded Welsh number one left the room. But Marion excused herself and left.

With just the four of us, something in the atmosphere instantly changed. Maybe Felicity and I should also leave? But I didn't want to blatantly insult the two men.

"I've got an idea," I said cheerily. "Why don't we invite the other crews to join us?"

Captain Roberts stared at me, an unfathomable expression in his dark eyes. He watched while I picked up the white phone and asked reception for the room numbers of the other Dan Air crew.

Within five minutes, Janet Pearson, flounced into the room followed by a slew of young hosties. From Janet's attire—a brushed cotton floor-length nightie and woolly socks—I wondered if she had dragged herself out of bed. With her cropped brown hair and big blue eyes, she emanated such a serene wholesomeness that she had always reminded me more of Julie Andrews from the *Sound of Music* rather than an air hostess. So, I was even more shocked to see her married boyfriend join her. Was he a member of her flight crew or were they not bothering to hide their relationship any longer? At least *he* was wearing clothes. As a training captain, I supposed, he was required to show a modicum of decorum, extra-marital affair or not.

Christopher stood and offered Janet his chair.

"Oh my God, you wouldn't believe what happened on our flight yesterday!" she announced to the room. Once she knew we were all settled and ready to listen, she began. "So, there we were on the Comet with a full load of Scottish hooligans, and we've started the descent into Gatwick. We're about 3,000 feet off the ground, so not too-oo far away from landing when these drunken louts at the overwing decided they needed some fresh air so they..."

A hush descended on the room as Janet leaned forward.

"...removed the two overwing emergency exits!"

"*Wha-a-a-t!*" everyone cried in unison.

Janet sat back in her chair. "Exactly!" She raised her hands, in a what-are-you-going-to-do gesture. "They pulled both hatches inwards, but thank God, they didn't jettison them! That would have been one helluva flight report, two Comet doors landing on the A23!"

"What were they thinking?" I envisioned the men in their drunken exuberance—even on the descent the aircraft still flying at about 250 miles per hour—sticking their heads out of the plane and throwing up ...or just taking a nice deep breath or ...climbing out onto the wing.

"These Neanderthals don't *think*!" Janet retorted. "But let me tell you, it got very noisy." She laughed. "At that speed, the wind was *howling* inside the aircraft. All the debris in the cabin was flying about. People were screaming, probably convinced they were going to be sucked out, or that the rumours were true and all Dan Air planes crashed so they believed they were on their way to meet their maker."

"What did you do?" a hostess from the other crew asked.

"We put the doors back in and calmed the passengers." Janet shook her head again. "But those things are bloody heavy. Haven't lifted one since emergency training."

"Did you have them arrested?" Felicity asked.

"God, yes! But the police show up automatically for the football flights now and take them away in handcuffs. Somebody always needs to be arrested for *something*. Just two days before that we had an even worse incident."

Felicity took the bait. "What happened?"

"Oh, we had to get the crash axe out for this one." Janet smiled and indicated with a familiar gesture to her boyfriend—who we weren't supposed to know was her boyfriend—that she needed a refill. "Going into Glasgow, this man took off all his clothes and was running up and down the cabin naked, flashing the purple veins on his balls."

Maybe Janet wasn't like Julie Andrews after all, I thought. The girls in the room gave a collective gasp. Dick and Christopher just smirked.

"*No-o-o.*" It was my turn to be horrified "What did you do?"

"We all ran into the galley. I got the crash axe out of the flight deck and waved it at him from behind the galley curtain. I threatened that if he came anywhere near us or the flight deck, that I wouldn't hesitate to use it ...on a certain part of his anatomy. He ended up just sitting down and ranting to himself. He got arrested, of course, but the police came on board and made him put his troosers back on before they clamped him in handcuffs."

More people suddenly spilled into the room, and there was a cacophony of voices as crews greeted each other and poured drinks. Meanwhile, weariness and the soporific effect of my two whisky and cokes were beginning to make me drowsy. I sat back on the bed and leaned against the wall to watch the others socialize, then surrendering to my habit of what Felicity called my *doing a Natasha,* I curled up quietly in the corner and closed my eyes.

Playful screams erupted in the room. I opened my eyes. Felicity had returned with another bucket bulging with ice, and cubes were flying through the air as people threw them at each other. I saw Dick toss an ice cube at Felicity, which landed in the vee of her blue shirt. She screamed as the cold water trickled down her front and a dark blotch spread between her boobs.

"Roight then," she said, grabbing a handful of cubes and pushing them down the front of Dick's white cotton shirt.

He gasped with the shock of cold. "Look what you've done!" he exclaimed, grinning, pointing to a large wet stain on his broad chest.

A few of the later-arriving crew backed to the edges of the room. Felicity and Dick seemed to be the only participants in this game now. He grabbed her by the arm and wrestled her onto the bed. Through my weary haze, I saw that he was attempting to tuck some ice cubes behind her shirt collar and down her back. All in good fun, it seemed. Felicity was kicking her legs in the air, her inimitable high-pitched laugh slicing through everyone else's suddenly quieter conversations. I moved off the bed, not wanting to get in the way of their antics—or get hit by low-flying semi-melted ice.

Then, as if suddenly coming to his senses, Dick sat up and inspected his shirt. "Look what you've done!" He wasn't laughing now. His brown eyes were dark with anger.

The atmosphere suddenly changed, and I looked around. The room was empty! Probably sensing the drop in room temperature—and not just from the ice— everyone had quietly left, even Christopher. Felicity and I were the only ones left with Dick.

"Look what you've done to me," he barked again. "And the bed's all wet."

"Well, you've done it to me, too!" Felicity pointed at her own water-sodden shirt. She was still giggling.

"I'll have to get changed now." He stood abruptly and disappeared into his bathroom.

Felicity and I exchanged *uh-oh, we're-in-trouble-now* looks.

"We should leave," I whispered.

We got off the bed and moved towards the door just as Dick emerged from the bathroom, blocking our way. My friend and I stopped dead.

Tricky Dicky was naked except for the hotel's skimpy white bath towel around his lower body.

Oh no. We had heard about certain captains' changing-into-something-more-comfortable routines and letting-the-white-towel-accidentally-fall-to-the-floor trick.

I gulped.

He grabbed me and pulled me to him, his black chest hairs perilously close to my nostrils, his skin reeking of stale alcohol.

"You're not leaving, are you?" he purred in my ear, but his voice was edgy with anger.

"Yes," I said. "*So-o-o* sorry. We have to..." I pushed against his six-foot-two-inch frame, but he wasn't letting me go. I placed my hands on his even-hairier arms, attempting to disentangle myself.

Felicity, now standing on our left, said firmly, "Let her go!" He relaxed his grip slightly, but still held me around the waist.

She grabbed my arm. "C'mon." she said, pulling me out of his hold. "We should get to bed."

Once we were standing outside his room in the relative safety of the corridor, we both exhaled.

"What about *my* bed?" he growled.

We glanced back through the still open door. He was standing in the centre of the room, hands on hips, contemplating something, the white towel around his waist, the only barrier between us and a horrible memory. *Please God*, I thought, *don't let the towel drop.*

"It's all wet," he whined, waving an arm at the bed.

Felicity sighed, exasperated. "Okay," she responded, as if speaking to a four-year-old. "Why don't you have my room and I'll bunk up with Natasha? She has a spare bed. I'll move my things."

A fair offer, I thought. But he still stood there, mentally debating his next move and staring ...at me. Then he came out into the corridor, and once again, slid his arm around my waist, nudging me toward his room.

Felicity tugged at my arm and he finally released me. We ran down the shadowy corridor illuminated by faux Victorian street lanterns. Once we were safely inside 300, my room, we collapsed on the two single beds, laughing.

"Daft bugger!" Felicity said, reverting to her imitation of a west-country accent.

I giggled, releasing some of my own tension.

"What's 'is problem, I'd like ter know?" Felicity continued, sounding like Farmer Giles. "I offered 'im a dry bed, didn' I?"

"I don't think that's what 'e was after," I said in the same accent.

"No, 'e wanted you, my luv. I told you, you're a little *femme fattle*!"

"Why do I attract all the creepy ones? One minute he seemed to be having fun with you and the next he turned nasty. But," I added, "I don't trust him. You will sleep here in the other bed tonight, won't you?"

She nodded "Alroight, my luv."

A noise in the corridor made us both pause.

We listened. A raised voice, a woman, Scottish. Then a man's voice, muffled. And the voices were getting louder. They were coming from the direction of Dick's room. We looked at each other, frowning.

Felicity went over to the door and cracked it open. I watched as she peered down the long, carpeted hallway.

"What's going on?" I hissed.

She shook her head. And then we both heard, "What are yoooo doin' in the corridor without your troosers?" A woman's voice. Was she a Dan Air girl or just a poor hotel guest who had happened upon our deranged captain? "It's nae right, yoooo prancin' 'round the corridor in your knickers. You should get back in your rrroom and put your wee troosers on."

More indistinguishable words were spoken by the male.

"What's he saying?" I whispered.

Felicity peeked out. "He's standing there in the middle of the corridor in his knickers and yelling about his wet mattress." She paused to listen. "He wants to know where we are. He's demanding we come back and remake his bed 'cos it's cold and wet." She stepped back into my room. "I'm not sure, but I think he's become unhinged." She slumped down on the other bed. "Do you think I should go back and offer him my room key again?"

"We could," I said, feeling vaguely guilty, "but I don't like the idea of him sleeping next door to us."

We both paused, thinking.

"I know," I said. "We'll go down there together and give him your room key. But first, you get your things in here. And Felicity," I added, "please let's not go in the room. Just hand him the key and run."

A few minutes later we peeked down the dimmed hallway. All was silent.

"Maybe he's gone to bed," I murmured, hopeful.

"Hmm?" Felicity said, pondering. "Doubt it. We better go and at least offer him the key."

Leaning into each other for protection, we crept toward room 323. His door was closed. We breathed a sigh of relief and turned to scurry back to our own rooms.

"What are you two up to?" Tricky Dicky's voice boomed from behind us. Both of us dreaded turning to perhaps see our fearless leader in his knickers—or worse still, *not* in his knickers.

Felicity, the brave, took a deep breath and spun around. Then I did the same. My cheeks flushed with embarrassment, but Tricky Dicky seemed to be unabashed standing there in his white Y-fronts, advertising his family jewels.

"Er ...er ...we ...," Felicity stammered and then burst into a fit of giggles.

I couldn't help myself. Her laugh was infectious, and I began giggling too, and couldn't stop. Despite knowing that we would pay for this somehow, perhaps with our very jobs, the two of us fell into each other and couldn't stop laughing.

"This is *not* funny," he snapped. "How am I supposed to sleep on a sopping wet, cold bed?"

Between guffaws, Felicity held out her room key. "Here. I'm sorry," she offered, not an ounce of remorse in her voice. "Why don't you take my room?" She tried to sound more respectful. "I've cleared my things out. It's clean and dry."

Tricky Dicky surveyed the large key hanging from its wooden fob as if it was dripping with ectoplasm. "If you were *really* sorry, you would come in here and change the bedding!" he snapped. Then he leaned forward and grabbed my wrist. "Come on."

Felicity stopped laughing and grabbed my other arm. "She's not going anywhere with you," she told him.

Was I about to become the rope in a tug-of-war? Tricky Dicky and Felicity glared at each other for what seemed like an eternity. Then he released me, turned back into his room and slammed the door shut, the sound reverberating down the otherwise silent corridor.

Back in the sanctuary of 300, Felicity sighed. "Ah well, we tried. There's nothing else we can do."

As I fell asleep, I pushed away nightmare images of a naked Tricky Dicky chasing me doon the corridor without his troosers.

Why was that bell ringing? *Someone make it stop.* I opened my eyes. Where was I? A hotel room? But where? Oh yes, Glasgow. I sat up. The white phone next to the bed was making that obnoxious noise.

The long body in the other twin bed was still sleeping, a tousle of browny blonde hair just visible above the bedcovers. Felicity! The drama of the previous evening came gushing back. Tricky Dicky. As I picked up the phone, I noticed that the bright luminous green digits read 7:45 am. We weren't flying out until 2:00 p.m. Who would be calling us at this hour?

"Natasha?" Our number one's voice sounded uncharacteristically stern.

"Yes. Is that you, Marion?"

"We need to talk. Can you and Felicity meet me in the hotel restaurant as soon as possible?"

Uh-oh.

Marion was probably one of the most easygoing and funniest number ones in Dan Air, so I was a little disturbed by her dour tone.

"Oh ...okay. Yes, I'll wake up Felicity. We'll be down in half an hour."

"Make it snappy."

"Yes. We will."

Twenty-five minutes later, Felicity and I were sitting opposite Marion who was just finishing her toast. My stomach was doing cartwheels, so I rejected the breakfast menu and just ordered tea.

"Well," Marion began, "you probably know what this is about, don't you?"

I didn't like the way she looked straight at me. I hadn't participated in the ice cube fight. Mystified, I shook my head.

"Captain Roberts isn't very happy with you."

"Why?" I asked. What had I done, except maybe howl with laughter at him in his underwear?

"He told me that you invited two other crews to his room without his permission and then you all started," she said, tossing an accusatory glance at Felicity, "an ice fight."

"But" I protested, "Captain Roberts gave me permission to invite them." *Or had he?*

Marion held up her hand to stop me. "He has asked me to let you know that unless you apologize, he will take further action."

"*What?*" Felicity interjected. "Apologize for what? *He* was the one running up and down the corridor half-naked," she told Marion. "And what further action would that be anyway?"

Marion just looked at her as if to say, *do you really need to ask that question?*

I gulped as I really, really loved flying. Until the end of the summer, when the airline would decide whether we were worth keeping as permanent staff, Felicity and I, along with over a hundred and twenty other newly trained stewardesses were still under evaluation. If he chose to, Tricky Dicky could put something, anything, on our files and cause us to lose our jobs. His unjust accusation made me angry.

"No, I'm not going to apologize for something I didn't do," I said. He was being a bully and I wasn't going to stand for it.

"Are you sure?" Marion Albright asked, still in her calm voice. "I will have to go back to him and tell him that."

"But I *did* ask him if I could invite the other crews over. He was standing right there as he heard me call the front desk and get their room numbers. He would have objected if he didn't want me to. And then when Felicity brought the ice, he participated in the fight! What's his problem?"

Marion rolled her eyes as if she had dealt with this tedious situation a million times. "I think we all know what his problem is. I wasn't there, but I suspect he wants to make you pay because he didn't get his wicked way with you."

"Oh." So that was it.

"If I were you, Natasha," she added more softly, "I would just apologize to Captain Roberts and appease his wounded male ego so we can all get on with our day."

The thought of having to say "I'm sorry" for something I hadn't done had always irked me. Being number four in a family of five, my siblings had often blamed me for their misdemeanours. Maybe *I* was still pouting over childhood injustices. But Marion had a point. Give the man what he wants and let's get on with our day. After all, I did love my job.

"Okay," I said. The only way I could be at peace with this unfairness, I told myself, was to accept that I was dealing with a fifty-four-going-on-four-year-old captain. He was emotionally a child and would have to be treated as such.

"Thank god for that," Marion exclaimed, breaking into a smile. "I know it's not fair, but he can get very, very nasty. I think you're doing the smart thing, Natasha." She pushed her chair back. "I'll go and tell him. Wait here."

Felicity and I stared at each other. "I feel bad for you, little buddy," she said, touching my arm. "It should be me he's mad with for getting his bed wet."

I nodded, a little stunned. "But Marion's right. He didn't get his way, so he wants to punish me."

Marion returned quickly and sat back down at the table. "He said he would accept your apology."

"That's jolly decent of him," Felicity retorted.

"But he wants to hear it from you, Natasha," Marion said. "He's sitting in the lounge area."

I groaned as I got out of my chair. Felicity stood up.

"You stay here, Felicity. He only wants to see Natasha."

I felt sick, repulsed by his power games and afraid of being alone with him.

"But she's not safe...," Felicity began.

"Christopher's there with him," Marion said, as if the first officer's presence would be reassuring.

Great. I thought. *Two of them!* At least, in a public area, I should be physically safe.

When I entered the unoccupied lounge next to the hotel lobby, Tricky Dicky, his pipe in his mouth, and Christopher Wolsesley were sitting on a long low couch against a far wall. They both stared at me, awaiting my performance, as if I was about to audition for a play. What a farce!

While Captain Roberts remained smugly silent, I could see a vague twinkle in the first officer's eyes. Maybe he was thinking if *he'd* propositioned me in his knickers, I would not have turned *him* down!

I viewed the captain as I would a child. "I understand," I began, "that you would like me to apologize to you?" Disdain dripped from my voice.

"Do you think you need to apologize to me?" he asked imperiously, sucking on an unlit pipe.

No! But here we go. More games.

"Oh yes. Absolutely," I exclaimed. *Oops, perhaps that was a tad too sarcastic.*

"What for?" He sat up straight, switching his pipe to the other side of his mouth. This, I could see, was going to be like the Spanish Inquisition. *Off with 'er 'ead,* was probably coming next.

"Well," I began, a tad exasperated, "Marion told me ..."

"I don't care what Marion told you," he shouted, standing up and beginning to pace in front of the couch, his hands behind his back, holding the unlit pipe. He stopped pacing and angrily pointed the pipe at me. "What do you have to say for yourself?"

This man wasn't just a four-year-old, I realized, but a looney-tune. In the book *Airport* I had just finished reading, the writer described why and how captains frequently "lose it." Perhaps the author had met Tricky Dicky.

"I'm very sorry," I offered aloud. Not sure for what, but I am sorry. God. Let's just get this over with please. Christopher was trying to contain his mirth. *I'll rattle his knobs and switches one of these days,* I thought.

"You're *sorry?*" Tricky Dicky waved his pipe at me, screaming out the last word. "*Sorry!* That's just not good enough!" He began to pace again.

What did this man want? Oh yes, that's right. Well, he wasn't going to be getting any of *that!* And he knew it. Instead, he was going to make me suffer.

"What else can I say?" I pleaded. Exasperation was starting to wear me down. Though on the verge of tears, I refused to let this ogre see me upset. Christopher suddenly empathized with me and muttered something to his captain.

"Listen," I began. "I'm sorry I invited the other crews to your room though I was sure you had agreed to them coming. I'm sorry they got into an ice fight which soaked your bed..." And, I was so tempted to say, I'm sorry that I laughed at you in your knickers. I'm sorry I was so repulsed by you and indicated that even if you were the last man on

God's earth, I still wouldn't have nooky with you. "I'm very sorry, Captain Roberts," I added with as much sincerity as I could muster.

Addressing him with his title seemed to break his dark mood. He stopped pacing, sucked on his dry pipe and then sat down. For a few minutes, he leaned forward, scrutinizing me as if I was the errant child in the school principal's office.

"Very well then," he snapped.

I waited.

"You can go."

"Thank you." I exhaled, turned and went back to the restaurant.

I would still have to see him, I realized, on our return flight that afternoon. Maybe Marion would let me work in the cabin and not the galley, so my contact with him would be minimal.

When I re-entered the restaurant, Felicity and Marion looked up anxiously.

"How'd it go?" Marion asked.

I shook my head. For some reason, I felt sick with an unidentified shame. He had regained his power by chucking the humiliation back to my side of the net.

Game, set and match to Tricky Dicky.

As we boarded the aircraft later that day, the cockpit door was open. Tricky Dicky was standing just inside the flight deck, struggling with a piece of equipment on the bulkhead behind his jump seat. When I looked back again a minute later, I realized he had placed an oxygen mask on his face and was taking a few "whiffs." There was only one reason why he needed an intake of oxygen right before the flight. He had been drinking within the eight-hour pre-flight no drinking limit.

He caught me staring at him. Our eyes connected and there was instant understanding, the balance of power restored. He quickly closed the flight deck door.

In that brief moment, the full sad picture of who Tricky Dicky was fell into place. And I could only feel sorry for him. At the time, it never occurred to me that, for the sake of everyone's safety, I should have reported him. I had something on *him* now. For him to lose his job, and perhaps his license, would have been far more devastating. As we flew to Munich and then back to Gatwick, I prayed that we would make it. Perhaps for my own emotional and physical preservation—if it was possible—I could request never to fly with him again.

Tricky Dicky and I only had one more encounter. On that flight, he either pretended not to know me or—due to the death of many of his alcohol-soaked brain cells—he had completely forgotten the incident. He was, I reasoned, just like a fart in a teacup. When the hot air dissipates, there's nothing left but a bunch of dried-up old leaves.

5

RIGHT ON THE NOSE

"Do you want to go flyin'?"

Julia's Yorkshire accent on the other end of the line was unmistakeable. It was only nine o'clock in the morning and the sun was shining into my living room on this bright August day.

"Very funny!" I said. Although summer was coming to an end, Julia's boyfriend Adrian, who was in charge of Dan Air's crewing schedules, was still rostering us for 10 days-straight, duties including doubles and night-flights. We were all exhausted. The last thing I wanted to think about on my day off was flying, or Adrian.

"Ee, lass. I'm not jokin'. Adrian has got his PPL, but he needs to get in some flyin' hours for his commercial pilot's licence. He's offered to take us up in the Cessna over to some aerodrome near Stanstead to do some take-offs and landings. And then later, we're going to have a bit of a party back 'ere."

"Can Adrian really fly?" I had been so busy resenting Adrian for the way he lorded it over all of us using the power of his rostering to allow or void romances, parties or concert tickets, I had never envisioned him being anything else, especially a pilot.

"Aye, 'e is!" Julie responded, proudly.

Flying in a light aircraft might be fun for a change, I thought. At least, I wouldn't be serving teas and coffees. "Pauline's comin'," Julia added, as an extra incentive.

Our mutual friend always made me laugh. "Okay."

"We're taking off from Shoreham, so we'll pick you up in 'alf an hour. And you'll come to the party later?"

"Aye, 'appen," I teased. After spending a day flying in a Cessna with Adrian, I might need a cocktail or two or three.

"Are we doing the right thing?" I whispered to Pauline as we buckled up in the backseat while Adrian was busy with exterior checks of the Cessna 160.

"Gawd knows." Pauline giggled nervously. "But it's too late now."

Julia climbed into the front seat and buckled up. "Ee, you look like two frightened little rabbits. 'E's very good, you know," she said, proudly, foraging in her handbag for her compact. Even on her day off, Julia presented the perfect magazine ideal of an air hostess, constantly checking her make-up. "Ooo, I 'ate me bags," she said, holding up the small mirror to her face and poking at the grey patches beneath her eyes.

"What causes that anyway?" I asked. Even with layers of face powder, I had noticed that she couldn't disguise the almost black shadows.

"Me adenoids." She scrunched her face into a funny grimace. "I could get an operation to clear them up and get the bump in me nose removed, but it would cost 10,000 pounds. The National 'Ealth System won't cover cosmetic surgery."

It had always surprised us that Julia had not been snapped up by British Airways when she had applied there. With her long luxurious blonde hair perfectly quaffed into a chignon on top of her head, her regal posture and her immaculately manicured fingernails, she emanated the quintessential air hostess. But maybe BA didn't take her because when she opened her mouth and spoke in her broad Yorkshire accent the illusion of upper-class refinement was dispelled.

The other shocker about Julia was that in the very early days of her flying career she had fallen for Adrian. The sophisticated Julia could do so-o-o-o-o much better—or so we thought.

Now the couple were living in sin in an old but spacious terraced home in Horsham, not a mile away from me and we had to finally accept that Julia's adoration of Adrian must be the real deal. His charm escaped us, but as my mother often intoned, "There's no accounting for taste." Good thing for Adrian.

"All set?" he said as he climbed into the pilot's seat. He donned his headset, giving Pauline and me a cursory glance, then beaming at Julia. We felt that he only tolerated us because we were her friends.

I nudged Pauline and was tempted to cross myself, but I didn't want to taunt Adrian. My rosters might then be forever cursed. Pauline and I just exchanged looks of *What the hell are we doing?*

He turned on the ignition and the propellors started whirring.

"Here we go, ladies!" he said.

"Hey, who are you calling a lady?" Pauline joked, but he couldn't hear her through his headset and over instructions from the tower. He began to steer the light plane toward the runway ready for take-off.

The small plane, which after the solidity of a jet aircraft felt as fragile as balsa wood, bumped down the pitted runway. Adrian pulled back the stick and we were airborne. Beneath us, the patchwork of the Sussex countryside lay all around, and I exhaled. We were up. So far so good.

The loud drone of the single engine made it challenging to talk. Unlike cruising at higher altitudes in a jet where we mainly saw only cloud formations or clear blue sky, being able to see the scenery below felt more like real flying. Every now and then, Pauline and I just nudged each other and pointed to things we saw below. After a while, I relaxed and began to enjoy the flight.

Soon we were winging our way over central London, looking down on the Thames. With the sun shining on the water, it looked like a silver ribbon curving its way through the city. Big Ben, the Houses of Parliament and other landmarks were easy to spot from that height. Then I remembered, we weren't on any air traffic radar. London airspace, I knew was busy. I peered nervously around to see if any other aircraft were within spitting distance, but I only saw light cloud cover. After we left the city behind, we were once again flying over countryside. We must be over Essex now, I thought.

Adrian said something to Julia we couldn't hear. She turned around and shouted, "We'll be landing in about ten minutes."

Now that we were nearing our destination, I was beginning to change my impression of Adrian. He did seem to know what he was doing, after all. Perhaps he *would* make a good pilot.

As we began the descent, all I could see ahead was a flattened track of grass, at the end of which was a grey Nissen hut. Other light aircraft were parked, at odd angles around the building, as if the pilots had suddenly abandoned their planes and made a dash for what ...shelter, the bar? Then I realized, this was the airfield where we would be landing. I looked at Pauline. The worry in her eyes reflected mine. Oh my God, we were going to land on grass!

As we neared the ground, I could tell, even before Adrian put the stick forward—and even as a non-pilot—that something about his approach was not right. We were either going too fast, or we were too high to put the plane down, especially on this uneven surface. I felt a pain in my right arm. Pauline had clutched my wrist, her nails digging into my skin, her eyes wide with fear.

We were still at least four feet above the ground, when Adrian let the plane drop.

Bang!

Julia screamed.

"Oh, no!" Pauline cried and clung to me. "We're all going to *di-i-e*!"

My teeth rattled in my head, and my back felt the massive jolt. I grabbed Pauline's other hand and we hung on to each other. She's right, I thought. We're going to die.

We waited for the undercarriage to collapse under the impact ...but instead we were bouncing up and down, up and down, tilting this way and then the other. Would we keel over?

Adrian cursed and pulled the stick up again.

The plane lifted and righted itself.

Oh no! He was going to try again. Julia covered her face.

The Nissen building wasn't far away now. Oh God! We were going to end up diving nose first into it, killing us and whoever was in there!

Pauline whimpered, "I want my Mummy!" half-joking, half-terrified. She and I huddled into each other, my head on her shoulder, her head on mine. We scrunched our eyes shut, not wanting to see what was coming.

Silence ...then bang again onto the unforgiving ground. *Ugh*! So, this is what a crash feels like, I thought. Even if we don't die today, my teeth are going to embed themselves in the top of my brain.

Then the plane lifted yet again, this time not so high and tilted to the left.

"No! Please God, No!" Pauline cried.

Silence.

I opened my eyes and peeked ahead, afraid of what I would see.

The Nissen hut and its rounded corrugated iron roof was less than fifty feet away. I held my breath.

The plane was hovering just above the grass. Adrian let it drop to the ground again and, this time the bang was not so harsh. This time, the plane clung to the ground and bumped and jostled along the grass. Then the plane stopped. Just ten feet away from the door of the Nissen hut, we came to a standstill. Adrian switched off the ignition.

We all sat immobile, not moving an inch. I exhaled.

"Sorry about that girls!" Adrian said cheerily, removing his headset. "I misjudged it slightly. It's always tougher landing on grass."

"Bluddy 'ell," Julia muttered.

Pauline and I could not speak.

"Why don't you go and have a drink while I check the plane?" he said, pointing to the hut.

"Th-that's a bar?" Julia asked.

"Oh, thank God," Pauline finally spoke. We unlatched from each other and fumbled with our seatbelts. My fingers, I noticed, were shaking.

"Well, at least it's not far to get a drink," I said, as I tumbled out of the plane, so grateful for terra firma. "My legs are really wobbly."

"Ee, I thought I was about to meet me maker and land *in* the bar," Julia added.

"I would get down and kiss the ground," Pauline smiled, "but I don't want Adrian to know I was that scared."

As we entered the bar, we were surprised to see so many tables occupied at lunchtime. The patrons all turned to look at us. What were they thinking? Why did we look so pale? How lucky we were to still be alive? Or would we be crazy enough to get back in that plane with that unseasoned pilot and fly home? Because, I realized, that's what we would have to do.

We found an available round metal table, the metal beaten, probably salvaged from some WW II aircraft. In shocked silence, we chugged down double brandies.

"Bluddy 'ell," Julia said again, still in shock. Pauline and I exchanged looks. We did not want to criticize Adrian's lack of landing skills too much. After all, as much as we didn't like him, he was our friend's boyfriend. We would let her do the lambasting. "Ee, I don't know about you," Julia finally spoke. "But I don't bluddy well want to get back in that thing!"

Pauline and I exhaled, relieved she felt the same. "Neither do we!"

There was another silence as we contemplated our options. Here we were, out in the middle of the Essex countryside, not even sure where, so how else could we get home if not in that deathtrap? Julia and Adrian were hosting a party tonight. The reality of the situation sank in. Whether we liked it or not, we would have to get back in that plane with Adrian as the pilot.

"Want another drink?" I offered.

Both women nodded.

"If I'm going to die today," Pauline muttered, "I don't want to feel a thing."

"It'll be better landing at Shoreham," Julie said, as I stood to go to the bar.

"Why's that?" Pauline asked.

"Because it's a paved runway," she replied, not really convinced of her own reasoning.

As I stood waiting for three more large brandies to be poured, I wondered. If we land like that on concrete, it's going to hurt a helluva lot more than grass.

By the time Adrian entered the bar, we were on our third brandy and unrestrained giggly hysteria had sent in. Everything Adrian told us—that the undercarriage had not been damaged, that he had refuelled the aircraft and that he had another engineer give the plane a good overall check—we found hilariously funny. To his credit, rather than being annoyed or impatient, he seemed to forgive our silliness. I'm sure he knew that he could have killed his first passengers.

"Time to go, ladies," he said, helping Julia stand up.

Slightly sozzled, and as numb as if we were climbing into our own coffins, we fell, still giggly and with suppressed terror, back into the plane. Through my tipsiness it occurred to me that Adrian's sober demeanor was not only because he hadn't imbibed any alcohol, but that he had also scared himself. If he had lost confidence, would he be able to execute a safe landing at Shoreham?

The flight back seemed to take an eternity. The effect of the alcohol had now worn off, the giggling had ceased, and we all sat in stupefied silence, each with our own thoughts of whether we would come out of this adventure alive.

But Julia was right. The landing at Shoreham was much, much better, even smooth. Adrian had redeemed himself ...somewhat.

As the couple dropped off first Pauline and then me at my home, I said, "Er, thank you for ...an exciting day. See you later. I can't wait to see your renovations."

The dusky summer evening was still warm when I arrived at Julia and Adrian's older terraced home. Julia was standing, at the kitchen counter, chopping vegetables, a flowered frilly apron looking incongruous over her Chanel-like cream dress, while Adrian was outside talking to a collection of guests.

I waved my bottle of brandy at her. "Where do you want this?" I asked.

"Just dump it in't punch," she said, then gave me an inquisitive look. "Natasha, 'ave you recovered from today?"

"Oh, aye," I smiled, mimicking her accent. "It were a grand adventure, but I do 'ave to tell ee, I thought we were going to land nose first into that bar!"

She smiled. "Aye, we might've all done face plants and got rearranged faces. Me, I wouldn't mind a new nose." She paused and said more seriously. "Adrian did feel bad, yer know, that 'e scared us all like that."

"Well, he owes us some good night-stops then, doesn't he?"

"Aye, 'appen," She smiled sardonically and carried on peeling and chopping.

The crystal bowl on the table was already half-full, the colour of the punch looking a little dubious. But I did as I was bidden and added the brandy, wondering which spirits were already in the murky fruit-laden concoction.

"I like the renovations," I commented, looking around the kitchen.

Julia rolled her eyes. "It were a lot o' bluddy work, but I'm glad you like it."

Instead of the old sash windows, there were now French doors leading to the patio. A brand-new gleaming white sink, a massive fridge and a snazzy-looking oven adorned the back wall with a door in the corner leading somewhere.

"What's that?" I asked. "A larder?"

Julia frowned. "No, chuck, it's a downstairs loo."

"Nice. And the room's much lighter," I said. But I noticed how the large slate flagstones covering the floor were still uneven, and a tad dangerous. "Are they meant to be like that?"

"Ooh, yes. Me, I didn't want them. Too bluddy cold, but Adrian insisted." She waved a carrot she was peeling at me and said in her posh accent, "It's very trendy, don't you know."

Other members of the flying fraternity were already gathered outside. I stepped onto the dimly lit patio, nearly spilling my glass of punch as my heels caught in more uneven stones. Hosties, members of crewing, customs staff, ramp agents and some flight deck crew were clustered in small groups exchanging their latest flying dramas. Pauline was lamenting the most recent gross injustices of crewing loud enough for them— as they were standing right behind her—to hear. I joined her, but when they moved away, I asked. "How are you feeling after today's little event?"

"Bloody lucky to be alive!" she whispered, looking around, to make sure that Adrian wouldn't hear. "But you have to give it to him. If that had been me, I would never have wanted to pilot another plane. And we *were* the worst passengers."

"Yes, I saw another side of him today. Maybe he's not so bad after all."

When the air cooled and the dark night crowded in, the party moved inside. The guests—oblivious to the combination of hard spirits in the punch—were now on their second or third glass. No one appeared to be feeling any pain ...yet.

To a kitchen now packed with people, a slurring Julia broadcast to a quasi-drunken audience that she was going to the loo. People turned, shrugged and went back to telling jokes and relating airline fiascos. She then disappeared into what I had first thought was the larder, slamming the door behind her.

Suddenly from inside there was *a thunk, thunk* sound and a small scream. People stopped talking as we all glanced toward the loo door and frowned.

Adrian, who had been leaning against the sink, was the first to be alarmed. He went over. "Julia!" He knocked. "Are you okay?" he shouted through the door.

Another thump, then a muffled grunt came from inside.

"Open the door!" he called, concerned and rattling the handle. A hush descended over the kitchen. Everyone gazed at the door and waited.

"Julia! Julia! Open the door!" Adrian called authoritatively although we could hear a trace of panic in his voice.

We waited.

A clicking noise broke the silence. The door opened very slowly.

Julia emerged with both hands covering her face. Blood was dripping through her fingers. She was making a snorting noise. Was she crying or giggling?

"Oh God." Adrian gently pulled her toward the kitchen sink. He rummaged through a drawer and found a clean towel. "Put your head back," he instructed.

But Julia's head lolled forward, and she pushed Adrian and his towel away, protesting. "Ooo, ai'm all right, Adrian." Her voice sounded garbled, and her hands still covered her nose. "Don't make such a fuss." Stark red blood now splashed down onto her creamy white dress.

As he placed the towel firmly over her nose again, I was surprised by his tenderness.

Weakly attempting to fight Adrian off, she said, "I just tripped on't flagstone and banged me nose on't sink."

While he ministered to her, two of his friends stepped up and stood on either side of Julia, supporting her as she teetered back and forth between them.

"Let me look," Adrian said, prying her hands away from her face.

I gasped as I saw more blood and how Julia's nose was swollen into a distorted shape.

"Oh God!" he groaned. "I'm taking you to the hospital."

Assisted by one of his friends, Adrian led the still protesting and very drunk Julia out of the kitchen.

The buzz of conversation immediately started up again as if nothing had happened and the party went on into the night, though the drinking slowed, and we all treated the flag stone floor with a little more respect.

The next time I flew with Julia was two weeks after the party. Something was different about her face. I couldn't place it at first. When I looked closer, I saw that her nose was changed ...smaller, somehow. I finally realized the bump was gone, and the grey bags had completely disappeared from under her eyes. She appeared even more the perfect stewardess.

"You look...," I began. How should I say it...? "Good, really good."

Julia smiled, somewhat abashed.

"What happened at the party exactly?" I asked. "Last time I saw you, you looked like a vampire losing her life force."

"E-e-e, lass." She wagged a finger at me. "I was very, very naughty. I 'ad a we-e-e bit too much to drink and tripped on a stone in 't loo. Then the sink came up from nowhere and hit me right on the nose."

"Those bloody sinks. Always jumping out at you."

"Ooh, I know."

"Did it hurt? It looked really painful."

"Nah." She grinned, ruefully. "With all that wicked punch inside me, I didn't feel a thing. But ..." She grinned, smugly. "I did save meself 10,000 quid."

"How?"

"Well, I broke me nose, so when they put it back together, they fixed it and I got a free nose job! Some'ow it took care of the other problem, too. Me adenoids. Look." She pointed to beneath her eyes. "No more bags."

"Less painful than a plane crash then, to get your face rearranged."

"Aye, 'appen," she nodded, remembering our day.

"So it just goes to show, doesn't it?" I said.

"What's that?"

"It pays to drink."

"E-e-e, ba gum, lass." She nodded, grinning. "You hit it right on the nose."

6

NEAR MISSES

November 1974

In the early evening of Tuesday, 4th November 1974, sleety rain was slashing against my living room windows, the sound of it making me shiver. It was the proverbial dark and stormy night, and I was on night standby which meant from 7:00 that night to 7:00 the next morning, they—the infamous crewing department—could call me out for a flight. At just ten past six, I was warm and cozy in my home, preparing my dinner and watching the evening news when the phone rang.

Not knowing who it was—my boyfriend, Julian, my psycho mother, crewing, or a friend—I gambled and picked up the phone. Too late, I realized that there were still 40 minutes before I was officially on standby.

"Miss Rosewood?"

Uh-oh.

The familiar grating voice of a young lad in Dan Air crewing was the first clue to my immediate future.

Tricky bastards! Why didn't I wait until seven? My only question would be where and when they were sending me? Groaning inwardly, I droned, "Yes?"

"We would like you to do a Stuttgart."

Would you now? Stuttgart. But I'm so comfy, and now you want me to go out into the cold, dark night.

"Departing 2100 hours," he was saying. "Flight number 5748." As if sensing an imminent argument, he added, "We need a German speaker."

Resigned, I muttered, "Okay. I'll be there."

One hour later, I was waiting in an empty, cold crew room when Ursula arrived. Not only was she the number one, she was also German. Crewing had lied. Two language speakers were unnecessary.

Anita and Elaine, the other two stewardesses entered the crew room and the four of us soon exited airside. As we walked toward the Comet, yellow lights from the terminal shimmered on the black, shiny, wet tarmac, highlighting the sleety rain that was still falling at a 45-degree angle. The plane was like an ominous black bird sitting there. I shivered —but not because of the cold. Something didn't feel right.

A total of four stewardesses and three flight deck—or fright deck as we liked to call them—had been called out for the Stuttgart. Being a tad superstitious, I was never comfortable when crews were pulled together at the last minute for ad hoc flights. There was something fatalistic about it ...as if the Universe had some dastardly plot afoot.

"Qvasi Modo iss our captain," Ursula announced as we entered the cabin.

"At least he's fun," I commented, unlike some other captains I had come to know in my time with Dan Air who could be lascivious, mean, neurotic or too superior to fraternize with us "girls."

Captain Jack Kendrick, was a short dark-haired, bearded man from South Africa with a slight hump at the top of his spine, probably caused by a bad case of scoliosis. His sense of humor, however, combined with his professionalism inspired respect in many crew members, myself included.

The Comet had just landed, and cleaners were already aboard so the cabin was still luxuriously warm from the previous flight. Once preparation for the imminent 119 homeward-bound Germans began, I went into robotic mode, carrying out my designated pre-flight duties.

One hour later, I was droning *"Guten Abend. Guten Abend. Guten Abend,"* as passengers ducked through the forward door into the galley.

"Gut'n Abig," some responded, in their local Schwabish dialect, peering around the shadowy galley and then entering the lit cabin.

As we taxied, the galley slave for this flight, Anita, and I were seated on the forward jump seat. We listened to the captain's South African accent as he made his pre-take-off PA. "I wonder if he knows we call him Quasimodo," I asked her.

Anita shrugged. "It's better than calling him the Hunchback of Notre Dame."

Isn't that the same person, I wondered. Flight crew could be scathingly cruel sometimes.

The aircraft accelerated down the runway and lurched into the air. With the number four, Elaine, by her side, Ursula sat at the back of the plane on the rear jump seat wearing the mandatory headset. As part of her number one duty and emergency procedures, she listened to ground control, air traffic control and dialogue between the captain and first officer as they took off and recited their post take-off checklists.

At the front, Anita and I paid attention to the routinely changing tones of the engines as the Comet climbed higher and higher. I exhaled. Everything sounded normal.

In the 1 hour 45-minute flying time, we served drinks, miniature sandwiches, two teas and coffees and offered sales of duty-free items. On this night, despite the inclement weather, there was no turbulence. All passengers—mostly mature middle-class Germans returning from vacation—appeared content.

For landing, in the unlikely event of an emergency and needing to facilitate a hasty exit, the curtain separating the galley and cabin was pulled back and secured so—from our jump seat—we could see the first few rows of passengers in the dimmed cabin.

The plane landed softly.

And then it happened.

Or rather, it *didn't* happen.

I looked at Anita and frowned.

Why was there no reverse thrust?

Normally braking was applied as soon as the aircraft touched down. But not now. The plane was careening at full speed of approximately 175 mph down the runway. Stuttgart wasn't a major airport, so I knew this airstrip wasn't long enough to allow a runaway plane. I envisioned the racing Comet ploughing into the terminal's glass windows.

We still weren't braking.

Something was wrong. Very wrong.

As if hearing my thoughts, a loud roar and whining sounded outside the aircraft. All brakes were suddenly applied at once; reverse thrust, flaps, ailerons. Like one of those Tom and Gerry cartoons where the cat comes to a screeching halt and his bum sticks up in the air, the Comet felt as if it might also go ass-over-teakettle.

I automatically put my head between my knees and covered my head with my hands—the brace position—or as we call it, kissing your ass goodbye.

Around us, there were bangs and thuds as metal oven doors flew open and crashed down onto stainless steel counter tops, coffee pots clanged against each other in their stowages, cupboard doors swung wide spilling loosened coffee grounds and tea bags onto the already grimy galley floor.

I told my knees this is it! We are going to collide with another aircraft on the runway. We are going to die in a ball of fire. No-o-o!

I clenched my whole body and waited ...and waited for the inevitable crash.

Everything went quiet. An eerie hush descended over the plane. The hush seemed to go on and on. Had we died and didn't know it? Tentatively I opened my eyes, uncurled myself from my brace position and looked to my colleague. We both frowned, waiting, confused. The plane was still moving, just not as fast.

I peered into the cabin. Passengers in the front row were white knuckling their armrests, clutching each other, eyes wide with alarm.

Their expressions mirrored my thought. *Bloody hell!* What was that? Or as these Germans might say, *Gottfriedstutznochmal! Was ist los?*

Anita and I unfastened seat belts and stood, allowing the jump seat to snap back into its flush position against the galley bulkhead. Before passengers would trudge through the mess, Anita hurriedly scooped up the coffee grains as best she could while I closed cupboard doors and righted fallen coffee pots. Through the galley opening, I could see Ursula making her way down the cabin, hanging onto the hat rack, her thick red hair piled high accentuating her now ashen complexion.

She burst into the galley. "*Mein Gott!*" she hissed. "Zat voss too close!"

"What happened?" I asked. Through the headset, she would have heard the cockpit's conversation on landing.

Without answering, she pushed me out of the way and snatched up the handset to make her landing PA before the aircraft came to a final rest.

Normally passengers couldn't wait to disembark, but this night they just sat, stunned. Then on hearing Ursula's instructions, they snapped out of their daze, unlocked their seat belts and stood to retrieve their belongings.

I beckoned to the first row of now-standing passengers to come toward the front exit. But they just stood there, as if still confused, uncertain what to do. I pointed again to the galley door. "*Moechten Sie hinausteigen?*" Would you like to disembark?

"*Ach, vielen Dank.*" Thank you, many said grateful for instructions. They finally exited, ducking their heads as they left.

"*Schoene Landung.*" Nice landing, others commented, perhaps thinking that zooming down the runway at full tilt and then slamming on the brakes at the last minute was quite normal. Or were they being sarcastic?

"*Ja, Ja. Sehr schoene.*" I grinned and nodded, thinking that agreement was the best policy.

I couldn't wait to ask the captain *what the hell was that?*

When the last passenger was out of the door, I heaved a sigh of relief and went to sit in the first row of seats. Then Anita and Elaine joined me. Before beginning our usual routine of preparing the galley and cabin for return passengers, we all needed a few minutes. The flight deck crew were still huddled in the cockpit.

Ursula whooshed from the flight deck into the cabin, clutching her clipboard with her paperwork attached.

I started to stand, but she waved a hand. "Ssit!" she ordered. "Vee are not going anyvhere," she added and disappeared again down the back. "I haff to count ze bar."

What did this mean?

Captain Kendrick suddenly appeared, the hump in his slumped shoulders even more prominent, the colour of his face almost matching his white shirt—as if he had just seen his life flash before him. Was he trembling? And why was he wearing his jacket and coat?

"What happened?" I demanded, surprised by unbidden feelings of anger.

He shook his head. "You don't know how lucky you are to be alive," he muttered as if talking more to himself.

"Why?" I asked, not really wanting to know.

"Come and look."

He led the way out of the galley forward door onto the front steps. "See that?" he said, pointing at the tail.

I followed his gaze.

"Oh my god!" I was trying to absorb the implications of what I was seeing. I looked back at him.

His expression mirrored mine—disbelief and horror.

The tail plane illuminated by its own landing lights, was *dangling* from the plane's main fuselage by one metal strut.

I peered more closely. The triangular tail looked as if a giant frenzied can opener had attacked it. Large grey/black gouges distorted the red, white and blue airline logo, now mangled beyond recognition.

"But ...what ...don't you need a tail to steer the aircraft?" I asked Jack, incredulous.

"Yiss," he muttered, still in a state of shock, his native South African accent sounding even more nasal. "The tail plane is usually attached by three struts to the fuselage. The two top ones have ...snapped."

"How long has it been like that?"

"Could be since Gatwick," he responded dully. "It's a miracle ...we're all alive."

"But ...how could you take off without a rudder?" My meagre understanding of aerodynamics was that the tailplane was sort of crucial in the take-off process.

"Well, everything was normal at Gatwick ...and on take-off. It must have happened once we were on autopilot." His accent was getting stronger by the minute, his voice husky, breaking with emotion. He was probably in shock, thinking how, there but for the grace of God, 126 souls could all be dead now. "The first officer did the landing," he explained, "but then he told me he had no control. So, I took the plane, but I couldn't steer it either."

"I have control" is the usual message passed between pilots to confirm who is actually flying the plane. If the first officer had suddenly told the captain, "Take control," that meant he was physically unable to fly or his controls were inoperable.

"Fortunately," Jack continued, "there were no crosswinds tonight and he landed straight on the runway ...so thank god, there was no need for correction. I couldn't get any response from the rudder either, so we had to just let it roll. If we had braked, we risked needing the rudder and ..."

My God.

"...if there had been crosswinds, we would have gone awff the runway," he continued. "The wheels would have sunk into the grass, and we would have rolled over in a ball of fire."

Ball of fire. Gulp. Why did he have to give me *that* image?

"Needless to say," he said, shoving his hands in his pockets and hunching his shoulders against the cold night air, "we will be staying in Stuttgart for a few days."

A few days! But we don't have any civvies. Just our airline uniforms. Just yesterday, tired of carrying never-used spare knickers and emergency toiletries in my crew bag, I had removed them. Murphy's law!

Jack retreated into the aircraft. I followed. Ursula had just finished counting and sealing the bar at the rear and was at the front donning her coat and hat.

"Secure the aircraft well," the captain told her. "The plane could be here for a long time." He disappeared into the darkened flight deck where the subdued voices of the first officer and engineer could be heard in a serious discussion.

An hour later, the seven of us were sitting in a Bavarian-style restaurant in a Stuttgart hotel, our home for the next few days. Jack and his two crew had disposed of their epaulettes and appeared in white shirts and black trousers, while we simply showed up in our white blouses and blue tunics with coats slung over our shoulders. With not an airline badge in sight, we were still not sure that the other patrons believed our attire wasn't an airline uniform. We didn't care. We all needed a stiff drink.

Once our *wienerschnitzels* had arrived and we were on our second beverage, I asked Jack, "How long do you think we'll be here?"

"A while. All Comets are being grounded worldwide right now." He shrugged. "I think it's metal fatigue. If I'm right, it could happen to any other Comet with the same number of flying hours."

"Dan Dare"—famous for its cheap maintenance practices—had apparently hauled the ancient but graceful Comets out of a museum, declaring they still had a few more flying hours left in them. Maybe not.

"Didn't the ground engineer see anything amiss at Gatwick?" I ventured. Maybe it was a silly question. How could anyone have seen anything in the black rainy night?

The captain frowned, gave a half-hearted shrug and glanced briefly at the flight engineer. "It's difficult sometimes," he said, then focussed on cutting his veal. "There will have to be an investigation. These planes are old."

What was he not telling us? We all knew that any extra time on the tarmac cost the airline thousands of pounds in airport fees. A lot of pressure was placed by the airline management on cockpit crew to take off punctually, even sometimes with technical problems. As if flight deck crew didn't have enough to worry about.

"We are so bloody lucky there were no cross-winds tonight," David, the first officer finally spoke, shaking his head, still not able to believe his luck. "If there had been, we would have been ketchup on the runway."

As if on cue, a bosomy waitress appeared in her dirndl. "*Moechten Sie noch was trinken?*"

"Is anyone going to have another drink?" I asked.

They all nodded.

For our three-day unexpected stay in Stuttgart, the airline oh-so-generously splurged for each crew member to purchase one toothbrush and one extra pair of underwear.

"That's outrageous!" Anita grumbled. "If we were working for British Airways, we would have been given a whole set of civvies and toiletries."

"Oh, I kno-o-o-w," I responded, launching into my mock gossipy tone. "But don't get your one pair of knickers in a twist. It could have been much worse. We could have been burned to a crisp and not needed *any* clothes."

To confirm my point, the following day we heard that fierce crosswinds had begun to howl across Europe. As Monty Pythons would have declared, "We were lucky."

Anita did have a point, though. Our uniforms, which we wore from Tuesday until Friday—despite handwashing our blouses—weren't very fresh by the time we boarded our flight back to England.

As the captain had predicted, we didn't fly home on our Comet, nor with the flight deck crew. They were ordered to stay with the aircraft in Stuttgart while the whole tail mechanism was inspected, x-rayed and repaired. They also had to write copious reports for the CAA inquest that would follow.

On Friday evening, with ferocious crosswinds still howling across the continent, we boarded a British Airways Trident to bring us back to Heathrow. Passengers surveyed us, frowning at our less than smart-looking Dan Air uniforms. Ursula sat next to me in the center of the cabin with Anita and Elaine in the row behind us. Despite the Tridents being much newer aircraft and BA having a good safety record, Ursula was twitchy.

As we began our descent, she grabbed for my hand. "I haff a bad feellink," she hissed, her eyes wide, peering through the windows at the mass of orange lights twinkling in the dark west London suburbs below.

Judging by the turbulence, the winds were still bordering on 75 mph as we neared the ground. The lower we descended, the more the Trident was buffeted up and down and from side to side. All four of us knew that with high crosswinds and to ensure a good landing—even with a full load—the pilot would have to "bang it down." We were sitting mid-cabin, right above the undercarriage and we would feel the worst of it. I sat back, tensing myself for the harsh impact.

And he did bang it down.

Reverse thrust was engaged.

Ursula and I exchanged smiles and exhaled.

Then another loud bang ...and another.

Ursula grabbed my hand again, her eyes wide with fear.

The aircraft lurched and lifted precariously to the right.

"*Aaagh!*" she cried, squeezing my hand even tighter.

People around us gasped, screamed and moaned.

The plane teetered back to the left.

More screams rippled through the cabin. White knucklers clung to armrests, passengers held onto friends and even strangers in seats next to them.

A hush descended in the cabin.

Everyone held their breath.

Twenty long seconds passed.

The Trident finally settled back to its center of gravity on the runway and continued at high speed. A rhythmic, double-thudding came from below.

Ursula and I exchanged frowns. "Burst tires!" we exclaimed in unison.

The plane eventually decelerated and taxied off the runway.

Ursula's nails had been embedded in my palm, but the pain didn't register until she released me, and I saw the tell-tail crescent marks in my hand.

"Zat iss two accidents!" Ursula exclaimed. "Do you sink zere's goink to be a ssird?"

She was reading my superstitious mind about plane incidents coming in threes. "I think this *is* my third," I told her, remembering my recent horrific bang-bang landing in Adrian's Cessna.

As we taxied, our British Airways hostess approached and informed us that we had to report to Heathrow operations for the details of our flight back to Gatwick on a light aircraft.

Ursula and I looked at each other.

"Zey must be jokink," she exclaimed.

She was right. Fly on a small plane? In these winds? Behind us, the two other hostesses chatted amiably between themselves, oblivious to our sense of foreboding.

Thirty minutes later, battling against gale force winds and clinging to our hats, we were led by a ramp officer across the tarmac to a waiting Cessna 175. To our horror the light plane was tipping from side to side in the howling gusts. Even as we climbed up the few little steps, the wind almost lifted the small plane off the ground. They can't be serious, I thought. This thing will never take off, or worse, be able to land.

We only half-listened to the Italian captain as he delivered his emergency briefing in the Cessna. "The emergency exit-a is in-a the aircraft-a ceiling." Ursula and I glanced at each other frowning. Should we get off right now? Or was this going to be her number three and my fourth incident? The fatal one.

The four of us clutched our bags, watching out of the window as the plane's wings visibly flexed in the wind as if the flimsy machine was antsy to lift free of its chocks.

Suddenly the radio crackled. The captain turned back to his flight deck panel and picked up the handset. We listened to the muffled conversation, holding our breath, hopeful.

Il Capitano nodded and said, "Roger-a." He turned to us. "I am-a very sorry," he addressed Ursula, "Operations-a said-a we can't-a fly. The winds are-a too high for-a take-off. You must-a get a taxi back-a to Gatwick."

"*Gott sei Dank!*" Ursula muttered.

"Thank God!" I echoed her.

As we were propelled by the wind across the tarmac back to the terminal, still clutching our hats to our heads, I shouted to Ursula, "I count this as the number three near miss. We should be safe now."

"I hope zat you are right," she shouted back, grimacing.

For the following week, I informed crewing daily, through my pseudo-nasally voice that I had a really, really bad cold. In reality, I just couldn't bring myself to fly. Instead, I sat on the couch in my living room, staring at the wall, the captain's words going around and around in my head. "We could have ended up in a ball of fire."

Six days later, though, the shock had dissipated, and I was back at the airport checking in for a flight—on a BAC 1-11.

Our near miss was the talk of the crew room. The airline rumour machine confirmed that Jack's first intuition about metal fatigue had been correct. Five other Comets around the world—after being grounded and inspected—were found to have metal fatigue in the struts of their tail planes. Two of them could have crashed on their next flight if our Comet hadn't been the first to survive a potential disaster.

Nine months later there was an enquiry. As I had originally suspected, the blame was laid squarely on the ground engineer who apparently did see something "unusual" on the tail plane. Perhaps he was compelled by someone in authority to give an "all clear". Perhaps the flight engineer chose to dismiss it, or *he* was also ordered to ignore the warning.

While the rest of us got away with our lives and just one pair of knickers—albeit in a bit of a twist—both flight and ground engineer, sadly or justifiably, lost their jobs and their licences.

7

CLOSE ENCOUNTERS
OF THE HARRIET KIND

January 1975

Oh no! I groaned inwardly as I checked in for the Naples flight and saw that Harriet Coulsdon was my number one.

Harriet had no sense of humour. Tall and big-boned with short, straight brown hair and a very intense stare, she emitted more the aura of a Wormwood Scrubs prison warden rather than a glamorous air hostess. What had I done to crewing for them to make me fly with her so much? Whatever the reason, I knew that while operating with her, keeping *my* sense of humour was the only way to mitigate my misery.

When the other member of our crew arrived, the Italian Mariabella, she begged me, "Ah Natasha! Please-a, let-a me work-a in-a the galley. These Italians-a, they drive-a me-a crr-ra-z-ee!" Whenever Mariabella and I flew together which—as I was the only other Italian speaker in the airline—was frequently, we often negotiated who would hide in the galley and who would face the mob in the cabin. Even though I wasn't thrilled at the thought of working with 89 rambunctious Italians—and Harriet—I caved.

As we traversed the Alps, the duty-free cart was loaded to the gills, and like an onslaught of marauding octopuses, men, women, children —and nuns—reached out and grabbed cigarette cartons, bottles of alcohol and perfumes.

"*Eh, eh, Signorina, Signorina!*" Our Italian passengers yelled, frantically waving as if we couldn't already see them. "*Eh, Signorina, Whisky, Whisky. Cigarette! Cigarette! Profumo!*"

Reminiscent of a school ma'am with a ruler, Harriet smacked their hands away from the goods and snapped, "Stop it! Stop it!" I was more aware of how the Italian men were undressing us with their eyes and shamelessly salivating. While the sexless Harriet appeared not to notice, my skin was crawling.

When we got to row 13 with the drinks service, Harriet frowned at the young Sophia Loren-type who was sitting in the middle seat with a hunky Italian man on either side. The men's shirts were open down to their hairy navels displaying their thick cheap gold chains and what they apparently thought were their sexy tanned and rippled muscles. Harriet grew even more agitated, tutt-tutting under her breath as she saw the man in the window seat kissing and canoodling with Sophia. Even though they were sitting in what should have been Harriet's row to serve, she leaned over to me and muttered, "Natasha, take care of those ...people."

Once the last row had their drinks, we pulled the trolley back toward the galley. I noticed that Sophia now had her hands all over the man in the aisle seat! And Harriet—who was glaring at Sophia very intently— became more than usually uptight, her cheeks flushing a deep red. Feeling Harriet's strong disapproval, Sophia and Romeo number one cowered under her stern glare. Why were they so afraid of her? True, she was a little intimidating, but why should they care?

Back in the galley, as Mariabella and I dismantled the trolley, I asked Harriet, "What's going on between you and the three in row 13?"

"Ufff," she snorted. "They're disgusting!"

Yes, maybe they were into a ménage-a-trois but that was hardly the crime of the century, I thought. People can do a lot worse on planes, like plant a bomb or ...die. "Why? What have they done?"

"Well," she huffed, her cheek twitching, "the three of them were on my Naples to Gatwick two weeks ago at the beginning of their holiday."

I waited and watched, fascinated by Harriet's various facial tics because whenever she was upset, as well as the twitch in her cheek, she would scrunch up her nose or her nostrils would flare. Mariabella and I exchanged suppressed grins.

"I noticed how that *girl*," Harriet continued, spitting out the last word, "was all over one of the men, the dark-haired one in the window seat. And later," Harriet looked away, her skin flushing pink, "I'm not even sure if ...you know ...well ...that she wasn't giving him a ...well ...you know..."

"Oh ...tha-a-at." I nodded, saving her the embarrassment of uttering the words blow job. Of course, it wouldn't have been the first time there had been hanky-panky under a blanket, but Harriet seemed personally affronted. Had she ever had sex, I wondered?

"Eh, it's a better-a to make-a love than-a war. No?" Mariabella posed to Harriet.

Our intrepid leader shrugged and commanded, "Natasha, start handing out snacks."

After what seemed far longer than a two-hour, forty-minute sector, we began our descent into Naples. I cleared empty plastic glasses and other debris from the cabin while, Mariabella began the Italian PA. "*Signore and Signori, ci sono pregati...*" Harriet was ahead of me at row 11, glancing at laps, checking that all seat belts were fastened. She turned suddenly and with a look of consternation, glared at me.

I frowned and moved closer to her. "What's the matter?" I whispered.

With eyes wide, cheeks flushing and lips in a tight thin line, she inclined her head toward where the Italian trio should have been sitting. 13B and 13C were empty. Sophia and Romeo Number Two were missing. The first Romeo was nonchalantly looking out of the window as we descended through the rapidly changing white clouds.

I frowned. Where could they be? I glanced up and down the cabin. They weren't behind me or in the galley. As I looked past Harriet, no one was standing at the rear of the plane. There was only one place they could be. The loos.

"Maybe they just needed to go to the toilet before landing?" I suggested. Even as the words came out of my mouth, I sensed something else was going on. Harriet and I exchanged looks. "But ...I thought she was with Romeo in the window seat?"

"*Exactly!*" She harrumphed, turned and stomped down to the rear.

This, I have to see, I thought, and followed closely with my tray still in hand.

When Harriet arrived at the rear, with me tight on her heels, only the portside toilet was showing the red *Occupied* indicator. With noises coming from within and understanding dawning, Harriet glared at me. "Really!" she snorted with disgust. "That slut was supposed to be with *that* man," she waved a hand at row 13 where the first lover was still calmly sitting. Was Harriet more concerned about the lack of loyalty between these Italian sex maniacs, or about what they might be doing not twelve inches from us?

"They have to sit down for—," Harriet started to say when a rhythmic banging began behind the thin door, followed by a soft moaning.

We stared at each other; eyes wide. Harriet's face was even ruddier now.

I tried not to smile at her oh-so-straight-but-twitching face. "Harriet, what do we *do?*" I asked, feigning horror.

Without answering, Harriet turned and with clenched fist banged on the toilet door. "Excoooose me!" she yelled through the flimsy partition. "Sir, Madam, you need to return to your seats *now*. We're landing soon."

"Ah! Ah! Aaaaah!" came the girl's orgasmic response, followed by even louder thuds and bangs.

"How *dare* they ignore me!" she snarled, almost apoplectic.

I suppressed a giggle. Then through the last row of passenger windows, I glanced down below at the familiar Neapolitan suburbia coming more into focus, getting larger by the second. How much time did we have before landing?

Harriet's nostrils were now flaring. I expected her to begin pawing the floor and for smoke to come out of her ears. Instead, she took the pen clipped to her uniform apron and inserted the nib into the hole in the *Occupied* sign, sliding it to the left. Realizing with horror—or was it delight—that she was about to open the door, I stepped quickly behind her so I wouldn't get the whole picture in full technicolour.

The green *Vacant* tab was visible now. She pulled the door open and gasped.

My curiosity won out. With Harriet's large frame blocking my view, I moved to stand beside her so I could see.

Oh my God!

A naked hairy Italian bum was stuck up in the air, pumping up and down. His trousers were tangled around his ankles while the woman's bare legs were clenched around his naked, hairy back. Her long, straight blonde hair was splayed over, of what appeared to be, bared breasts. With eyes closed in bliss and her uninhibited moaning, she seemed oblivious to the two gobsmacked stewardesses standing staring at their half-naked contortions over the unsanitary toilet. As if in tandem with the now noisy aircraft engines—reminding us of our imminent landing—the Italian began pumping faster as the girl's moans reached an even higher crescendo.

Unabashed, Harriet stepped forward and with one of her squared, thick fingers she stabbed the bare-backed Italian on his hairy shoulder. "Excoooose me!" she shouted above the noise. "Sir! Sir! We are landing. You have to go back to your seats *now*."

It had the desired effect. With a dual groan, and like balloons deflating, the contortionists immediately slumped into each other.

I was not sure who to feel sorry for—the *coitus interruptus* couple being yelled at by the thundering Harriet or the virginal Harriet witnessing this scene of a writhing bare-bottomed body entwined in another over the airline toilet. This was not a pretty picture that either of us would be able to erase.

Now the man was standing, full frontal, glaring at Harriet. Another not-so-pretty image.

"You need to ...get back to your seat," she said, covering her eyes with her hand. "And ...oh, for God's sake, pull up your trousers!"

"Yes," I mumbled. "The passengers are already flying Dan Dare. They don't need any more frights."

Ignoring my attempt at humour, Harriet stood firmly rooted to the spot, her lips sealed in a thin line while, in the very tight space, the couple struggled to put their clothes back on. When we stood back, allowing them to return to their seats, the girl tossed her hair over her shoulder. She gave Harriet an evil look, muttering Italian curses under her breath, as if the stewardess had just been discovered cavorting with *her* boyfriend.

Harriet stomped up the cabin after the couple and stood over them as they resumed their seats and fastened their belts. Romeo Number One turned and conversed with Sophia and Romeo Number two in friendly rapid-fire Italian as if the three of them had just reunited at a café.

When we returned to the galley, Mariabella was already sitting on her jump seat with her seat belt on. The flaps were coming down. We were close to the ground now. But Harriet, who should have been making her way to the rear and taking her position on the rear jump seat for landing, still stood in the galley, her cheek twitching and hand on the flight deck door handle—for support, I suspected—while she processed what she had just seen. How would she write this event up in her flight report? I wondered.

"What's-a goin' on-a?" Mariabella asked.

"Port toilet. Shenanigans," I told her.

"Ah-h-h." Mariabella nodded understanding. "Did-a they ask-a you for a certificate-a?" she asked Harriet.

Harriet frowned. "What for?"

"Qualifying for-a the Mile-High Club-a."

Harriet stared at Mariabella, confused. She obviously had never heard that some passengers set out to have sex on a plane at 35,000 feet as something to brag about. There was a rumour—and probably just a rumour—that one airline issued certificates to their nympho passengers who qualified for this dubious feat.

"Whaddya meana?" Mariabella jumped in. "No-a certificate! Why-a not-ta?" She raised her hands in despair, but there was a twinkle in her eyes as she turned to me. "Ah, these Italians-a! They drive-a you crazy!"

But our duty with Harriet wasn't over yet.

On the inbound flight to Gatwick, there was a mixture of Italian and English passengers on board.

"Any chance I can go up to see the cockpit?" one English fifty-something, tall, slim man, had asked me during the drinks service. "I'm just getting my private pilot's license and I'd love to see it."

"I'm sure it won't be a problem," I responded as I passed him his ginger ale, "but I will have to check with Captain W-w-w-willie." I still could not say that man's name without stuttering and blushing.

The captain was just finishing his lunch when I entered the flight deck. "Is it all right if a trainee private pilot comes up?" I asked.

"Oh goodie," he responded. "I might get some intelligent questions. Yes, bring him up."

I went into the cabin and invited Mr. Tall and Slim to follow me. We had just arrived in the galley, and the passenger had his hand on the flight deck door handle when Harriet burst through the curtain.

"Where do you think you're going?" she roared at him.

He turned to look at her. "Well, I ...I ..." the poor man stuttered, clearly instantly terrified of Big Harriet and looking to me for support.

"He's just going to visit the flight deck," I told her calmly.

"Did you frisk him?" she snapped at me.

"What? ...No!"

"Didn't you hear about the Chicago flight where a man got into the flight deck with a gun?"

I was too stunned to answer. Of course, we knew about hijackers, but this man was more like a birdwatcher than a mad man. "Well, I don't think that's ..."

Before I could say "necessary," Harriet had turned the mild-mannered man around and slammed him face first against the flight deck door. She was rubbing her square thick hands down his upraised arms and all over his slim back. I watched in horror while, with his face turned in my direction, his left cheek was squidged against the flimsy fibreboard. With eyes scrunched closed, he grimaced, probably trying to block out the invasive mauling. When Harriet arrived at his hips, I saw the man flinch as she unceremoniously squeezed first the outside then the inside tops of his legs and then groped all the way down to his ankles.

Oh, no! Had the sexy Italians stirred something up in the sexless Harriet?

Mariabella and I were in shock. We could only stare, incapable of saving the man from this horrendous indignity. We exchanged looks as if to say, *What the hell...?* If frisking passengers before entering the flight deck was a new airline policy, we hadn't been informed. And wouldn't it have been easier just to refuse him entry?

Once Harriet had molested his entire body, she stood up, panting, apparently satisfied. "Okay, you can go in now," she told the stunned man.

He glared at her, brushed himself off as if ridding himself of slime, quickly groped for the handle and gratefully backed into the cockpit and the safer company of men. Once inside, he firmly closed the door behind him.

"Don't let anyone on the flight deck again without frisking them." She addressed both of us.

Mariabella and I exchanged another frown. Was Harriet completely losing it?

A few weeks later, I flew with Captain Willie again. As we sat at the front of the plane on turnaround, waiting for passengers to appear, he asked, "Remember that Naples when Harriet frisked the trainee pilot?" He smiled grimly.

"How can I forget?" I said. "Poor man. Even I felt violated."

"Well, apparently he didn't enjoy the experience and complained."

"Quelle surprise!"

"Harriet got hauled up to the office."

"Oh? What did our intrepid leader say?"

"Jane Philoughby suggested that perhaps Harriet should take a rest from the pressures of being a number one for a while." Captain Willie stood up and stretched.

"Oh no! How did she react to being demoted?"

"She begged Jane to give her another chance. Jane relented but gave Harriet a warning."

"To do what? Get a sense of humour?" I commented. "You can't do this job without one."

"Personally...," He turned to go back into the flight deck, "...I think a good roll in the hay might do her more good."

Hmmm? Why did men always think that sex was the answer to everything?

But in the light of events to come, maybe he was right.

Just weeks later, another Harriet story emerged which made us all wonder if her intensity wasn't becoming her downfall ...literally.

She was rostered for an early morning Palma. In the shadowy dawn before engineers had powered up the Comet with lights, heat and electricity, the cabin crew were deposited at the bottom of the aircraft stairs. Instead of waiting for power to light the interior of the aircraft, Harriet, ever keen to get the job done, led her crew up the metal stairs.

Unbeknownst to her, the ground engineers *had* arrived and were on the plane. But the cabin lights hadn't been turned on yet. As Harriet ducked into the dark galley, she would not have seen that the square black lid covering the electrical bay access—which was usually flush with the galley floor—had been removed. She could also not know that the ground engineer, who had been busily checking the electrical hold below, was just about to emerge from the abyss and poke his head above floor level into the galley.

Before the engineer could—literally—give her a "heads up" that he was there, she stepped into the open black hole and landed on top of the stunned man. They both panicked. He, suddenly saddled with the hefty Harriet on his shoulders, buckled, while she in her confusion wrapped her long and heavy legs tightly around his neck almost strangling him.

Although he didn't enjoy this close encounter of the Harriet kind, the young engineer survived. He did have to wear a neck brace for a time and apparently endured nightmares of hefty women falling from above and choking him. Poor Harriet was more badly wounded, and not just with her pride. She scraped her shin on the sharp metal edge of the electrical hold, and blood spewed everywhere. Shaken and with thirty stitches in her leg, she was forced to take time off.

It has been written that our personality determines our fate, so it wasn't a big surprise when just two weeks after the landing-on-the-engineer's head event, that Harriet's story continued in the same vein.

In those non-union days, Dan Air overworked all their staff. We cabin crew often joked that the airline needed death certificates to prove that we were not fit to fly and even if we did die, they would probably demand a second opinion. So, despite Harriet's injury, the airline did not let her rest for long.

Just ten days after her accident, crewing needed a qualified number one—just to sit onboard, they said. Harriet would not need to operate or do any work, but her presence would satisfy the CAA (Civil Aviation Authority) requirements and make the operating crew legal. Crewing neglected to explain how, in the event of a full emergency, the incapacitated Harriet would be able to get herself and 89 passengers out of a burning aircraft!

Ever the dutiful employee, she caved into crewing's haranguing and —with the permission of the chief stewardess— and despite a nasty gash all the way down her left shin—got on the flight. Even behind her thick support stockings, the long wound pulled together by thirty ugly black stitches was still visible.

Being in a pressurized cabin put extra stress on her lesion so what happened next was inevitable. Halfway through the flight, Harriet bent down to unlock a bar box. That's when her stitches burst. Blood gushed forth! Passengers, horrified at the gory scene, immediately wondered if she had recently been injured in an air crash! After all, with Dan Air's *un-safety* record, flying disasters were the first thought on passengers' minds.

The brave Harriet finally did get her needed time off, but all she could do was lie on her sofa with her leg elevated and wonder if Jane Philoughby was right. Were the gods trying to tell her something? Should she stop taking herself and her job so seriously? Maybe she should give up flying?

Perhaps she *would* have been better off working with the convicts at Wormwood Scrubs. At least there, she would not have been admonished for frisking all those hairy inmates and they, at least, might have enjoyed close encounters of the Harriet kind.

8

BRUSSELS MIX UP

May 1975

"Miss Rosewood?"

My hand tensed on the black telephone. What did crewing want with me on my day off?

"Ye-e-s?"

"This is just to give you notice that your standby on Tuesday has been changed to a VIP Brussels day-stop."

"Oh." I exhaled. *Nice!* These more luxurious VIP flights were few and far between, so I was always flattered to be chosen. "Thank you," I said. For me to be grateful to crewing was also a rare occurrence.

The airline seemed to like me these days. Only two weeks earlier, I had been called up to the office. As I waited in trepidation to enter the chief stewardess's inner sanctum, I had wondered what had I done? Had Tricky Dicky finally registered a complaint? Once inside, Jane Philoughby had informed me that, as part of a loan repayment from British Caledonian, Dan Air had inherited four additional BAC 1-11s. Consequently, they needed more seniors. Out of my initial training group of twenty seven hosties, I was one of the four who had been selected for early promotion to number one.

"Aren't you happy?" the secretary in the outer office had asked as I sat and waited for the other three to emerge and we would be told when and where to report for training.

"Well ...yes," I lied, not wanting to appear ungracious. But this would mean, for a mere additional two pounds per week, I would take on all the extra responsibilities of the cabin, passengers, crew, monies and emergencies. The really bad news was that I would only fly short haul now. My dream of flying the 707s, being able to visit my brothers in Canada and see more of the world was disappearing over the horizon.

"Check-in 07.00 hours for the Brussels," the man in crewing was saying. "Returning within eight hours or whenever they are ready to depart."

"Who are the VIPs?"

"Er ...some insurance company."

Not Elton John then, or even someone remotely exciting. "Thank you," I repeated, making sure that I didn't sound like I was groveling. As I resettled in front of the idiot box, I thought, it should be an easy flight with a leisurely day of shopping or sightseeing in Brussels.

But once I saw the check-in sheet on Tuesday morning, I wasn't quite so excited about the day. The crew was comprised of the ever-so-stern training-captain Don Samuels who barely ever cracked a smile. And oh, what a surprise! His girlfriend, Janet Pearson—who nobody was supposed to know was his girlfriend—was the operating number one. And the first officer was ...oh no ...Christopher Wolsesley, or Mr. Knobs and Switches, the goofy, bearded, married pilot who frequently accosted me in the galley.

The third crew member was a TBA, to be advised. Please God, let her be fun so I don't have to be alone with Christopher or explore Brussels on my own.

Two minutes later Janet flounced into the room with her usual Julia Andrews *The-Hills-Are-Alive* exuberance. "Good morning, Natasha." she trilled. "I'm so glad you're on this flight."

The real reason for her joy, I knew, is that she would be spending a whole day with her amour, and she knew I knew about their relationship.

When Marion Albright arrived and announced she was on the Brussels, too, I was surprised, but also apprehensive. I hadn't flown with her since my Tricky Dicky debacle. Crewing must have wanted to impress these passengers with three number ones—Janet, Marion, and myself, a training captain and a goofy but experienced first officer.

"Hello, Marion." I felt myself blush.

"Natasha!" She grinned. "So Tricky Dicky didn't get you fired then?"

"No," I muttered.

I decided not to tell her that on that fateful Glasgow night-stop, minutes before beginning our return flight, I had witnessed Dick Roberts on the flight deck, an oxygen mask over his face. Flight deck crew members took "whiffs" for only one reason: to infuse their brains with oxygen after having imbibed alcohol within the regulated eight hours of duty. He was now aware that I had caught him in the act and, that instead of him endangering my job, I could cause him to lose his. That leverage I would only use if he ever tried any more shenanigans with me.

"Nope. Still here," I told Marion, holding my head high. "Actually, I've been promoted!"

"Well done!" She patted me on the arm. "Well, that'll either get you into trouble or keep you out of it."

Janet picked up the black ops phone in the corner of the crew room to get the final flight details. "Oh, no!" she groaned, her joy deflating. "Well, what shall we do?"

Marion and I exchanged looks and frowned. What could go possibly wrong with a Brussels?

"Belgium's going on national strike today," Janet informed us as she hung up. "Everything's shutting down. If we don't get there before 10:00, we may be walking to the hotel."

"Bloody 'ell," Marion exclaimed, her earthy Welsh accent coming through. "There's always something, isn't there?"

After transport took us out to the 1-11 sitting on the tarmac, we prepared the aircraft for our VIP passengers with classier touches: pillows with linen covers instead of the usual thin tissue-like fabric, real napkins instead of no napkins, colorful fresh fruit and gooey cheeses arranged on silver platters instead of frozen cakes in plastic trays, real china instead of plastic cups, and champagne flutes instead of plastic glasses. If only our service was like this all the time.

While we were carrying out our respective pre-flight routines, the flight deck crew arrived in the galley. With a terse "good morning," from the captain and a knowing wink from Christopher, they both disappeared into the flight deck. I didn't understand the attraction between the exuberant Janet and the moody captain but as my grandmother would often intone in her northern accent, "There's nought so queer as folk."

Twenty minutes later the cabin looked fit for the Queen.

Janet leaned out of the front door and called down to the ramp officer waiting below on the tarmac. "You can bring pax." Clutching his clipboard, he spoke into his crackling walkie-talkie, gave her a thumbs-up and climbed into his van. The fifty-two men and three women VIPs soon arrived holding slim briefcases, and much more expeditiously than usual, were seated, belted and ready for take-off.

In the short flight to Brussels, the service would be more challenging for the three of us to serve champagne on trays and not trolleys, offer gourmet appetizers individually instead of handing out stacked snacks and sell duty frees by personal order and not from a cart. But operating with two other seasoned hosties, we worked almost telepathically together, and our service was seamless.

By the time the aircraft came to a halt in front of the terminal at *Aeroport de Bruxelles*, it was just 9:10 a.m. The passengers had been warned that if they wanted their bus to take them to their destination, they were to disembark quickly.

"Where are we staying?" I asked Janet while I packaged some cheese and fruit to take with us to the hotel.

"Brussels Hilton, right in the centre of town. It's the only hotel that's staying open and that's only because of the political bigwigs. Everything else, including all the restaurants are shut."

Just then, a Belgian ramp officer in a blue uniform, reminiscent of Inspector Clouseau, arrived at the top of the stairs. "Weee 'ave to leeve immediatement. Ozerrwise, ze taxis will not worrrk."

None of us were eager to stay on a cold aircraft for the day so we quickly donned our uniform hats, coats and gloves and climbed down the stairs. After the captain had locked the front door of the aircraft, he and Christopher followed in another taxi.

"What are we going to do all day?" I asked, while our leathered-interior Citroen sat waiting for traffic lights to change.

"I'm tired," Janet said. "I'll probably just rest."

Marion and I exchanged knowing looks. *Nod, nod. Wink, wink.*

"How about you, Marion?" I asked. "Shall we take a look around Brussels?"

"Oh, I dunno." She yawned. "These early morning flights are killers, aren't they? I'm going to me bed for a couple of hours." She glanced at the small box of gourmet goodies sitting in my lap. "We could meet for lunch in your room, why don't we?"

"Of course."

Driving into the centre of the deserted city, we saw a lone man closing up the roller shutter on his shop and a young girl running as if to get off the street before an asteroid hit the planet. The emptiness was eerie. Maybe the world *was* coming to an end and we were the only remaining survivors. I was sorry that I would not be able to enjoy the normal hustle and bustle of this capital city.

The Brussels Grand Place Hilton Hotel sat in the center of a downtown square surrounded by stately old buildings. The driver of the large Citroen deposited us on the pavement at the glass front door and drove off in a hurry. At least *he* had plans for the day.

"*Bonjour! Bienvenue a la 'ilton.*" A young man in a smart navy uniform behind the front desk greeted us in the quiet hotel. "You are stayeeng *juste* for zee day, yes?"

"That's right," Captain Samuels confirmed. Janet and I leaned against the counter surveying the luxurious mirrored lobby. Marion and Christopher were in conversation behind us.

"*Monsieur le Capitaine,* for you numbair 313," he said, handing him a key with a massive wooden fob attached.

I won't be throwing a room key like that in my handbag in error, I thought, but that was probably the idea.

"*Et pour les mesdemoiselles,* Miss Pearson 306 and Miss Rosewood 312." The front desk agent obviously had not been apprised of Janet's affair. If he had, he might have put them together with adjoining doors. But my room number was right next to the captain's while Janet's was further down the corridor.

"Oh ...Miss Albright," he indicated to Marion waiting bedside me, "I am sorree. Before I give you zee key, I need to check somessing wiz 'ousekeepeeng."

Marion shrugged and continued talking to Christopher.

The captain, Janet and I left Christopher and Marion waiting at the front desk while we headed through the grand empty foyer to the lifts. Once inside the elevator, I stood in the back-left corner while Janet stood on the opposite side, leaning against the mirrored wall. Her eyes were shiny, probably in anticipation of her tryst. As the lift whirred up to the third floor, the stoic captain remained stiffly planted at the front, his back to us, intently studying the lighted lift panel.

Behind his back, I lifted my key fob to show her my room number then wordlessly offered it to her. She frowned, not understanding. I pointed to the room number on the massive fob. Realization dawned. She beamed. Without speaking, we quickly exchanged keys. I would now be in 305 and she would be next to the captain in 312.

The lift pinged and the doors opened.

We all stepped into the corridor, looking for the direction of our rooms. Determined to maintain his professional decorum—and keep what he thought was his secret—the captain announced, "Ladies, unless you hear otherwise, I'll see you in the lobby at 1600 hours."

"Okay," Janet and I chimed in unison, both amused by his pseudo-officiousness.

We watched as he strode down the corridor and disappeared into his room.

"Do you want to take some of this food for your lunch, Janet?" I offered. "There's lots."

She peeked into the box and shook her head. "No, that's okay, Natasha. I've brought my own delights." She giggled. "But thanks, anyway," she said as she flounced off. "See you later."

As I walked to my room, I wondered why I was being party to their deceit. While I didn't condone cheating—especially as my father's affair had caused the devastating disintegration of my own family—I had to remember they were both grown-ups and—with or without my approval—they would continue their affair anyway.

When I entered Room 305, I was delighted to see the expansive king-sized bed, the luxurious shag pile carpet and the spacious bathroom stocked with perfumed soaps. Too bad we're only here for a day, I thought. But what was I going to do with myself? First things first. I'll get out of my uniform and have a nice shower.

As I emerged from the bathroom, in my "civvies," there was a soft knock at my door. I groaned. It better not be Christopher Wolsesley—dressed in his usual unsexy safari outfit and hoping to seduce me. But when I cracked the door open, I was not the only one who was surprised.

The ever-so stern Captain Samuels was standing in front of me, now in civvies, grinning like an excited schoolboy about to get his lollipop. He was bearing gifts of some kind, but I was so stunned by the transformation of his never-before-seen handsome smile that I didn't notice what he was carrying.

When he saw me, his grin instantly faded.

"Oh," he said.

"Oh," I said and frowned. Janet obviously hadn't told him of our exchange. I pointed to my right "She's thatta way. Room 312."

"Oh ...er ...thank you," he said, blushing. He turned and left.

Oh dear. Now he knew that I knew his secret. I closed the door.

I went back into my room. Hmm. What to do? Maybe I'll sit out on the balcony and read, I thought. I hadn't opened Erica Jong's book *The Fear of Flying* yet, and at least I could enjoy the view of Brussels.

The white phone sitting on my bedside table rang. Now what?

"Natasha?"

"Yes." I recognized Marion's concerned tone.

"Um ...er ...I don't know how to put this, but is something going on between you and the captain? I mean you know he's already having an affair with Janet, don't you?"

"Marion! What do you take me for?" I said a little too sharply. After the Tricky Dicky episode, she was apparently convinced that I was the airline bicycle. Then I realized that Marion must have seen the captain knocking at my door.

"I swapped rooms with Janet so they could be closer, but she forgot to let him know."

"Ah. Well, that's all right then. You are a bit of a femme fatale, you know?"

"Oh, please! I have a lovely boyfriend, and I'm not into old captains."

"That's okay then. Just making sure, don't you know."

"You still want to come to my room for lunch at 12:00?"

"Of course."

As I hung up, I wondered if Marion had really believed my version of the Tricky Dicky story. I *had* been the innocent, hadn't I?

I picked up my book again.

The phone rang.

"Natasha?"

This time it was Janet. Was she going to accuse me of stealing her man?

"Are you having an affair with Christopher Wolsesley?"

"Wha-a-a-at?"

"It's okay. You can tell me."

I laughed. "What on earth makes you say that?"

"Well, he just called my room ...which he obviously thought was your room ...and began whispering sweet nothings. By the time I let him know that I wasn't you and that he had the wrong room, it was too late."

I sat on the edge of the bed. "Did you tell him which room I'm in?"

"No. Did you want me to?"

"God, no!"

"That's all right then."

I heard the captain's deep voice in the background, his tone uncharacteristically tender. "See you later," Janet cooed and hung up.

I grabbed my book and headed for the balcony. The view of Brussels with its stately old buildings, sporadic patches of greenery and other not-so pretty industrial parts stretched out in a flat patchwork to the horizon. I was only on page three when I heard another knock at the door. Now who would this be? If only they had peepholes in the doors so I could know. This time, when I opened up, I wasn't surprised.

"Oh," I said.

"Ah," he said.

"Ugh," I muttered.

"There you are, you little minx."

Before I could protest, Christopher pushed his way into my room, closing the door behind him.

He strode past me, as though he'd been invited in and looked around, inspecting the room. I pulled the handle on the door to leave it slightly ajar. Meanwhile, Christopher plunked himself on the edge of the bed. Grinning inanely and playing with his red, raggedy beard, he patted the floral bedcover beside him. "We can't let this lovely king go to waste, now can we?"

I gazed at the hairy arms emerging from the green and brown short-sleeved safari shirt and his safari shorts with a myriad of pockets and the inevitable woollen knee-high socks he always wore stuffed into open-toed sandals. All that was missing was his pith helmet. He belonged in the jungle with Dr. Livingstone, not in a five-star hotel in Brussels. But I knew he was harmless. If I had called his bluff and returned any amorous moves, I predicted that he would run like an antelope fleeing across the Serengeti.

"Christopher!" It was all I could do not to laugh at him. "You can't stay here."

"Oh, com'on." He grinned, baring not very white teeth. "You know you like me."

Was he mistaking my suppressed laughter at his ridiculous, upper-class-twit behavior for flirtation?

"Christopher, you know I have a boyfriend and you are married. You have to ...."

To my surprise, the amorous first officer stood up, strode toward me and wrapped his hairy arms around my waist. Instinctively I pushed my hands against his chest.

At the same moment, I heard a knock.

Surprised, Christopher glanced over at the door and loosened his grip.

I twisted around to look behind me.

"I'm early, but I was wondering if you wanted to..." Marion was standing just inside my door, her mouth wide open. "Oh Natasha," she said, using my mother's I'm-so-disappointed-in-you tone. "I thought you said..." She turned to leave.

"Marion! ... Wait!" I pushed Christopher away from me and ran over to the door. Before she could exit, I gently closed it.

"Really, Natasha. It's none of my business," she said, waving a hand, averting my face and instead fixing her eyes on the fire drill notice on the back of the door. "If you want to fraternize with the whole flight deck fleet..."

"But that's just it, Marion. I *don't*. I have a lovely boyfriend at home and really..." I said, pointing at Mr. Safari. "Really, can you see me ...you know ...with him? I mean *really*?"

Marion surveyed Christopher in all his sexless glory and smiled. "Well, yes, you do have a point, don't you ...?"

"He pushed his way in, and he just won't leave," I insisted.

"Christopher, get out and leave Natasha alone," Marion ordered in her flat Welsh tone.

Like a rebuked puppy, with the proverbial tail between his legs, Christopher walked obediently toward the door and, without looking at either of us, left the room.

"Thank God you came in when you did, Marion. Thank you."

"Christopher's just a harmless twit," she said, walking over to a pink armchair and sitting down.

I sank onto the bed. "I thought so, too, but he won't take no for an answer."

"Now that's the second time in two short months I've had to rescue you from flight deck. What is it that's so irresistible about you, Natasha?"

"I don't know. It's embarrassing."

"Tell me something ...."

"Yes. What?"

"What perfume do you wear?"

"Yves St. Laurent. Rive Gauche. Why?"

"Oh, I don't know. Maybe I should start wearing it."

9

BOMB!

June 1975

"There's a bomb threat," the unemotional phone voice of the airline Ops man droned as my cabin crew of two waited behind me in the grubby crew room. I, as the number one hostess, and as pre-flight routine demanded, was checking in with Operations for any idiosyncratic flight details. A bomb scare was what you might call an idiosyncrasy.

"We were told the bomb is for a German destination," he continued. "We think it could be a Berlin flight ...Your Berlin flight."

Lovely! I thought as I stood holding the cold, shiny, black phone receiver in my now sweaty palm. "Who's taking responsibility? The IRA?" As if it mattered. A bomb was a bomb.

"No idea, luv," he replied wearily. "Just passing on the message."

Why did these dramas always have to happen when I had a lovely date planned with my new boyfriend, Julian? "Will you tell the passengers?" I asked.

"Nah. They'll get the drift when they get thoroughly frisked. Boarding will take a while."

That means a long delay. But I hadn't heard the worst yet.

"Will they be bringing the sniffer dogs on board?" I enquired. Cabin crew were used to seeing huge German shepherds straining against their master's leashes as they snuffled under seats, searching for drugs or explosive materials. Who knows what nasty smells lingered there? Sometimes I wondered if that constituted cruelty to animals?

Ops Man hesitated. "Well, actually, there are a few German flights today, so the police want you girls to check your own aircraft."

Wha-a-at?

"Well," he reasoned, "you are much more familiar with all the nooks and crannies of the plane, aren't you, luv?" The endearment at the end included a good-luck-with-that-one tone.

Wonderful! We knew the airline considered cabin crew expendable but not quite *that* expendable.

"And what exactly do we look for?" I asked, remembering James Bond movies with large-dialled alarm clocks, a mass of multi-coloured wires and loud ticking noises accompanied by bright red digital numbers counting down seconds. But even in 1975, bombs had become far smaller and more sophisticated than that. An explosive big enough to blow up a plane could be disguised as anything as small as a lipstick—or so I had been told by a first officer.

The man sighed helplessly. "Beats me, luv. But you'll know if something isn't right." His faith in us and my intuition was touching but misguided. "Transport's on its way," he intoned, reverting to his Ops Man routine airport-speak. "Have a good flight."

If we make it off the ground.

I turned to the two pristinely dressed young women who were sitting and chatting amiably behind me. "Guess what, girls?"

As the three of us were driven across the grey tarmac in a huge bus, I thought about the word "bomb" and was instantly transported back to my experience in London two years before.

Just as Peter, my-then boyfriend and I were entering the Earls Court Boat Show, armies of Bobbies were evacuating everyone, including themselves, from the large round building because of another bomb scare. Despite my protestations, Peter had insisted that we go into the exhibition hall and return our borrowed passes. In the eeriness of a hall filled only with deserted boats, I stopped dead in front of a sleek fifty-foot pristine white yacht, just feet from his friend's exhibition stand. Something about its stillness had sent shivers down my spine. While I had stood transfixed, Peter had carried on,

returning the passes. His mission accomplished, we had then hurried along
the underground tunnel and out into the light of day.

We had just stepped outside the circular building's glass front doors and
onto the top step, when behind us we felt, more than heard, a giant thud.
We turned to look. The walls shook, the glass rattled and inside dust flew ...

"Whisky X-ray!" the transport driver yelled, as he pulled up close to
the bottom of the front stairs of our 89-seater aircraft. The BAC 1-11
sat waiting for us. Would it also be our coffin? The three of us climbed
up the metal stairs and deposited our crew bags on the empty front seats.
Both stewardesses looked at me expectantly, waiting for instructions, as
if I knew what to do. Hmmm? Yes, how does one organize a bomb
search?

"Let's split the plane into three sections," I began, trying to sound as
if hunting for fragile explosives was a regular part of my pre-flight
routine. "I'll check the flight deck and galley. Belinda, you take rows one
to fifteen. Dorothy, you take it to the back, the rear ventral staircase and
the two loos. Make sure you check the hat racks all the way down on
both sides."

"What exactly are we looking for?" Belinda, the freckled redhead
enquired in her gentle, lilting Irish accent.

Hell, if I know, I thought. "A bomb could be very small, like a pen
or a lipstick, a roll of newspaper, anything that shouldn't be on the
aircraft."

"What do we do if we find something?" Dorothy asked.

Run like hell is what I wanted to say. "Don't touch it, just tell me.
Then I'll call ops to get the dogs out."

They both nodded mutely, apparently accepting my fake confidence, and turned to carry out their duties. Was their calm manner
simply shocked acquiescence or abject terror?

Had the company warned them during training that bomb-hunting
was part of their job description? Not likely! If the airline had a union,
we would have been at home by now with our feet up, sipping on a nice
cup of tea. But too late to argue now. There were 89 physically and emo-

tionally ruffled passengers in the terminal, waiting to get home to Berlin. And we had a bomb search to do.

In the cramped galley, I poked through empty cupboards and in vacant stowages. Belinda, my number two—who had begun to scour under cabin seats, pulling out life jackets and peering into less-than sanitary ashtrays in the seats' armrests—called out, her voice carrying through the empty plane. "Now why would they want to bomb a Berlin flight?" she complained. "To be sure there's more trouble in Belfast right now."

"Man is not to reason why" were words that frequently rolled around in my head when on this job.

"Or an Eilat flight?" Belinda continued. "There's more strife in Israel."

I had the urge to make a bad joke, as the English are wont to do, about how maybe the Irish got Berlin confused with Belfast and put the bomb on the wrong plane but thought the Irish Belinda might not appreciate my humour. And anyway, those IRA people were to be taken seriously. The Irish Republican Army called it "The Troubles" and wanted the English out of Northern Ireland "somethin' fierce." They had already bombed a few English locations to show us their feelings about our occupation, but the English were a little thick in this matter and were stubbornly refusing to budge.

"Oh, who knows?" I stepped into the cabin. "Maybe some nutcase from World War ll still wants revenge on the Germans. Or maybe it's a Commie who resents the Berlin wall? Then there's the *Baader-Meinhof* Gang, though I don't know much about them. The possibilities are endless. It only takes one lunatic."

I left her with those cheery words and turned to begin my search on the flight deck. A man in oil-smeared green overalls sat in the captain's seat, playing with knobs and switches, carrying out the regular pre-flight ground checks before the captain and first officer appeared. I hoped that the flight deck crew were just busy filing their flight plan and not being cowardly, awaiting the "all clear."

"Good morning," I said, hoping he was, indeed, a ground engineer and not a lone bomber.

Dan Air was a large airline with a fleet at Gatwick and other bases: Glasgow, Manchester, Bristol, Cardiff, Aberdeen and Berlin. Some of the ground engineers I recognized by name, some by face and some not at all. "Don't mind me," I told him, smiling. "I'm just looking for a bomb." He nodded as if I had told him it was raining outside. But he had his earphones on, a clipboard on his lap and seemed to be listening for a noise, as if tuning a piano. He turned to face forward again and continue what he was doing. Maybe I should ask to see his airport pass? I thought. While I'm wishing him top o' the mornin', he could be in the process of sabotaging the aircraft controls. But an airport pass didn't mean validation either. One stewardess had replaced her picture with photograph of an ape. It took three months for security to finally notice the picture wasn't her.

Apart from the engineer, the flight deck seemed to be undisturbed. An array of quasi-meaningless dials in front of the captain's and co-pilot's seats stared back at me. But I doubted whether a bomber would leave a note with a big arrow on it: "Bomb planted here." More panels of switches and dials on the ceiling above them all appeared to be normal. I glanced at the centre console that housed crucial electrical equipment. How would I know if something had been tampered with? I peered over the engineer's left shoulder and looked down into the side pockets where flight crew kept charts, checklists and other manuals. Nothing unusual there, nor on the co-pilot's side. A supernumerary jump seat was stowed behind the captain's and against the rear bulkhead of the flight deck. I yanked on the cold metal handle, sliding it out from its vertical location. Sometimes trashed cups and other paraphernalia would get trapped in that rear corner.

All I could see now was a spare headset hanging off the bulkhead and a couple of thick black books. More manuals. With the engineer sitting in the captain's place fiddling, I wouldn't be able to search underneath either of their seats. Oh well.

I left the engineer testing for the sound of something.

The galley was still void of catering supplies. Caterers would not bring anything on board until we had completed our bomb search. Who could blame them?

From my crew bag on the front seat, I retrieved the brown envelope that contained the in-flight paperwork so I could begin my report. As always, I filled in the flight number, destination and names of crew members. What would I write this time? "Bomb found ...loud bang ...."

Behind me in the cabin Dorothy was just three rows from the rear so she was almost done. Belinda was a little slower but perhaps a little more thorough, being from Ireland and all. And although she was from southern Ireland, far away from Northern Belfast and the ongoing war, who knew if she had witnessed bombs exploding or lost loved ones in the Protestant-Catholic debacle. Having lived in London with constant bomb scares and explosions, I knew people developed a way of coping. Denial.

"All clear." The engineer's voice came from behind.

"Oh, goodie," I responded. I had hoped that he would tell us the aircraft had an "A" defect and we couldn't fly. But even a stuck emergency exit, a dodgy undercarriage or a fragile hydraulics system—all "A' defects—wouldn't have stopped this no-frills airline from taking off.

Dorothy, who had entered the galley, shrugged. "Couldn't find anything."

Belinda followed. "Well, if there's a bomb, I can't find it," she said, as she put some debris in a garbage bag.

"So, let's assume there isn't one," I commented, not really relieved, as I poked my head out of the door to report our status. The tarmac was deserted. No ramp agent, flight deck crew, ground engineers or baggage handlers. Not surprising, but not heart-warming.

"Have you ladies done a Berlin before?" I asked my two crew as we waited for the cowards to appear.

They both shook their heads.

"Well, I should warn you," I began, "you may know that the city is an island in the middle of East Germany, so to reach West Berlin we have to fly over East German airspace. There are only three flight paths or "corridors," one from the south, north and west. Once in the corridor, all western aircraft must descend to ten thousand feet. The lower we fly, the bumpier the ride. And judging from these clouds, who knows how bad the weather will be by the time we reach German airspace, so we have to be quick on the service."

"What are Berliners like?" Dorothy asked.

"Well, usually they're friendly. But very few of them speak English. Maybe it's because since 1961, they have been somewhat isolated behind a 12-foot plus wall. Too bad we're not night-stopping. West Berlin is very exciting. And, oh, the food is fantastic! At night, you can hear American helicopters whoop-whooping overhead. Berliners seem to be oblivious to being enclosed by a wall punctuated with East German gun-pointing soldiers."

Belinda's eyes grew large with alarm.

"Oh, don't worry," I said. "The guns aren't pointed at you."

"Well, who then?"

"Poor East Germans who are desperately trying to escape. Once across the wall, all the defectors have to do to claim freedom is run to West German police station, declare political asylum and they are instantly westernized. If they can handle leaving their families—."

"Good morning!" A ramp officer in a crisp white shirt and black tie appeared at the top of the steps clutching a clip board and his walkie-talkie. "No bomb, then?" he asked.

"Yes, it's under 5A." I pointed to a seat in the cabin.

The ramp officer blanched.

"Want to dismantle it?" I asked. Then he saw my wry grin and exhaled.

"All clear," he growled into his crackling communication device.

The plane was immediately inundated with activity. Caterers loaded cardboard boxes. And, as if they had been lurking at the bottom of the stairs waiting for the "all clear," the captain and first officer magically appeared. Now we just needed our passengers.

"*Guten Morgen*," an older bespectacled male passenger appeared in front of me in the galley. Although he was smiling, I could tell from his slightly stunned gaze that he was recovering from the recent invasive body search.

"*Guten Morgen*. Where are you sitting?" I asked, checking his boarding pass.

Perhaps Berliners were so used to living with a constant military presence is why they didn't flinch when they got onto a threatened plane. Or were they just crazy? Who was I to question their sanity? They would have also been informed that if they didn't board, they would endure another two hours of unloading baggage, identifying their own belongings and then re-boarding. No one wanted to be "the one" who caused all that grief or to appear cowardly in front of others.

Once the ramp officer confirmed that all passengers were inside the aircraft, I began to tally "heads."

In seat 3B, just three rows ahead of the forward galley, I noticed a larger, sixtyish woman. Her husband was squeezed in the window seat next to her. She appeared to be your average *hausfrau* returning from her English holiday, clutching her voluminous black leather handbag on her lap.

"Nine, ten ...," I counted as I reached her seat. She leaned into the aisle, grabbed my hand and whispered, "*Fraulein, ich muss mit Ihnen sprechen*/ I must speak with you." "*Es ist dringend*!/ It is urgent," she hissed. "But not here," she added, throwing a furtive glance at the people in front of her. Her big eyes, behind humungous, old-fashioned glasses, seemed to be fixated on the young man and woman sitting in the front seats, 1A and 1B while their two young children—a well-behaved girl of eight and a boy of ten—sat in the row behind them. Why was she ogling them like that?

"*Ja. naturlich*," I responded. Something in her manner, wanted to make me giggle. "But we're taking off. Can it wait until we're in the air?" Had this *Hausfrau* decided she was now an M15 agent out to catch the bomber?

Disappointed that I wasn't responding with the same sense of urgency, she sat back in her seat. "*Ja, Ja. Hoffentlich.* Yes, yes, hopefully," she huffed as if to imply I may regret not taking her seriously. She probably wanted to have the family arrested before take-off, hailing her as the heroine.

She cast another evil stare toward the couple, tightening her grip on her handbag and stiffening as if to say, 'I'm not going to let him out of my sight!"

As I finished the head count of 89, the *hausfrau* had still not peeled her eyes away from the young couple and their children. Could the parents feel her intense gaze boring into the backs of their heads?

"Full load. 89 pax," I reported to the ramp officer. "Looks like no one's escaped leaving suspicious luggage in the hold then," I added.

"Yeah, a missing passenger is kind of a dead giveaway with a bomb scare." The ramp officer laughed, handing me a copy of the ship's manifest. "Have a good flight!" he called over his shoulder as he hurried down the stairs.

I closed the front port door behind him and went into the flight deck.

Captain Ron Davis was tall, dark, handsome, and greying. He was known to be a bit of "an old woman," but as we cabin crew often reiterated, "There are old pilots and there are bold pilots but there are no old bold pilots." This captain, I knew, planned on living a long time.

"89. No babies," I called, handing him the manifest. "What's the flight time?"

"One hour twenty," he said taking the sheet and barely turning around. "There are some heavy winds over Germany so it will get bumpy as we fly the corridor."

Oh joy. We better get our service done quickly in case we have to sit down for half the flight, I thought. "Thanks for the warning."

Being the language speaker, I stood in the galley and gave the pre-flight address in German and then in English while Dorothy and Belinda stood at the front and middle of the cabin, acting out the safety demonstrations. As usual the passengers—except the lady in 3B—ignored the girls in their yellow lifejackets.

During take-off, as I sat at the rear of the plane behind 89 heads, I pondered why people react so calmly to threats. Was it stoicism, bravery, denial or sheer stupidity? I decided my talent was denial.

Once the wheels were up and the *No Smoking* sign was extinguished, I stowed my rear jump seat behind the last passenger row and donned my navy apron. Even before I extracted my paperwork from my crew bag, the *Hausfrau* from 3B was at my side.

"The *Fasten Seat Belt* sign is still on," I explained in German. "You should still be seated."

"*Ja, Ja,*" she responded dismissively, her massive handbag hanging from her arm. "But I must speak with you."

"What is it?"

"You see the man and wife in the very front seat?" As if I didn't know who she meant, she pointed to the front of the aircraft.

I nodded.

"Well, I know they don't look like it but they are the terrorists!"

The earnestness with which she spoke struck me as funny. Struggling to keep a straight face, I asked, "Really? What makes you think so?"

"Well, I saw their pictures in the paper a few years ago. *Ja, ja,* his hair is a different color and sure, he's a bit shorter and with his children now, but I know he and his wife are the terrorists."

The *Fasten Seat Belt* sign extinguished and several passengers got out of their seats. They were headed to the rear of the aircraft where we stood by the two loos. To my shock, one of the people coming our way was the man in 1A. *Oh no, The terrorist!*

"What do you think I should do?" I asked her, attempting to show respect.

"*Ja. Es ist klar. Sie mussen der Polizei in Berlin Bescheid lassen!*" she exclaimed. "*Er ist sehr gefahrlich. /* It's obvious. You must let the West German police know. He is very dangerous."

"Yes, of course. I'll tell the Captain." My acquiescence seemed to satisfy her, as if she had done her duty.

Looking up the cabin, I could see that "the terrorist" was getting closer. The *Hausfrau* was still leaning into me, whispering, her back to the cabin and unaware of the oncoming encounter.

"What would you like me to do?" she asked, just loving her part in this drama.

I put a hand on her arm. "Why don't you just return to your seat and keep a *very* close eye on him. Please let me know if he does anything suspicious." The man was getting closer. I whispered. "And thank you for that information. I'll let the captain know straight away."

"The terrorist" was almost upon us. Perhaps he would tap her on the shoulder and say "Boo!" The twinkle in his eye told me that he was aware of our conversation and was enjoying the joke. Thank God. A German with a sense of humour!

"*Okay. Ist gut*," she replied, gravely as if we were running a resistance movement. For a scary moment, I thought she might salute, but instead she smiled, happy. She turned to go back up the cabin and instantly collided with her nemesis. Flustered, she struggled to regain possession of her unruly handbag. The man behaved as a perfect gentleman and stood back, calmly waiting while she pushed past him and hurried up the narrow aisle.

He grinned at me as he disappeared into the port toilet.

Remembering our potentially restricted time in which to serve passengers, I quickly trudged up the cabin. Should I tell the captain about "the terrorist?" Better to be safe than sorry. He would probably laugh, too, but it would be off my plate and be his responsibility.

As I reached the galley, Dorothy and Belinda were setting up the drinks trolley. Carefully, I pulled the curtain across so that passengers would not be able to see our movements or hear our conversation.

"Just so you know," I whispered to the two girls, "the lady in 3B has informed me that the lovely couple sitting in the front row, 1A and 1B are terrorists."

"And would the children be their accomplices now, to be sure?" Belinda asked.

"Yes, they would need help," Dorothy added, giggling.

"I'm just off to warn the captain of the danger we're in," I told them, "then we'll begin the service."

When I opened the flight deck door, Ron and the first officer appeared to still be dealing with post-take-off procedures. I waited. Finally, Ron settled back in his seat. I tapped him on his epaulette. He removed his headphones and gave me a cursory glance over his right shoulder.

"Want to know something funny?" I smiled.

Ron grunted. He didn't have a big sense of humour so I cut to the chase.

"The lady passenger in 3B has warned me that the lovely young couple in 1A and 1B and their two children in 2A and B are dangerous terrorists. The lady told me that she recognizes the man's face from a newspaper years ago, even though he now looks completely different. She wanted you to contact the West Berlin police and have him arrested."

"What do you think?" he asked.

Great! He's putting the onus on me. "I think it's funny. They look like a Disney family ...but you never—."

"Okay then." The captain had decided something, but I wasn't sure what. He seemed a little distracted, as if he didn't care about any terrorist. My job was done. The passengers might all turn into terrorists if we didn't serve those drinks soon, I thought. I left the pilots to their real jobs, flying the plane.

Once the drinks were served, we dished out quasi-frozen sandwich triangles and cake. By the time we were serving beverages, we had already descended to ten thousand feet. The plane was now bouncing up and down and jerking from side to side, making pouring the hot liquid into passengers' cups—without scarring them for life—challenging.

"Can you please hold your cup over the aisle?" I asked one lady passenger mid-cabin.

She silently complied. I glanced at her white face. "It's okay," I reassured her. "This turbulence is nothing. It's always this bumpy when we fly along the corridor into Berlin."

"Oh, I'm not afraid of that," she responded in an American drawl. Then she pointed out of the aircraft window.

Off the tip of our wing was a large black sleek military aircraft. I recognized it as a MIG jet. It was flying so close I could almost see into the pilot's eyes. On an instinct, I turned around and sure enough, on the starboard wing, there was a duplicate aircraft. Were they there to keep a beady eye on us, to make sure we didn't stray from the corridor into prohibited East German airspace? Maybe the ominous presence was something to do with the bomb scare? Or "the terrorist?"

The military jets had accompanied us before. If we veered off course, even slightly, there could be trouble. The thought was a tad unnerving knowing that—without any just cause and with 89 plus five innocent crew on board—they might decide to shoot our plane down.

"They are just there to guide us along the corridor," I told the frightened woman, as she carefully placed her filled coffee cup on her lap table.

She nodded, but not comforted she glanced again at the jet.

The captain's voice came over the public-address system. "Ladies and gentleman," he began, "we are expecting the turbulence to increase in the next while and until we land in Berlin. Cabin crew, prepare to take your seats."

As I took my coffee pot up towards the galley, I glanced at 3B. The *Hausfrau* was still sitting in the same position, clutching her bag and not taking her eyes from "the terrorist" as if her staring at him would act as handcuffs and keep him in his seat. She returned my look and nodded. The man was talking to his wife while their children played a word game.

Once in the galley I pulled the curtain across. "We have to sit down so I'll do a landing PA now," I told Dorothy. "Stow everything." She nodded and took the coffee pot from me. I picked up the PA system and roughly translated into German what the captain had just said. There was a groan from some of the passengers as they realized they wouldn't be getting a second cup of coffee or be able to get to the loo.

The aircraft shook and bounced. Dorothy and Belinda quickly collected picked-over snack trays while I checked that seat belts were fastened.

"Cabin secure," I called into the cockpit. Ron, busy with controls, didn't hear me, so I stepped forward and tapped him lightly on the shoulder, giving him the thumbs up.

Dorothy and Belinda took up their positions on the double jump seat in the galley while I negotiated my way down the bumping aisle to my rear seat. I strapped myself in and through the windows observed the ominous black military jets as they continued to fly alongside our plane.

Could MI5 *Hausfrau* be right about the Disney couple? Sociopaths were often extremely good-looking people. I had been fooled before. Maybe I should be taking this German woman more seriously?

Memories of that day in London and being in the hushed silence of that exhibition hall ran through my mind like a bad slide show. I had been right to feel leery of the white yacht. Later, back at Peter's flat, we had seen the carnage on TV, the bomb had been planted in the yacht's cabin. Just a few more minutes and we both would have been ...

A loud clunk-clunk-clunk sound told me the undercarriage was unfolding. The MIG jets had, as far as I could see through the small ovalesque windows, disappeared. There were two airports in Berlin, one east, Schonefeld, the other in the West, Tegel. Unlike other airports which are mostly located out of the main city and in some foggy land bowl, Tegel—probably due to restricted space within the walled city— sat in the middle of German suburbia.

On our final approach, we were flying precariously close to—or that's how it appeared— some of Berlin's unsightly old buildings. We could see apartment occupants sitting at their kitchen tables watching us. Our wing tips dipped between their balconies, nearly touching their multi-coloured laundry strung out on lines, waving in the breeze like flags. One day I was sure we would land with people's clean knickers hanging off the edge of our wings.

We were almost down.

I hoped now, as I had hoped that day in London before almost being blown to bits, that today's drama was over. But now, like then, something told me we weren't quite done.

The aircraft's tires hit the ground with a minor bump. Despite the plane's landing speed of 135 mph, I unleashed my belt and hurried to the front of the aircraft where over the PA, I instructed passengers to remain seated. Even before I was finished, the red light illuminated on the forward panel, summoning me to the flight deck.

"You rang?" I shouted over the noise of reverse thrust. The first officer was completing landing procedures.

"We're night-stopping." The captain turned and announced without preamble. He was grinning.

Darn. My date with Julian!

"Why?"

"We're U/S. *Kaput.*" He precipitated my next question by saying "Radar. And they can't get the part until tomorrow, so we may fly back empty."

Nice.

"I hope you girls have your clean knickers with you." He smiled for the first time.

I wouldn't have enlightened him either way, but with Dan Air's tendency for aircraft going U/S, I usually carried an overnight kit.

The radar must have been the issue that the ground engineer had been checking at Gatwick. He obviously hadn't fixed it. Maybe that's why the MIG's had been with us. Without a radar, perhaps we *had* strayed out of the corridor into East German airspace.

As the plane slowed, I asked the captain, "Did you call the West German *Polizei* about our dangerous terrorist?"

He smirked. "I've been a little busy."

How would I inform our German MI5 Agent that she had not been taken seriously? Tact, lots of tact.

When I exited the flight deck, passengers were already standing, stretching their cramped limbs and reaching above their heads to retrieve coats and bags.

The Disney family would be the first to get off. Our MI5 agent would follow.

Once the airport finger was affixed to the front door, a German official appeared and before passengers could disembark, and as part of the routine, he asked for the passenger manifest.

"You vill also haff to count ze bar und submit paperwork before you can leaf ze plane," he commanded and then waved, signalling that passengers could now get off.

As they stepped forward, the Disney couple smiled at me, the joke still fresh. "*Hofftentlich, finden Sie Ihren Terrorist.* Hopefully, you find your terrorist," he said, a little smugly as he passed by me.

On hearing his voice for the first time, I was shocked at how creepy he sounded. "*Ja, Ich, auch.* Me, too," I said, an icy feeling shimmering up my spine. I watched as, still grinning, he shepherded his wife and children off the plane.

MI5 *Hausfrau* and her husband were the next people to get off. "*Warum lassen Sie Ihm weg?* Why are you letting him go?" she addressed me, hurt and mystified.

"Don't worry," I told her. "*Ich habe den Kapitain informiert.* I gave the captain the information."

This ambiguous statement seemed to satisfy her. "*Ja, das ist gut.*" Still clutching her monster handbag, she pulled her husband off the plane and disappeared into the finger.

As the limousine transported us to the Ambassador Hotel, I wondered if the *Hausfrau* had been right. Later, as I rinsed out my uniform blouse in the hotel's bathroom sink, I thought about that day in London.

Only five hours after the first Earls Court bomb had exploded, we were just exiting a pub less than one hundred yards away from Grosvenor Square when we heard the sickening thud of yet another bomb. The leaves of the trees right in front of us had rustled as dust from the blast settled. Ashes gently blew through my hair and settled on my cheeks. As we discovered on the news the next day, the bomb had been planted under a car outside a private home and triggered when the unsuspecting member of the House of Lords had turned on his car ignition. Without the luxury of a warning, the poor man had died instantly.

Once I had freshened up, and disguised my uniform by donning a pink sweater, the three of us waited for the two flight deck crew to appear in the lobby of the Ambassador on Berliner Strasse.

"This might be your only Berlin night stop," I remarked to Belinda and Dorothy. "While you have the chance, you should see the Kurfurstendam."

"The what?" Belinda frowned.

"It's the main street in Berlin, just around the corner."

"But it's raining," Dorothy protested.

"We'll take a taxi. You should see the ..."

Just then the lift door opened and Ron and Peter stepped out.

"I'm just going to show the girls the Ku'Dam," I told the two pilots. "We'll meet you at the *SchnitzelHaus?*"

"*Bitte hier anhalten,*" I told the taxi driver as we approached the bend on the one-way brightly lit thoroughfare, the orange lights from the numerous street lamps bleeding across four lanes of busy and shiny wet streets.

"What is that?" Dorothy asked, peering out of the rain-streaked window across the road at two illuminated buildings, their multi-colored windows shining like kaleidoscopes into the night.

"The tall hexagonal building is called the "lipstick," I told her, "and the shorter squatter one is called the "powder puff. They're churches."

"What's that dark building in the middle?" Belinda asked, seeing the burned-out ruin still mottled with bullet holes sandwiched between the two hexagonal constructions. Without any spire to reach skyward and with half of the front wall missing, the tower appeared incongruous between the two sleek new buildings.

"It's the old cathedral which was bombed during the war. It's called the *Kaiser-Wilhelm Gedachtnis Kirche*. It means Church of Thought."

"Why didn't they demolish it?" Belinda muttered. "It's so ugly."

The taxi driver turned and said sombrely, "*Uns zu errinnern.*"

"What?" Dorothy looked at me.

"To remind us," I told them.

"Of what?" Belinda enquired softly, still staring at the charred walls.

"*Dass es nie wieder passierieren werde,*" the driver added.

"To never let it happen again," I offered.

"Then dat's a good name for a church then, isn't it?" Belinda sighed. "Church of Thought."

At the *SchnitzelHaus*, both pilots were already drinking from huge beer steins. In true German style, the Dirndl-attired waitress served up huge slabs of meat on planks of wood accompanied by the best potato salad I had ever tasted. As we began to grapple with our dinners, we recognized the two men that entered also as Gatwick flight crew, Captain Jo Dempster and First Officer Dan Ranger. We invited them to join us.

"How come you're here?" Jo asked as he sat down." I didn't know another crew was night-stopping."

"Our radar went U/S," Ron told him as he finished swallowing a large bite of meat.

"Yes," I added, "we had quite the flight."

"What happened?" Dan, the perennial flirt, winked at me.

"As you know, we had a bomb scare at Gatwick, then we were pursued by MIGs, probably because we had a defunct radar and were straying into East German airspace. Then a German passenger was convinced that the lovely-looking family in 1A were the *Baader-Meinhof* gang, the terrorists"

Captain Dempster dropped his fork and stared at Ron.

"I hope you reported it," he said, not smiling.

"What? The terrorist? No!" Ron was defensive. "We had radar to worry about over the East German corridor. And anyway, Natasha told me they looked like the Disney couple."

"So do the *Baader-Meinhof* gang." Jo was accusatory. We all stopped smiling. "The leaders are a couple," he continued, "and they were based in Berlin."

I gulped. The man's creepy voice.

"The woman helped her partner escape from a Berlin jail," Jo continued. "They haven't been seen since. *And* they could easily have children by now."

"But the silly buggers wouldn't be plantin' a bomb on their own plane, would they now?" Belinda ventured softly.

"Hardly!" Jo snorted. "They're not suicide bombers."

"No need to take it out on my crew," Ron retorted.

"You all do seem to think it's a big joke." Dan, Jo's first officer, piped up protecting his captain.

"Well, I think we can relax now," Ron responded, taking a slug of beer from his stein and sitting back. "No harm done."

"Oh really?" Jo put down his knife and grimaced at all of us. "For your information, a live bomb *was* found on a German flight today. A Berlin out of Gatwick. Our flight."

10

BENT OUT OF SHAPE

July 1975

"But I don't have any night stop clothes," I groaned at the man in Ops.

It was Boxing Day, and I was checking in for what should have been a quick Gatwick-Milan-Gatwick, back in good time for my boyfriend, Julian's family Christmas party. But now the voice on the phone was saying that, instead of returning to Gatwick that evening, we would be staying in Glasgow and not returning until the following day. Ops man and I both knew that although I was feeling bent out of shape about this change, no amount of whining from yours truly would change anything. Whether I had my pajamas, toothbrush and jeans to change into or not, I would still be laying my head on a Scottish pillow that night.

Ensuring that Ops man would notify Julian of my delayed return, I turned to face my crew. Madeleine, the French anorexic red-head was sitting on one of the low plastic-covered chairs with a make-up mirror, checking her oh-so pale complexion and poking at her already beautiful, perfect hair. I only knew her by reputation for being a non-eater. The third member of my crew sat next to her, my friend, Pauline. At least, she, I knew would guarantee a fun flight.

"Don't worree, Natasha," Madeleine responded when I complained about our unscheduled night stop. "I 'ave a drrress you can borrrrow."

I surveyed her bony, meatless frame. "Thank you, Madeleine, but I don't think your dress will fit." It didn't matter how often I went on diets, I was slim, but with my hour-glass figure, I would never achieve "skinny."

"Ah yes, but eet strrrretches."

"It will have to. Com'on let's go."

While Madeleine opted to be galley slave, Pauline and I worked cohesively in the cabin, checking emergency equipment and replenishing seat pocket contents. An hour later with a full load of mostly Italian passengers, we were in the air and on our way to Italy. Because the three of us were experienced, without having to do much talking, we slipped into an easy routine offering passengers drinks, snacks and duty frees. Occasionally when we were in the narrow galley, I would brush up against Madeleine's very bony elbow and shudder. Maybe, I thought, having a little flesh on my bones wasn't such a bad thing.

On landing at Milan, we waved a *Buon Natale* to our departing passengers. When the last person had disappeared down the steps, the captain emerged from the flight deck. The tall, lean and funny Bob Charlesworth was one of our most popular pilots, but as I looked up from doing my paperwork, I saw that, tonight, Bob was not smiling.

"Natasha. Can you get the girls together?" he commanded.

Uh-oh. "Okay."

I went down the back to retrieve Pauline. She was furrowing through her crew bag. "Captain wants to see us," I told her.

"Oh, what *now?*" With hand on hip, she responded in mock indignation. "Don't tell me he wants me to fly the plane again!"

We both chuckled. With Dan Air, anything was possible.

Back at the front, we joined Madeline who had just stepped out of the galley where she had been obsessively cleaning coffee pots. When we were all sitting in the front row of seats, Bob stood over us, grimacing as he prepared to deliver what was probably bad news.

"Ladies, I'm afraid the airport is going on strike."

"Didn't Ops call the Italian Dial-A-Strike to confirm?" I asked, only quasi-joking.

"Actually, they did, but they're also on strike," Bob grinned, sardonically.

"What does zat mean?" Madeline asked.

"Well, we have refueled, we have minimal catering and we have air traffic, for a while anyway, but we don't have aircraft cleaners, baggage handlers or ground staff to check-in passengers."

"So, what are you ...?" I began.

"Well, you can certainly say no, but I'm asking you as captain, and so we can get these Scots home, that we all pull together as a team and...," he took a long, deep breath. "Well, the airline is willing to pay you one hundred pounds each if you will clean the aircraft, including emptying ashtrays, help with baggage and then check in passengers."

Bob surveyed our crestfallen faces. The first officer appeared behind him observing our reactions and frowned. He didn't like it either. By addressing all of us at once, Bob was making it difficult for any of us to refuse.

"*Quelle horreure!*" the delicate Madeleine declared.

"Ashtrays!" Pauline scoffed. "E-e-w!"

"One hundred pounds!" I repeated, thinking of accelerated savings for my home-to-be. "Dan Air's getting generous. But what choice do we have?" I asked Bob.

He shrugged, both hands in his pockets. "You don't really. We have to take-off, and soon, before air traffic controllers leave. If we work together, we can get it done in an hour and a half. Or we'll be stranded here for God knows how long."

I turned to the others. "What do you say, girls? Let's do it."

Both my crew nodded and slowly got up. "Pauline, grab a sick bag and start at the rear with loos and ashtrays. Madeleine, can you start at the middle and work towards the rear, I'll do the front."

"Ugh. Could it get any worse?" Pauline moaned as she moved down the back.

Bob exhaled. "Thank you, ladies." He grinned at the first officer and turned to leave. "Dave and I will go and sort out the baggage."

"*Ah, mon Dieu*," the disgusted Madeleine complained as she moved from ashtray to ashtray. "I ssink we should 'ave glerves."

"In a perfect world, we would have, but I think we know that Dan Air nor the Italians are perfect."

"I like sssings to be perfect!" she huffed.

"Why are you working for Dan Air then, Madeleine! You could work for Air France."

"Ah, non. Zey are too perfect! I am not good enough for zem."

We were almost done when I heard thuds on the stairs and Bob bounded into the galley. "Okay, girls, when you're done that, I need two of you to come downstairs and help us load baggage."

"Wha-a-a-t? *We* have to load the baggage?" I asked.

"If two of you can climb in the hold, then Dave and I can pass it to you. It'll be faster and we have to make sure it's balanced. Ballast and all that."

As the number one, and knowing that Madeleine was too delicate for the oily, greasy, dusty interior of the forward baggage hold, I turned to Pauline, "We can do it, can't we?"

With the lighted terminal in the background—no doubt full of impatient, Scottish travelers—the captain put his hands on my waist and facing him, he hoisted me up onto the edge of the hold. As elegantly as I could, I swung my legs over the sill and kneeled, waiting for the first suitcase. As Pauline climbed into the dark, cramped space beside me, I hoped that we wouldn't end up with blackened knees and ripped stockings.

The two men pushed the suitcases onto the hold's sill. With Pauline behind me, we both maneuvered the suitcases—according to Bob's instructions— as far forward as possible. After twenty minutes of being on my knees, I felt a new respect for baggage handlers, but then I remembered, they used a conveyor belt to do their dirty work.

"Okay, that's it." Bob shouted finally.

"Thank God for that." Pauline breathed. "And people think that being an air hostess is so-o-o glamourous! If only they could see us now, on our knees, groveling in a dark and dusty baggage hold!"

I allowed the First Officer to lift me down off the sill and onto the ground while the captain helped Pauline. We both brushed the dust off our uniforms and inspected our grubby knees.

"Okay, let's check these passengers in now." Bob said, rolling down his sleeves and marching off towards the single-story terminal.

"I think we need to just clean up a bit and put on our jackets and hats." I called after him. "We'll be right there."

"Okay." Bob marched away, his long legs taking lengthy strides across the tarmac while the first officer went to the rear of the plane, presumably to begin exterior ground checks.

Madeleine was still straightening the cabin and adjusting the head covers as Pauline and I— probably looking like we had been rolling around in a gravel pit—appeared in the galley.

"*Ah, mon dieu.*" Her long, bony fingers fluttered around her freckled cheeks at the sight of us. "*Les pauvres!*"

As I brushed my hair and put it up again in its topknot and Pauline wet a paper towel and washed her knees, I told Madeleine, "We're going to the terminal to check in passengers now. Is the cabin ready?"

"*Mais, oui! D'accords.*"

When we arrived in the shadowy, mostly unlit terminal, the crowd of people were standing in large groups, quietly resigned to this situation. *Thank God.* Seeing us, they all turned and stared, emitting a group exhale. Bob stood behind the brightly lit check-in desk. The white lights shining down from above framed his silhouette, gave him a white aura, making him appear almost like an angel.

"I don't know how to check passengers in," I told him.

"All you have to do is," Bob addressed both Pauline and I, "check passports against names on tickets and then check the name on the ticket against the passenger manifest and tick it off." He handed me a sheet of names. "And then hand out a boarding pass with the end ripped off. As long as the names and numbers match, that's all that counts. We just have forty minutes so be quick. Okay?"

Pauline and I nodded as we stepped behind the counter.

"Ladies and Gentlemen," Bob called out to the crowd. "Natasha and Pauline here will check you in. Please have your tickets and passports ready. The last time slot for take-off is in 40 minutes. To speed up the process, please be as cooperative as you can be. Once checked in, come directly to the aircraft just outside this door."

Luckily, the Scottish passengers had a sense of humour about Italy and their infamous, on-going strikes. Soon all of them were seated on the BAC 1-11 and ready for take-off. All was well.

The one-hour, forty-five-minute flight from Milan to Glasgow was surprisingly quiet. While we could only offer tea, coffee and biscuits, I wondered if the alternative—being stranded in Milan without a hotel or food—had scared them into gratitude and exhaustion. Most passengers slept.

Just before we began the descent, Madeleine, Pauline and I stood in the galley, shaking our heads at our still-grubby knees but happy that we had all earned an unexpected wad of cash on tonight's flight. Suddenly the F/D light flashed red on the galley panel. *Now what?*

When I entered the cockpit to find out what Bob wanted, he and the first officer seemed to be unusually busy on the controls.

"Yes?" I called out over the noise of engines.

"We have a failed hydraulics system." Bob reported. "Number two system is still working but we don't know for sure until we land if we have a locked undercarriage or working brakes."

Bloody hell! Going instantly into emergency mode, I asked, "Shall I prepare pax for a pre-meditated crash landing then?"

"No, but just in case, make sure the girls know their drills. We may need to do an evacuation," Bob said, sounding as if he was casually ordering his landing drink, and not as if we were about to die in a ball of fire.

I stepped back into the galley. But when I went to explain the situation to my two colleagues, I burst into uncontrollable giggles. Wondering what so funny, Pauline and Madeleine stared at me, probably expecting a good joke and not news of their potentially imminent death.

Pull yourself together, Natasha. Don't scare them. I told myself. There's nothing funny about crashing.

Finally, I regained control. "One of the hydraulics systems has failed so it might be a belly landing or brakes may fail. We are not going to inform passengers at this point, but we may have to do an emergency evacuation on landing."

"*Ah, mon Dieu,*" Madeleine hissed.

"Now I *really* need a drink," Pauline added.

"I want to make sure that we all know what we are doing. Madeleine, go through your evacuation drill with me, please?"

"Yes, of courrrse. I open ze port door and inflate ze chute and tell zem to go upwind of ze aircraft."

"Remember to check for fire outside first!" I reminded her. "And passengers must leave all possessions behind."

"Pauline?"

"Oh, bloody hell. I just open the door and boot them out." She giggled, too, then straightened her face. "Sorry. I man the starboard door, inflate the chute, tell passengers to sit and slide, sit and slide and then go upwind, especially if they have...you know."

Pauline was referring to the fact that in some dire emergency situations, mainly decompressions, passengers often let loose their bodily functions, passing wind or worse. The other vision I had was, like the movie *Airplane*, potentially we could crash into the airport terminal windows. Giggly hysteria threatened to overtake me again. "Okay," I said, struggling to keep a straight face. "Let's make sure the aircraft is as secure as possible."

"Ladies and Gentlemen," I began the landing PA, amazed at my own calm voice. "We are just about to begin our descent into Glasgow"— and hopefully not fire and brimstone—"so would you please return to your seat, lock your chair and table in an upright position"—and pray that the undercarriage also locks ...

Once the announcement was done, I reminded both girls to check the cabin for any potential missiles: knitting needles, glasses, pens and other sharp objects. I also reminded them to keep a smile on their faces while they did the cabin check.

When all passengers were belted in, and the cabin and galley locked down as much as it could be, I entered the flight deck.

"Cabin secure," I called out. Bob was still busy talking on his headset and without turning, gave me a thumbs up.

Madeleine and Pauline were already sitting on their galley jump seat, seat belts fastened. "Good luck, girls," I muttered.

Pauline glanced up at me, a wry grin thinly hiding her fear as she crossed herself.

"Yes." I took a deep breath. "And we thought cleaning ashtrays was bad."

"Oh, I kno-o-ow," she said, doing a nasally impression of Sybil from Fawlty Towers. "That'll teach me to complain about being on my knees," she said, her brown eyes wide. "Whenever I say, it can't get worse, it always does."

As I walked back up the aisle to my rear seat, I gave one more inspection of the cabin and prayed *Please God, Make the hydraulics work.*

When I passed the second row from the back, I heard the woman in 26A comment to her husband, "Eee, Fred. I'm going to be so-o-o-o-o happy to get to me bed."

"Och, aye," Fred nodded. "We'll be home verry soon, hen."

Briefly I thought of Julian. Would I see him again? While he was looking forward to a Christmas party, we were dicing with death.

Sitting alone on my jump seat, I cursed yet again that there was no communications link to the flight deck or forward crew on take-off or landing, the most crucial times of flight. How was I supposed to be responsible for everyone if I didn't know in each moment what was happening? I had another chat with God and asked if he would be so kind as to let us land safely—with or without an undercarriage and brakes —and bring us to a nice, gentle halt.

We were coming lower and lower to the ground. I paid extra attention to the varying droning noises at each level of descent. So far, things sounded normal. So far.

The aircraft banked around in a wide arc on the down leg. In my mind, I envisioned a speedy evacuation, ushering these older people down the rear stairs. But if the undercarriage collapsed, we wouldn't be able to use the rear exit and we would all have to go forward through the over-wing exits and front doors. At least with a belly landing, pax could just step out. No chutes needed. But if the plane was on fire... The captain can't think it's really dangerous, I soothed myself, otherwise we would have prepared the passengers as well. He's probably just being cautious.

I peered out of the port window. The aircraft now hovered just feet above the rapidly disappearing runway beneath. Was Bob bracing himself, wondering whether he should yet dare to touch down and risk an undercarriage collapse and ...a crash. I held my breath. The plane dropped. There was a tug as rubber caught and tires met concrete.

Immediately shrill sirens sounded from somewhere outside and behind the plane. Startled and curious, passengers peered out of port windows and saw a convoy of fire engines about 100 feet away racing parallel to us down the side of the runway. Our plane was still moving at a faster than normal pace.

The undercarriage must have locked, I thought. But would the brakes work? Could we stop, or would Bob have to let the plane veer onto grass and flip over?

"Oh, look Fred," the woman in 26A nudged her husband. "Look at all those fire engines! I wonder where they're going?"

Fred leaned forward and squinted into the night. Seeing the flashes of red with bells ringing and lights flashing, he said, "Ach, I've gawt naw idea."

Ignorance is bliss, I thought.

And if there was a fire, I was comforted to see those hunky firemen close by to help.

The plane jerked as the captain gently tapped on the brakes. I held my breath and waited and waited.

Finally, the plane slowed. We decelerated to a taxiing pace.

Phew!

Now out of danger, I got up and walked to the front. Madeleine and Pauline beamed up at me, with relief. They happily undid their seat belts.

"Ladies and Gentlemen," I began the PA. "We have now landed in Glasgow." I exhaled. By the skin of our teeth, I wanted to add. Should I mention the fire engines? Probably not. "Please remain seated until the aircraft has come to a final stop...."

Before returning to the rear to open the back door, I told Madeleine, "I know you don't drink, but you better pour extra strong landing cocktails for the crew, Madeleine. We all need them!"

At the rear, I retracted my jump seat back into its stowage. When the *No smoking* sign went off, I pulled open the rear door. Then I extracted the stair handle from its recess and pushed it downwards. Behind me, passengers were already standing up, retrieving their belongings from the hat rack, with Fred and his wife edging their way to the front of the crowd. As the rear ventral staircase unfolded and touched the tarmac, the sight that met us was a bevy of firemen. Before passengers could move, one of the helmeted-men clomped up the stairs, his bulky yellow uniform barely squeezing up the narrow ventral staircase.

"Are you alright, lassie?" the forty-something addressed me.

"Yes, thank you." I breathed. "Seems like the hydraulics worked after all."

Behind me, I heard Fred's wife gasp. "Hydraulics! Oh, ma Lord! Were th-the firemen for us?"

I turned to her. "Yes, it was just a precaution. We thought we had a problem but apparently...we didn't."

"Thank gawd for that." Fred muttered, clutching his chest.

The fireman looked around at the few passengers he could see. "Okay, if you dawn't need us then..." He turned and left. I stood back, indicating that passengers should follow him down the stairs.

Once all the passengers were off—and like Fred, remembering to thank God for listening to my prayers—I walked to the front anticipating in joining everyone, except the teetotalling Madeleine, in a strong Scotch and coke. But when Bob emerged from the flight deck, he already had his hat on and was fastening the buttons on his jacket. "Let's take our drinks to the hotel and celebrate," he urged. "I don't know about you, but I want to get off this aircraft."

In stark contrast to the surrounding older, grey granite buildings of Glasgow, we arrived at the more modern red-bricked hotel. In my room and even before I had a chance to take my shoes off, Madeleine had appeared at my door, clutching the dress she had promised me.

"Oh, it's beautiful, Madeleine!" I exclaimed holding up the bright red woollen dress. "It looks like you bought this in Paris." I had visions of stretching it irrevocably to the size of my curves and when she came to put it on her skeletal frame later, it would hang like a shapeless sack. "Are you sure? I don't want to stretch it so much that it won't go back into shape."

"Ah, pff." She shrugged her French shrug. "Perfection is not so important." Madeleine laughed, sounding surprisingly musical. "Aftair today, none of us will be ze same again. We 'ave all been bent out of shape, n'est-ce pas?"

11

THE CHEAP SEAT

August 1975

It should have been an uneventful flight. After all, we were just flying one short sector from Manchester to Glasgow.

The tour operator was Saga and to qualify for their trips, passengers had to be sixty-plus, though they were mostly much older. These passengers sometimes only made it one way—outbound. And some didn't even travel that far. The more infirm snuffed it in-flight— in the cabin or in the loos. And the inbound passenger manifest often included pine boxes, which were stowed in the cargo hold. Saga flights, and deaths, were one of my worst fears.

Today wheelchair passengers and those with other medical paraphernalia were taking the usually protracted time to board the 89-seater two-engine BAC 1-11. While Pauline organized her galley at the front of the plane, and the new girl, the Scottish Roberta, helped the passengers settle into their seats, I counted heads.

"Eighty-nine?" I confirmed with the ramp officer who waited in the galley, clutching his clip board.

He nodded. "Full load." He then poked his head into the flight deck. "All on board, sir. Have a good flight," he called and then disappeared into the airport finger.

"Roberta, will you bring up the rear stairs and close the rear door, please?" I asked the dark-haired Scottish hostess as I returned to the galley.

"Och, I've just dunnit," she responded. "It's closed."

"Oh, good." I appreciated a new girl that didn't have to be told the routine. "Just come into the galley a second and pull the curtain behind you."

Roberta stepped inside and pulled the blue fabric until it fully blocked the view of passengers, still settling into their seats and fumbling with belongings.

"The flight's barely 50 minutes," I informed my two crew, "and I doubt if we'll go above ten thousand feet. Service is a light snack and one tea and coffee. Any questions, Roberta?"

"Ach, hen. I think I knaw what to dooo."

"Good." I picked up the handset from the galley bulkhead and began the pre-flight announcement as both cabin crew—clutching oxygen masks and life jackets— positioned themselves forward and mid-cabin for the safety demonstration.

"Ladies and gentlemen ...," I began.

As soon as I had finished and while the aircraft began taxiing, Roberta checked that passengers' seat belts were fastened, beginning at the rear and moving forward while Pauline checked from the front.

Once the girls affirmed, "Cabin secure," I called into the flight deck.

Usually I would receive a thumbs-up from the captain, but he turned. "Rear door's not closed," he called over the noise of revving engines.

I groaned. Maybe Roberta didn't know what she was doing after all. "Okay, I'll do it."

While the junior stewardesses took their place on the double seat in the galley, I headed to the rear of the plane.

On the other side of the rear door was a ventral staircase through which passengers, cleaners, engineers—and sometimes firemen—boarded the plane. When the stairs were raised and closed, they folded flat into a panel which formed the underbelly of the aircraft's rear end. Between the flattened stairs and the rear door was a triangle of black space which was not, like the interior of the cabin—pressurized. I saw that the rear door with its round porthole window was indeed slightly ajar.

I pushed the door closed and pulled the handle up into its locked position. Hmmm? I thought, Why had Roberta raised the stairs, but not locked the door properly?

While trying not to disturb passengers in the last row, I yanked on my retractable jump seat from its stowed location behind the back seats. Once pulled out, the metal and leather contraption snapped from its vertical position down into a chair that jutted partway into the aisle. I sat and pulled my seatbelt tight around me.

As number one, I was never comfortable in this location just forward of the port and starboard toilets cozied up too close to passengers. In addition to being cut off from the rest of the crew, the noise of the two Rolls-Royce engines positioned at the rear of the plane would probably make me go deaf before I was thirty years old.

After take-off, once the *No Smoking* sign had been extinguished and I heard the *clunk clunk* of the undercarriage retracting, I stood up from my jump seat. Pulling the spring-loaded latch of my chair until it reverted to one vertical slab, I apologized to the lady on my right as I jostled the jump seat behind her chair.

"They don't let you sit for long, do they, dear?" she commented affably.

"You have no idea." In an attempt at Monty Python humor, I added, "On this job I 'ave to get up before I go to me bed."

"What?" The woman frowned and cupped a hand behind her ear. The engines were still surging for the ascent.

I just smiled and waved a dismissive hand.

As the aircraft continued to climb at a steep angle, I walked uphill to the front of the cabin to make my after-take-off announcement and start the cabin service.

But I only made it halfway.

A tight grip on my arm pulled me back.

From one of the aisle seats, an elderly lady was looking up at me. "I dawn't want to be a nuisance, dear," she said in a soft Scottish brogue, clinging to my arm, "but my husband went to the loo just before take-off and he hasn't returned."

I gazed at the eighty-year-old with a sinking feeling. Oh God, I thought, I hope he didn't meet his maker in the toilet.

"Don't worry, madam" I responded, knowing that there was plenty to worry about. "I'll go and look. Some passengers don't know how to operate the door handle."

That part was true. Once inside, passengers had to pull the toilet door inward to open the folding partition. In a very cramped space, some people suffered claustrophobia. The hostesses would often hear a loud banging at the rear of the plane and watch as the toilet door bulged out-ward while some poor panicking soul, in a desperate attempt to escape, was ramming the door off its hinges.

People were lighting up their cigarettes creating a haze in the cabin. The *Fasten Seat Belt* sign was still illuminated so passengers were in their seats where they should be. When did this man disappear without my seeing him? I hadn't noticed any empty seats on my way to the back. Maybe he had got up during the one minute I was in the flight deck giving the captain the cabin check?

I arrived at the rear and stared at both toilets. Both latches were green, indicating they were both vacant. But that wasn't proof of non-occupancy. Apart from the loud whine of the engines, I could not hear any sounds of movement from inside the compartment, port or star-board. Which one first? Holding my breath, I chose the starboard toilet.

Before opening the door, I knocked. "Hello-o," I called out, desper-ately hoping there might be a response, even a feeble one. I leaned into the door and listened. "Is anyone in there?" But there was no reply. *Oh God, here we go.* Tentatively, I pulled the door inward and peered in. It was empty. The toilet seat was down, the sink still clean, the soaps un-touched. No one had been in here. He must be in the other one, I thought.

Turning around, I followed the same procedure with the port toilet. Hearing no response, I dreaded opening this door. What would I see?

An old man slumped over the sink in the throes of a heart attack, or worse, a dead corpse sitting on the can with his "troosers" around his ankles.

I pulled the door inwards and stared. As with the starboard toilet, the compartment was untouched, pristine—and empty.

I scanned the cabin. The wife was still sitting in her aisle seat with no one next to her. Where could he be? Passengers can't get off aircraft! Maybe he went forward. That's it. I hurried up the aisle again, hoping the man's wife wouldn't stop me.

In the galley, the two junior girls were loading meals onto a trolley. But there was no stray passenger with them. I held open the flight deck door and peered in, but only the captain and first officer were in their seats, still completing their after-take-off procedures. I closed the door again.

"You won't believe this," I announced to Pauline and Roberta, suppressing my rising panic, "but a passenger has disappeared off the aircraft."

Both girls stopped and stared at me. "But he hasn't tried our gourmet snacks yet," Pauline joked, herself a veteran of Saga flights.

I wasn't amused. I grabbed the passenger manifest and searched for the passenger's name.

Pauline became serious. "But how the hell ...?"

"The man in 11D ...Mr. MacPhee, went to the loo before take-off and hasn't returned," I informed them. "And both toilets are empty!"

Roberta pulled back the curtain to peer down the cabin, but I snatched it from her and covered the galley opening again. I did not want the man's wife to witness all three stewardesses appearing flummoxed by her husband's disappearance.

"Mebbee the poor wee man got sucked doon the biffy," Roberta offered, giggling.

"This is not funny," I snapped. How would I explain *this* on my flight report?

"Maybe he's a ghost and slipped out the back," Pauline offered.

My eyes went wide "Oh my God, that's it!"

I pulled the curtain back. "Pauline, can you start the snacks service with Roberta," I requested, deliberately adopting my everything-is-under-control face before starting down the aisle.

I hoped to sneak by the man's wife in 11C until I knew if my theory was correct, but the woman caught me by the arm again. "Have you found ma husband, de-e-err?" she asked fretfully.

Oh, no! "I think so... Let me ...Just give me a minute, please," I said, hurrying on toward the rear. God, I hope he's not dead.

I arrived at the rear door. If my hunch was right, and he had fallen in there, the older man could easily have died of a heart attack, shock, an injury or fear. It was unlikely he was still alive. I braced myself, stood on tiptoe and peered down through the rear door's porthole into the black void.

I could see something white.

And it moved.

Oh God, the man *was* in there.

And he was alive ...so far.

I wasn't sure if the plane was pressurized, or if it was even possible to open the door in flight. This had never happened before. But as they were flying at just 10,000 feet, he probably had enough oxygen. Or did he? Could he survive lying prostrate on the rear ventral staircase for a fifty-minute flight?

In an attempt to comfort the man, I put my palm against the round window and gave a small wave. At least he would know someone was aware of his dilemma.

I must tell the captain. As I strode up the cabin, I stopped briefly at 11C. How could I tell this frail woman that her husband was flying in the cheap seat outside the cabin? He might not be in any immediate danger from the aircraft, but he could be seriously injured, or experiencing heart failure.

"Madam, we have found your husband and I believe he's ...okay ...and ...I'll be right back." I pulled myself away from the woman's grasp and squeezed past the snacks trolley.

"Captain Broadchurch," I started breathlessly once I was in the flight deck. "Would it be possible to open the rear door in-flight?"

"Why? You wanna get off?" He turned and grinned at me.

Good, I thought. He has a sense of humour. Could I be fired for allowing a passenger to fall into the rear ventral staircase? "Funny you should say that. Actually ...one of the passengers tried to get off."

"What?" Both captain and first officer turned to stare at me.

"He must have mistaken the rear door for the loo before take-off and stumbled in there. Then," I blurted, "when you told me it was open, I closed it ...but I didn't know..." Who would think to look there? Anticipating the question on their minds, I offered, "I think he's still alive..."

"Good God!" the captain snorted. "The plane is partially pressurized, so we can't open the door. He should have enough oxygen though. We'll begin our descent early, but we'll still have to wait until we land before we can open it."

"Oh." I groaned, empathizing with the terrible fright and noise the man must be experiencing. "How long till we're down?"

"About twenty-five minutes," the moustached ex-RAF co-pilot responded. "I'll ask for clearance for a lower altitude, but it won't make that much difference to the poor bugger."

"Request an ambulance," the captain reminded the co-pilot.

And a pine box, I was tempted to add.

As I left the cockpit, I wondered what I should tell the man's wife. The other two girls working the meal trolley were just past mid-section of the cabin. I went up behind Pauline and whispered the news in her ear. "I found him in the rear ventral staircase."

Pauline's eyes went wide as she registered shock.

"Is he oh-kay?" Roberta called from the other end of the cart. "Can we get him out o' there?"

I gave the new hostess a stern look, silently reminding her that passengers would be listening. But they seemed blissfully unaware of the drama that was taking place—and that's the way I wanted it.

Roberta blushed and resumed handing out snacks.

Now the fun part, I thought. I have to tell his wife that her husband took the cheap seat.

As I approached 11C, I knelt and looked into the woman's terrified eyes. "Mrs. MacPhee," I started, reaching for the frail hand. "We have found your husband."

"Oh?" The little lady inhaled. "Is he ...?"

"He's alive ...and he's not in any danger." I hoped that was still true. "He might be a little bruised ...." *And completely deaf.* "It seems he went to the loo like you said," I continued, carefully picking my words, "but somehow he went through the wrong ...." I did not want to give the woman a heart attack. Two deaths on my manifest would not look good. "As far as I can tell, he's all right but unfortunately, we can't open the door during flight."

"Door!" The woman clasped a wrinkled hand to her chest. "Where...?"

"Well, it's more like a hold," I reassured her, immediately cursing myself for letting the word "door" slip. "I peeked through the porthole, and I saw him move. We just can't get to him at the moment."

"Oh, ma gawd." The woman was undoing her seatbelt. "I should go?"

"No. Better you stay here." I gently squeezed the woman's hand. "The captain is going to descend to a lower altitude to make your husband more comfortable."

The woman's rheumy eyes misted with tears.

"We will probably take you both to get checked up when we land, so don't be alarmed when you see the ambulance meeting the aircraft."

"Aw de-e-e-rrr," she moaned, nodding and shakily pulling a lace handkerchief from her left sleeve to dab at her eyes. "Aw de-e-e-rr."

At the rear, I peered through the porthole again. I waved, but there was no movement now. Was he still alive? Anyone could die from the terror of being trapped in that cramped, black space with engines roaring into both eardrums. For his sake, when he fell forward into the raised staircase and before the unholy noise of take-off began, I hoped he had been knocked out.

As I sat on my rear jump seat for landing, I realized that the situation could be worse. Thank god, this wasn't a regular flight when they would have been flying for two or more hours at a fully pressurized 35,000 feet.

With no oxygen in the enclosed staircase and temperatures outside the plane at a chilly minus fifty-six degrees, he would have been a goner for sure.

As soon as the tires hit the tarmac, and with the plane still travelling at one hundred and thirty miles per hour, I wrenched my seatbelt undone. After pulling the large handle down, I opened the rear door inwards.

There, lying in the stairwell was a tall, slim man in a dark suit. His bony hands appeared frozen to the side rails of the stairs. In the shadows, I couldn't see whether his eyes were open or closed. *Please God, don't let him be dead.* I opened the door wider to allow more light from the cabin.

I heard a low moan and saw a slight movement of his head. His eyes opened slowly as if afraid of what he might see. My shape must have been silhouetted against the daylight in the cabin. Perhaps he thought he'd died, and he was being greeted by a haloed being?

"Mr. MacPhee?" I asked gently.

Then his face crumpled into a huge grin.

He was alive!

I laughed with relief. "Sir," I shouted above the noise of reverse thrust. "The plane is on the ground, but we are still moving. Are you injured?"

The man stared at me as if I were still a vision—and still uncomprehending.

"Mr. MacPhee, are you ...injured?" I bellowed. "Can you move?" I stretched out a hand. "Let me help you."

Tentatively he released one hand from the metal railing and clung to my outstretched wrist. Though he was frail, he pulled so hard I thought I might tumble into the stairwell on top of him.

"'Ere. Let me 'elp you, luv." A strong male voice came from behind. I recognized the burly sixtyish man from the rear row on the portside. He squeezed in beside me.

Mr. MacPhee released my arm and grabbed the rail again so I could step back and allow Burly Man to take my place. "Com'on, guv," he said as he crouched down. "You probably wanna get out o' there." Steadying his weight, he clamped onto both of the older man's bony wrists and gently pulled him forward.

Once the dazed man was inside the cabin, teetering and blinking in the light—and as we were still moving—he was gently placed on my jump seat where he could recover his equilibrium. I noticed a slight gash on his left temple which he probably suffered when he stumbled into the dark hole, face first.

The plane had now slowed. I pressed the stewardess call button in the last row several times. At the front, Pauline stuck her head around the galley bulkhead. I signalled for her to come to the rear to give her my instructions. "Can you do a PA and tell all passengers they will have to disembark at the front, so the ambulance can access the rear."

Before the airport nurses supported the elderly man and his shaken wife down the rear stairs, I teased, "Next time, let us know you want to fly the cheap seat. We could make you more comfortable."

"Och, does this mean I get a wee refund?" the man countered in his soft Scottish accent, chuckling.

"No, but you might be inducted into the Flying Hall of Fame."

"What for exactly?"

He obviously hadn't suffered any brain damage, nor had he gone deaf, I thought, relieved.

"Oh, you know." I smiled, hoping he would understand my flying humour. "Being the ideal passenger. Out of sight, out of mind and no complaining."

"Waill, norrrmally I would thank you for a good flight, but the stewardesses didn't come by with a wee drink so-o-h I hope yooo'll understand if I don't rave about the in-flight service."

"Understood."

He nodded, grinned and then allowed the nurse to guide him and his wife down the all-too familiar stairs and into the waiting ambulance.

12

ARE YOU QUITE MAD?

October 1975

On a late September Sunday afternoon under a cloudless blue sky, Julian and I arrived at the historical Shobdon Aerodrome. Located on the border between England and Wales, and surrounded by gorgeous green countryside, this old royal air force base had played a major role as a reception point for casualties first received after the Battle of Dunkirk in 1940. Then in 1943, the RAF's Glider Training School moved to Shobdon, preparing glider pilots for the Normandy and Arnhem landings. Aware of this history, I imagined how the too-young pilots during that World War ll era, climbed into their planes for their next dangerous and perhaps final mission.

But on this day, in the mellowing sun of a still surprisingly warm autumnal afternoon with light recreational planes buzzing around the sky, the place was now a hive of peaceful activity.

When last week I had announced to my favorite ex-RAF airline captain, Pete Bentley, our intention to come for gliding and flying lessons, and perhaps do a parachute jump, he had snorted, "Are you quite mad?"

"Learning to glide is safer than flying in a powered aircraft that could go down in a ball of fire," I had told him. "At least there are no engines."

"My point exactly," Peter scoffed, twiddling his handlebar moustache. "And what happens when you run out of thermals?"

"Land safely in a grassy field?" I said, grinning.

"You are definitely mad!" he huffed, as he stood and disappeared into the flight deck.

Julian and I had originally planned to go to Canada for our vacation, but Dan Air had suddenly changed their ticket policy. Now we had to be married for both of us to receive airline discounts and marriage wasn't in the cards just yet. The only alternative was for us to do something boring like go to Bognor Regis, lie on the beach and eat candy floss. We wanted some excitement.

Whether or not I would do a parachute jump was still debatable. My real motivation for being willing to throw myself out of a small plane was, I realized, to prove something to my boyfriend—or myself. We had this unspoken dare between us. If he could do it, so could I—or so I liked to think.

We parked our Ford Escort and walked the long driveway towards the main hangar where we had been instructed to register for our week's course in gliding and power flying.

"Look!" Julian pointed skyward.

In the clear blue sky at about two thousand feet, I saw two small planes flying while bodies leapt from the black holes in their sides into nothingness. We stopped to watch. One after the other, small figures way up in the air splayed horizontally, like green army plastic soldiers— similar to the ones my brother used to play with—fell fast. One by one, their parachutes inflated and with legs now swaying vertically from side to side, they floated down towards earth.

More figures kept coming out of the second plane. The last person to jump fell through the air and kept falling. Why wasn't he pulling his chute? Was something wrong? He fell faster and faster, barrelling toward the ground.

A wad of dark material attached to his shoulders by strings suddenly shot up into the sky and formed a narrow column above his head. His parachute!

"Bloody hell!" I hissed. "It's not opening."

"Oh no," Julian muttered from beside me. "His chute's roman-candled."

He was falling, faster and faster, the chute still reaching skyward in a narrow stream of black.

A small crowd had gathered around us. "Pull your emergency!" A man to my right cupped his hands around his mouth and yelled as if the poor, terrified person might hear him. The others chimed in. "Pull your emergency!" they shouted in unison, their words carried away on the breeze.

I gulped and watched. Suddenly a second swath of black/grey material shot skywards parallel to the first chute. The crowd gasped ...then groaned.

"Shit!" a young woman exclaimed, her hand shading her eyes from the sun. "He should have jettisoned his main chute first. Now both chutes are tangled up."

He was still plummeting to earth.

The man behind me muttered. "Poor bugger!"

I could not take my eyes off the parachuter who was now maybe five hundred feet from the ground and would hit the earth at what ...200 mph?

"God!" Julian muttered.

The crowd fell silent. Some people had covered their faces, unable to witness the inevitable horror. I looked down.

Thud!

Everyone gasped. One woman let out a small scream.

I looked up. "Oh my God!"

The still-falling man's shoulders were yanked upwards from the rest of his torso. It was as if someone had slammed on his brakes and drastically slowed his descent. Both chutes had blossomed!

A collective sigh of relief spread through the crowd.

"Lucky sod," one man commented.

"He'll need a stiff drink," another one said.

"'E'll be roight if he gets away with a broken leg," a cowboy-type man with an Australian accent added.

The figure was floating gently to earth now. He and his chute disappeared behind a beech copse beyond the hangar and out of sight. We couldn't see how he landed.

Assuming that the man had arrived in one piece and the drama over, the crowd dispersed. Julian and I carried on to the historical hangar. "Well, you can keep your parachuting," I told him.

He frowned. "What do you mean?"

"I'm not leaping out of any bloody plane. If that had happened to me on the way down, I would have died of heart failure before I hit the ground."

"Doesn't happen often," he said.

"Once would be enough. I think I'll stick to flying lessons this week."

"Chicken!" He smiled, showing white teeth.

"Gloat if you want but I'm still a *live* chicken."

Inside the shadowy space of the hangar a Tiger Moth sat in one corner, apparently being restored, the fiery paint design on its wings half-done. Next to it, another small power plane looked as if it had met with an accident, the propellers bent out of shape. The large hangar reminded me of many a World War II film, or was it that I could still feel the ghosts of too-young pilots about to take off on their potentially deadly missions?

A short, dark-haired, good-looking man in green fatigues was standing behind a table, signing in other would-be flyers. A crackling and hissing walkie-talkie sat on his make-shift desk which he intermittently picked up and spoke into.

We stepped up and introduced ourselves. Green Suit confirmed that Julian would only be doing gliding courses for the week while my lessons included both power and gliding.

"You know," the ex-RAF instructor told Julian, "if the weather co-operates, and we get lots of thermals, you could go solo by the end of the week."

"How many hours will he need to go solo?" I wanted to know, my competitive spirit rearing its ugly head.

"Depends on your aptitude. Anywhere from fifteen upwards," Green-Suit responded. He smiled and extended his hand. "Flight Lieutenant Greggson. I will be one of your flight instructors—on the gliders at least."

"Nice to meet you," I said, feeling comforted by his firm handshake. "How many other instructors are there?"

"Two, probably. James Norton and Gary Owen." The man faltered and glanced down as if he didn't approve of his two civilian colleagues.

Uh-oh.

"We'll begin tomorrow with some basic aerodynamics, meteorology and parachute training."

"What?" I exclaimed, "Parachuting!" The color must have drained out of my face. Green-Suit seemed to be amused by my fear.

"You are required by law to wear a parachute when you glide so it's just to teach you how to open it," he said.

"That didn't work very well for that man we just saw plummet almost to his death," I retorted, waving a hand behind me.

Green Suit tapped the walkie-talkie sitting silent on the table. "We just heard. He survived with a sprained ankle. Of course, it could have been much worse, and it happens so rarely ..."

"So they say," I commented wryly, glancing at Julian.

Once we had our full timetable, our blank logbooks and instructions for the week's course, Julian and I went to find the Bed and Breakfast we had booked nearby. Later that evening, over a delicious fish and chip pub dinner, I interrogated Julian—as if he were the expert after having done just one jump—on the parachute failure.

"When your emergency doesn't open or roman-candles like his did," he told me, "you are supposed to jettison the first chute and then, and only then, pull your emergency. As you can see, he didn't let go of his main chute and they both got tangled up. He was damn lucky that they unfurled at the last moment like that." Julian shook his head, still stunned.

I shuddered, thinking of what might have happened. "Why do you have to count to ten after leaping from the plane and before opening the chute?"

"So the chute doesn't get sucked into the engine or get tangled up in the tail plane."

"Oh. That makes sense."

"In fact," Julian took a swig of his beer, "there was a story of a man who was parachuting and his chute *did* get caught on the tail plane. I don't know if he didn't wait for "ten" or if there was a strong wind that blew him back onto the plane."

"Oh, no. What happened?"

"Poor sod. His chute got caught on the rudder. There he was being dragged through the air seeing his life flash before him and knowing that he was going to die. The story goes that he got a pen out of his pocket and wrote a message to his family on his bare arm!"

"Was it his will?" I asked.

"No." Julian laughed. "He wrote that he loved them."

"How awful ...and lovely at the same time." I took a large gulp of wine. "It must have been a gruesome death."

"No, he survived! So he was able to tell his family himself."

"How?"

"I heard that the pilot did some fancy flying at a higher altitude to dislodge the chute and then the man did parachute to safety with his message on his arm."

"Well, that's a nice ending. But it's amazing that the plane was able to stay airborne with him on the rudder.

"Exactly." Now that Julian and I were soon-to-be-pilots, we already fancied ourselves as aviation pros.

"I'm definitely not parachuting this week though. Or ever." I reminded him. "You win that one."

"It's only *you* who thinks we are in competition." Julian smiled. "But we're not, you know."

"Well, maybe not in competition exactly." I put my wine down. "But you do push me to do things that I would normally be afraid of doing."

"Excuse me." Julian was still smiling. "Who suggested the gliding holiday?"

"Well, I suppose I did." I felt myself blush.

"See. Who's daring who?"

That night as I tried to get some sleep, I wondered if I ever had to use a parachute, would I have the courage to let go of the first chute before waiting to see if the second one was also a dud. I didn't sleep well.

The next morning, at 10:00 hundred hours sharp, and like many trainee pilots before us, we sat in the very basic RAF hut on uncomfortable wooden chairs. Through the small, high windows, we could see that the blue sky had disappeared and light grey clouds hung in a low ceiling. Green Suit talked about millibars, ground pressure, thermals and explained all manner of things that even after 18 months of commercial flying, I had not learned.

He showed us diagrams of the glider controls and explained how each one worked.

The parachute training consisted of being shown the small rucksack-like appendage and then being told that the blue toggle was the main chute and the red toggle was for emergency use only. "In the unlikely event that the first chute doesn't open," our instructor intoned, "you must jettison the main chute first, wait for ten and then pull the emergency toggle."

Heard this before. Still not comforting.

"However," Green Suit added, "in this weather," he waved a hand towards the small windows, "you'll be lucky if you get much above fifteen hundred feet. The aerotow will take you up to one thou and from there, you'll need to find some thermals to gain altitude and stay up. Remember, you should be at the bottom of the down leg of the runway with a thousand feet of altitude to spare. The chute's not much good to you from that height anyway."

Oh, this just gets better. Maybe Captain Broadchurch had been right. Maybe I am mad. What was I thinking? But if I back out now, I'll never hear the end of it.

After lunch we were taken out to the runway and introduced to our glider. The sleek red, black and grey Czechoslovakian Blanik sat on the runway like a graceful bird, with one wing touching the ground, waiting for permission to go somewhere.

"You go first," Julian, said.

"Thanks," I muttered. Was he gentleman or chicken?

Green Suit handed me a parachute. "Put that on."

The light package on the back appeared too small to contain a huge chute that, if it deigned to open, would let me float blissfully down to earth. With shaking hands, I put the straps around my shoulders and waist, glaring at the ominous red and blue toggles. Maybe the ever-so tight packing was the reason they sometimes didn't open?

I slung one leg over the side of the Blanik, followed by the other and sank into the front seat. Although I had been in a glider before—as a passenger–I couldn't believe that I was actually going to pilot my own plane. Well, co-pilot anyway.

I stared at the stick and the controls in front of me as fear and excitement churned in my stomach. The instruments before me were far less complicated than on a commercial aircraft; an altimeter, air speed indicator, release handle for the aerotow, compass, speedometer and vertical speed indicator. So simple. No gyroscope, radar or radio. In other words, no instrument aids to tell you what was coming from behind or right at you. Once we were up there, we would be on our own, except for the birds. Green Suit had warned us that eagles and ravens viewed gliders as competition for their thermals. Sometimes, the raptors landed on glider wings and attempted to chew off the ailerons. The Rolling Stones song, "Hey! You! Get Offa My Cloud," took on new meaning.

Green Suit climbed in the back of my glider. The rope attached to the Blanik's nose was already hooked up to the two-engined aircraft in front of us. I noticed that its wingspan was about as wide as the gliders stretching far out to either side of the runway. From behind me, Green Suit reminded me of the instruments and their readings as he had taught us in the classroom that morning.

"Whatever you do, don't touch the stick until I tell you, especially on take-off. Once we are up, I will let you know when you can release the aerotow. You will just pull that yellow lever until it releases. Understood?"

I was tempted to say "Roger. Over and out," but Green Suit didn't seem to have a funny bone. "Understood," I replied.

My instructor gave a few more directions to the aerotow pilot. Was he the cowboy Australian I had seen yesterday? He nodded, stubbed out his cigarette on the runway, and looking like the very cool *Marlborough Man*, climbed into his cockpit. Green Suit slid the transparent, plastic canopy forward on our glider until we were sealed in our own see-through capsule.

The aerotow revved its engines.

"Ready for take-off?" my instructor asked.

"Yes," I whispered huskily.

Green Suit waved at someone standing on the grass beside us who then waved at someone standing by the aerotow who then waved his flag. The glider moved forward.

Here we go.

Julian stood on the grass and gave me a weak wave goodbye.

As the aerotow accelerated down the short runway, the rope between the powered plane and the glider stretched taut. The stick controlling the rudder in front of me was making microscopic movements as, behind me, Green Suit skillfully kept the glider aligned behind the powered plane.

And then we were airborne. The only thing between us and certain death was that taut twenty-foot rope.

We climbed higher and higher until I could see the patchwork of green fields, trees and farmhouses stretching out below and all around us. The wind rushed past our canopy making a shushing sound. We were up!

"Release the aerotow." The order came from behind.

"Did you say release the aerotow?" I called over the rushing sound of wind on plastic.

"Yes, release the aerotow."

I leaned forward and yanked the yellow lever towards me. With a twang—and like a coiling snake—the rope fell away and below and then recoiled into the power plane's recess. While the engine plane banked to the left, our glider soared higher on its trajectory.

Suddenly everything went quiet. The only sound was the hush of the air rushing by us. Heaven! Now this is flying! Much nicer than being in a deafeningly noisy old Comet or 1-11 on take-off when you can barely hear yourself think.

"You have control," Green Suit called from the back.

"What?"

"Take the stick," my instructor said. "You fly the plane."

Oh. Already? With the silence and the sense of flying like a bird, I preferred just to sit there. Okay. If you say so. Gingerly, I wrapped my fingers around the baton-looking rod.

"Look for thermals. Remember cirrus and cumuli," he said, reminding me of cloud formations that were signs of warm air currents.

In the low bank of grey, there was not a cirrus or a cumulus in sight. I pulled the stick toward me, attempting to make the glider climb, but it made little difference. Then I nudged the stick to the right and we began to tilt into a steep right bank.

"Oops!" I muttered and pushed the stick the other way. The plane tilted dramatically to the left.

"Gently," Green Suit chirped up from the back. "The glider is very responsive."

No kidding. We flew in silence for a while as I barely moved the stick in any direction, afraid of its sensitivity.

"See that straight road below us?" Green Suit asked from the back.

I peeked down to the right. For someone who was terrified of heights, I wondered at my willingness to fly. "Yes, I can see it."

"Fly along it. Keep an eye on your altimeter. We should be at the end of the downward leg of the runway at 1,000 feet. What are we at now?"

Altimeter, where are you? "Oh yes, er ...1256."

"Good."

I maneuvered the stick ever-so gently to steer the plane towards the landmark.

"Keep your eye out for other planes," the voice behind me reminded.

Oh yes. Other planes. I quickly glanced around in a 180-degree motion to check for movement in the cloudy sky around us. Would I be able to see pale gliders on this white/grey autumnal day ...before it was too late?

A light wind kept wanting to blow me off course so I kept correcting the path, sometimes over-correcting and then over-over-correcting.

The voice behind me went quiet. Too quiet. Had my instructor gone to sleep or worse had a heart attack and died? Oh my God, how would I get us down?

After ten minutes I couldn't bare the suspense. "Are you still there?" I asked, trying to keep the panic out of my voice.

"Yes."

Phew.

"You're doing fine," he added.

"I am grateful for your faith in me, but I like it better when I know that you haven't gone to sleep."

"I'm here," he said, giving me great comfort. "What's the altimeter reading?"

"1002 feet."

"Good. The runway is in sight. Can you see it?"

I peered through the canopy and down to the right was the long strip of brown. "Yes."

"We are going to begin the descent. I will take control."

With a mixture of relief and disappointment, I released the stick and watched as it moved forward. Down below, through a light mist, I saw the farmyards and the green fields loom closer. The plane, like a graceful bird, gently and noiselessly was descending parallel to the runway, gliding ever closer to earth. Before I wanted it to be over, and right at the beginning of the runway, the Blanik did a U-turn and landed on the unpaved but smooth runway.

Later that night, at our already favourite pub, Julian and I exchanged tales of our flights and instructors. Green Suit had told Julian he was a natural.

"Probably all that sailing you've done," I acknowledged. "You're more intuitive around the elements, especially wind."

Julian laughed. "So are you conceding that I might actually be better at something than you?"

"I'll give you this one." I grinned.

On Day Two, while Julian went with Green Suit in another glider, I was introduced to James Norton, a short man but older, greyer and less affable than my first instructor.

This time when we took off behind the aerotow, Mr. Norton explained the dangers of not keeping the glider exactly in the right attitude on take-off. "Most dangerous job, aerotow pilot," he announced. "If you are not right behind the plane, and below its wake on take-off, it's easy to pull the aerotow off its trajectory and cause a crash, dragging you down with it."

I gulped. While I knew that take-off for a plane was the most crucial stage, I hadn't thought about the delicacy of this operation.

When we were airborne and I had pulled the aerotow release, Mr. Norton told me that I could fly the glider. But this time when I took the stick, I felt a resistance behind my maneuvering. He's holding onto control, I realized. His lack of trust in me and the knowledge that I wasn't *really* flying the plane left me feeling cheated.

By the end of the week, however, I would learn to appreciate the play-it-safe Mr. Norton. Even after five hours in a powered Cessna, learning to take off and land, spiraling towards earth in a deliberate stall and pulling out and then experiencing gravitational pull or "G" forces in a dizzying spin, nothing could have prepared me for my final gliding instructor and his lesson.

Gary Owen's eccentric reputation preceded him. The very Welsh loud and flamboyant man was a famous ex-professional-rugby-player-turned-gliding instructor. Whether he was safe or not was debatable. Should I be excited to meet him, or scared? Our meeting, though, would be delayed.

On Day Four, we were informed that due to bad weather, low visibility and the absence of thermals, we would not be gliding that day. Instead, we were summoned to the training hut where Green Suit taught us more details about meteorological phenomenon and aviation skills Though we would have preferred to be flying up high. Julian and I enjoyed learning more theory.

On Friday, the last day of our course, we anxiously peered out of our B & B's bedroom window and were both thrilled to see blue sky punctuated with soft cirrus cumuli. Two hours later, we stood on the tarmac apprehensively waiting for the notorious Gary Owen to make an appearance. The quasi-sundrenched day had brought out more glider pilots—some of whom were women. One young thirty-something climbed in her glider and took off solo behind the aerotow. Would I ever be brave enough to go up all alone in a plane with just the wind and aileron-chewing birds for company? Probably not.

While we waited, a small truck rolled up to the hangar. Attached to its rear was a long narrow box. A bearded man climbed out of the passenger seat, shoulders hunched. Other glider pilots gathered around him.

Julian and I sidled over to the group and watched as the long box was opened to reveal a white glider, its wings removed and tucked neatly inside alongside the fuselage–a glider coffin.

"Are you okay?" a woman pilot enquired.

"Where did you land out?" my power instructor wanted to know.

"Bill, you did it again! Are you all in one piece this time?" This man slapped the bearded man on his back.

Though it was a friendly gesture, Bill grunted. "No broken ribs today, Fred. But the wheat field was in sight this time when I lost lift."

"Could have been much worse in a powered plane," I muttered.

"Yes." He nodded and grimaced. "At least there's no fire."

Exactly!

"Well, boyo, you must be my next victim?" Julian and I turned around as a booming voice preceded the large, solid man who had emerged from the transom hut and came over. As he reached us, he slapped Julian on the back, sending him lurching forward.

"You must be Gary Owen?" Julian asked, once he recovered.

"That's right, boyo." His smile was barely visible under his bushy handlebar moustache. "And is this your luv-er-ly young lady, is it?" he said, turning to me and surveying me like prey. "How many hours have you done in the glider, then, precious?"

"Five in the glider, four in the Cessna," I said, proud now that I had my very own flight log.

"And you, boyo?"

Julian pulled the small blue log from his back pocket to show him. "Er ...nine hours ...just in the glider."

"Well then. I think the young lady should go first, don't you, boyo? She's got a bit of catchin' up to do."

Before Julian could respond, Gary took me by the elbow and steered me toward the Blanik sitting inert on the runway, waiting for its next adventure.

As I slid the metal flange into my seat belt harness, Gary's voice bellowed from the seat behind me. "Well, Natasha, if you've already done five hours, you're almost a professional then, aren't you?"

I laughed. "Not quite!"

"Well, let's see how you do, shall we?" Why, I wondered, did the Welsh always speak in questions, the intonation rising at the end of each sentence for emphasis?

He signaled to the flag man that we were ready to go.

Marlborough Man started the engines, the rope tightened until it stretched ahead in a straight line, the glider nudged forward and picked up speed.

"You take the stick." The voice came from behind.

"What? But I can't ..."

"Yes, you can, Blondie. Just try it."

Oh my God. We're all going to die.

I wrapped my fingers around the yellow tip of the stick. The glider strayed slightly to the right, so I moved the stick to the left. The plane slid over to the far left until we were too wide of the aerotow. I moved the stick back to the right until the glider was barely behind the plane. I was over-correcting. We didn't have far to go before we would run out of concrete and the aerotow would rotate and take-off. I had to get behind the power plane.

I pushed the stick to the left again. Oh no! The plane veered far to the right ...and nearly went off the runway. "I can't do this," I yelled.

"I have control," Gary called out. Instantly I felt a slight pressure on the stick as he took over. I held my breath. Would we recover our position in time? He maneuvered the glider back in line ...just as the aerotow lifted off the ground.

The power plane rose up, pulling us up behind it. I exhaled. Shaking, I leaned back and let the aerotow take us higher with Gary, the mad instructor, at the helm.

Right after take-off and while the power plane was still climbing, I had a horrible thought. Gary might tell me to take control again. But he didn't.

"Pull the release," I heard and leaned forward to do the deed.

Twang! The rope fell away. Phew! Did the aerotow pilot know how close he had come to certain death on the runway? I hoped not. And now here we were, pointing skyward again.

Today the autumnal sun that shone—despite intermittent clouds—lit up the fields below in a carpet of luxuriant green.

The altimeter read 1276 feet when the voice came from the back once again. "So ...Natasha. You can take control now." This time, there was no pressure behind my microscopic movements—unlike my previous instructor. Gary was going to let me fly the plane. Once more, I felt the thrill of a new-found confidence. But this wouldn't last for long.

"See those birds up there? Starboard."

I looked up to the right and saw four unidentified blackbirds gliding round and around in an eight-foot diameter circle. They must have found thermals!

"Take the glider over there. See if we can get some lift, won't you?" Though apprehensive that the birds might attack our ailerons, I did as I was told. I pushed the stick gently to the left and then back towards me. The glider obeyed and rose, but one of the raptors must have seen the Blanik looking like a huge red and black striped bird and flew right at us.

Aaagh! The bird grazed the starboard wing. I held my breath. Silence. I peered to the right. It was gone. I peered below and saw that Big Bird had found other warm air currents where it was gliding, perhaps happy to rest its weary wings.

"Now stay in the thermal" Gary instructed. "Just keep going around until we gain some altitude. You don't want to go home just yet, do you?"

As we turned in a wide circle, I could feel the air beneath gently lift us like an invisible cushion. Below, the farmhouses, roads and patchwork of fields became smaller.

"This is my first thermal this week," I called back to Gary.

"Well, that's good, isn't it? You want to feel it, don't you?"

The sound of hushed wind on plastic could once again have lulled me to sleep. This was like sailing, but on air instead of water.

"Oh, I think we have a little problem to our left now."

As Gary spoke, I saw what he was referring to. Coming straight at us was another very large bird with a wide wingspan. Was it an eagle?

"I think it's time to leave now," my instructor said, with not a trace of amusement in his voice. "Just put the stick forward and descend about one hundred feet. That should get rid of the blighter, shouldn't it?"

The altimeter now read 1,367 feet. We had a little room to play with before we would have to begin the down leg.

Without much warning, I felt Gary's strong hold on the stick again. "I'll take it now," he called from behind and thrust the stick forward into a much steeper descent. The large bird loomed eerily close to the canopy before suddenly veering and disappearing from sight. When Gary finally levelled out, he asked, "So Natasha, you have done any stalls in the glider?"

"No. What? ...Stalls?"

Before I could finish the question, I saw the stick come right back toward me and the nose pointing almost perpendicularly up into the sky. The blood drained from my head, and I felt pressure going all the way down my body. My head, I was sure, was about to be sucked through my feet.

"Just a little "G" force, don't you know?" Gary explained.

I wanted to ask, "How many Gs?" but the muscles in my face were being sucked down into my chest and I couldn't speak. I knew that Dan Air jets were equipped to withstand 9 "Gs" of gravity. If this was just a *little*, I didn't want to experience any more.

Then without warning, the nose fell forward all the way down, pointing straight down toward earth.

"Ugh!" I groaned as the fields and farmyards spread beneath me. I was almost standing in the glider's cockpit. I heard scratching noises and realized it was the sound of my nails clawing at the canopy hoping to cling to something, anything to stop me from falling, or the feeling of falling. But the smooth surface offered nothing to hang onto. As the blood now rushed the other way, from my feet to my head, I froze, paralyzed by my fear of being suspended a thousand feet above earth.

"Now Natasha, can you see those lovely chickens in that farmyard just below, can't you?"

Hell, I can see their feathers! I thought. "Y-y-yes, I can s-s-see them," I whimpered. Now can we get this thing upright again, please!

"When you're a pilot, you've got to know what the plane can do," he went on, but I wasn't listening. I was just aware that I was pushing my feet against the nosewell, as if it would prevent me from plummeting to earth.

"You know that to stall a plane just means that you don't have enough speed-to-lift ratio so it's very important to know your stalling speed."

"O-kay." Whatever.

But if you do find yourself in a stall, all you need to do is push the stick forward and, well, you can see how we are picking up speed now, can't you?"

"Y-y-yes," I whimpered. We were falling toward the ground, closer and closer. The numbers on the altimeter were spinning fast-the wrong way-but Gary blathered on, oblivious to my apoplexy.

"Look at the airspeed indicator and tell me what it says, can you?"

"Er ...er ...airspeed indicator." I tore my eyes away from the chickens and refocused on the spinning instruments. Airspeed indicator. Where is it? Don't panic. "Er ..." As fast as the altimeter was dropping, the dial on the airspeed indicator was spinning in the opposite direction. Through a blur of tears, I told him the numbers.

"Just a little longer ..." he muttered.

Oh no. Just how close would we get to earth before he pulled up? I could not only see the chickens' feathers now, but also the colours of their eyes. There was nothing between me and that hard ground except a thin transparent plastic shield.

Then a miracle happened. The stick moved back toward me. The nose slowly came up. I sobbed with relief and sat back in my seat as the blood rushed once again to my face.

"I thought we might do some spins, but I think we can do that another time, don't you think, Natasha? Natasha? Are you there, Natasha?"

"Mmmm." I still could not speak

"All right, now. We can begin the descent. You take control."

The runway was just down there to my right. Now I couldn't wait to get down and out of this cockpit. In a daze, I grabbed the stick gently pushing it away from me. As we glided down to two hundred feet and we were poised for the U-turn onto the runway, I expected Gary to take over. But he didn't say anything.

"Don't you want to take it for the landing?" I asked.

"Oh, no. You can land it now, Natasha. Just keep going down and then ease up when you are about ten feet off the ground."

"But I can't," I whined. "I've never landed before."

"Well, it's time you did, then, isn't it? Come on, now. Natasha, you're a natural."

Natural what? Coward? Please don't make me do this.

"Point the stick further down, steeper. That's right," he urged as I aimed towards the green grass just before the runway began. "You're doing great, now aren't you?"

This man was either very brave, very stupid or quite mad. I decided on mad.

"Oh ...you're a little bit too far starboard, but it doesn't really matter if we land on grass. Just keep it going straight now. Don't correct. Now pull back. Pull back. *Pull back!*"

Rough green grass was rushing by us ten feet below. I was vaguely aware of several people standing outside the transom hut watching me land ready to leap inside and out of harm's way.

"Now ever so gently, let her down onto the grass."

Memories of sitting on the jump seat behind the pilots and watching them do numerous landings suddenly popped into my head. I remembered how they held the plane above the runway before gently setting it down at speeds of over 150 mph. We were probably just at 40 mph. I could do this. I pulled the nose up very, very gently and then tilted the stick forward again. The wheels made contact with the bumpy grass, and we rolled forward.

"Keep her straight now," Gary called over my shoulder. "We don't want the wings to tip now, do we?"

The glider obeyed, the wings stayed level until finally we came to a halt.

I exhaled. I did it! I landed the plane!

"You see, Natasha. I said you're a natural, didn't I?"

All I wanted to do was get out of the dam glider and get the bloody parachute off my back. Gary obliged by lifting the canopy and I spilled over the side. As I stood on terra firma, I realized how wobbly my legs felt.

Julian stepped forward. "How was it?" he asked. "I saw you doing stalls–."

"Is the bar open?" I snapped.

Gary Owen laughed and put a beefy hand on my shoulder. "She's a natural, you know. She did a great job, she did. Now it's your turn, boyo."

Thirty minutes later, as I sat nursing a scotch and coke, I watched the Blanik through the dusty windows of the small bar. The glider was visible at about thirteen hundred feet with my boyfriend in it, not only doing stalls, but flying upside down in rolls. I wondered how he would feel on his return—if he made it back.

An hour and a half later, when a blanched-faced Julian returned, I asked him, "So how was it?"

He shook his head. "I'll give you this one," he said taking a large gulp of his beer. "I don't think gliding is for me."

I smiled. Should I tell him that I would probably never get in a glider again either, or just keep this victory to myself? As we clinked glasses, I said, "Well, you can't win them all, now can you, boyo?"

On my return to Dan Air the following week, I flew with Captain Broadchurch again. "So," he asked when he saw me, "how'd you like flying planes without engines?"

"Gliding was lovely ...much more intuitive, but it seems to attract mad people. I think I'll just stick to the fun people who fly powered aircraft."

He smiled and disappeared into the flight deck.

13

NOTHING CAN GO WRONG, GO WRONG, GO WRONG ...

November 1975

"Bloody hell!" I cursed as I slammed down the hallway phone.

"What's the matter, Natasha?" Samantha called through the open door of our living room.

I joined my flat mate relaxing on the settee and flopped down on the armchair opposite her.

"Crewing won't give me the day off for Ellen and Greg's wedding," I huffed. "Well, they'll give me the day off, but I have to be on night standby."

"That's not so bad," she muttered, her face still buried in her *Woman* magazine. "They probably won't call you out."

"Easy for you to say." Samantha worked for British Airtours, and rarely got called out on her standbys. Just like the Comet aircraft that they had purchased from an aviation museum, Dan Air would also have us exhumed to squeeze another twelve-hours labour out of us.

Samantha glanced up. "Eee, it can't be that bad, chuck."

"You have no idea how bad it can get." But then again, neither did I.

Saturday, November 22, 1975, rolled around. The late morning sun shone on Ellen and Greg as they emerged from the small, grey-granite Norman church. The bride beamed as we all tossed confetti at her and her new husband. He, ever the stoic police detective, allowed himself a small grin. After a lunch-time glass of champagne, followed by a lengthy reception, I arrived home just before five o'clock.

As I put the key in the front door, the phone was ringing. Oh No. Praying it was anybody but crewing, I picked up the black receiver. I groaned as I heard a man's voice say, "Miss Rosewood?"

"Ye-e-e-s?"

"We need you for a night Tenerife."

Ugh. That's a twelve-hour duty! Should I "do an Emma" and try and get out of it? What story could I tell them? My pet leopard had escaped? I had been abducted by aliens? I had just come down with the bubonic plague? No, they had heard all the outrageous excuses.

"What time is check in?" I asked, resigned to getting no sleep on this night.

"Twenty hundred hours."

Oops! I realized that legally, I shouldn't have been drinking eight hours before my 7:00 pm standby duty, but I told myself, I only had one glass of champagne and that was about six-ish hours ago. Close enough.

As I donned my uniform, I dreaded the flight ahead. Not having had any sleep during the day, I was going to suffer through this lo-o-o-o-ng night.

The yellow lights of the expansive airline carpark highlighted a slight drizzle and only accentuated my dark mood as I began my long trek to Concorde House for check-in. The room was eerily empty except for one girl.

"Are you on the Tenerife?"

"Yes, I'm Philippa."

Her pristine uniform looked as if she'd just taken it out of the bag. I wasn't in the mood for dealing with a brand-new girl. "How long have you been flying?"

"One month."

"Oh." So not *brand* new, then. Maybe the third crew member would be more seasoned.

I went over to the flight sheet on the table to see who our third girl was. There were just two names, mine and Philippa's. Hmmm? I picked up the black phone to Operations. "Who's our number three?" I demanded.

"Er ...we have a slight problem." The young man sounded as if he expected me to reach through the phone line and throttle him. "You don't have a number three."

What? As so many other number ones before me had vented their frustrations on crewing, I sensed he was holding his breath waiting for my wrathful explosion.

Was it legal to fly with 89 pax and just two stewardesses? Not that Dan Air ever gave a flying toss about legalities. But yes, darn, it was allowed. The CAA stipulated that only one stewardess per 50 passengers was required. The challenge would be that the service would take longer, and if there was an emergency, we would have to adapt to different emergency drills.

"There's more," ops man was saying.

Now what? 89 paraplegics, Tricky Dicky for captain. Bomb scare? "What?"

"The aircraft is late in-bound and we want to keep your time slot so they've decided not to clean the aircraft."

"Ugh!" I imagined stinky full-ashtrays, stray bits of food on the carpet and God knows what in the loos.

"'Fraid so," Ops man said tentatively, still waiting for a blast down the phone line.

"Anything else?"

"There's good news."

"You're going to fuel the aircraft?"

Ops man snickered, relieved that I still had a sense of humour and he wasn't going to be the brunt of my anger—tonight at least. "You're positioning back."

"No punters on the inbound?" I envisioned being able to sleep. "Thank God!"

As Philippa and I walked across the tarmac flooded with more yellow lights, I learned that she had spent five years as a nurse at Guys Hospital. No wonder her manner exuded cool, calm and confident. If there was only going to be one new crew member instead of two, then I was glad it was her.

"Well, at least we have four hours to do the service," I told her reassuringly. "After they're fed and watered, they'll all probably go to sleep. Nothing much can go wrong."

Once we were on board, the empty aircraft looked as if there had been a food fight in the cabin. My grumpiness didn't improve when the catering arrived. Instead of a hot meal for this four-hour flight, tonight's passengers were going to be treated to triangles of ice-cold ham sandwiches.

"Why are these still frozen solid?" I challenged the caterer.

"Beats me darlin,'" the caterer said, slinging the light cardboard boxes into their galley stowage. "I fink dis was an ad 'oc flight, a rescue. The pax was supposed to fly BCAL."

"This is not good enough!" I snarled at no one in particular. "Only two girls, a dirty aircraft, frozen catering. These passengers will not be happy!"

"'Ave a good flight, luv." The caterer tossed the words over his shoulder as he fled the aircraft—and my wrath.

Philippa and I did what we could to make the cabin and loos look presentable before 89 holiday makers swarmed the steps. I stood at the front door and greeted each one with a "Good Evening," and a smile I wasn't feeling.

One fifty-something woman stopped and grabbed my arm. "My husband told me I should go up to the cockpit. Can you ask the captain?"

"Yes, of course. I can ask him," I told her. Some captains didn't like entertaining passengers in their hallowed space, while others reveled in the hero-worship of awe-filled visitors. Our captain, Ron Wilson, was a nice man, but he was also a stickler for protocol, and the other pilots considered him a bit of an "old woman."

"Don't forget," the woman snapped as she moved down the aisle.

"I won't," I replied, bristling at the nasty edge in her voice. Something about her demanding manner reminded me of my controlling alcoholic mother.

I watched as she and her two female companions settled into 9A, 9B and 9C. The rest of the passengers clambered onboard and sorted their belongings before plunking down into their seats.

"We'll do a drinks round first," I told Philippa, "then snacks, but hopefully they'll go to sleep before being subjected to cold food."

By the time we were in the air and the *No Smoking* sign had been turned off, it was only 9.20 pm. Whether she possessed common sense or was very intuitive, Philippa seemed to understand what was required of her. As we loaded the drinks cart, we fell into an easy flow of teamwork. Without a number three, Philippa and I would have to do double duty in the galley *and* in the cabin.

As we maneuvered the loaded drinks cart into the first few rows, with Philippa on the forward end and me on the aft, we grinned at each other. Passengers were already snuggling under their blankets and drifting off. If everyone sleeps, this might turn out to be the best flight ever.

As we arrived at row nine, I saw that Cockpit Lady was sandwiched between her two friends and laughing.

"What can I get you ladies to drink?" I asked, happy that they were already in the holiday spirit.

"Whisky and coke," she demanded.

"Would you like ice?"

"Yes. Lots."

I handed her the plastic glass, with a shot of whisky and a can of Coke.

"Give me three of those little bottles," she added, pointing to a box of Johnny Walker miniatures.

"And I'll take three gins," the woman by the window said.

"Give me the same," the friend in the aisle seat commanded, handing me a ten-pound note.

They probably want them for their hotel room, I thought as I passed over their bottles and gave the woman her change.

"You won't forget to ask the captain about me going up to the cockpit, will you?" the woman in the middle repeated, in my mother's who-the-hell-do-you-think-you-are tone of voice. The hard, flinty look in her eyes told me she didn't like me, but I didn't like her either. In twenty months of flying, having a personality clash with a passenger was a first for me.

"Once we've done the service," I responded with as much civility as I could muster, "then you can probably go up there." Maybe she was afraid of flying, I reminded myself and her aggression was masking her fear. "I have to check with the captain first." This seemed to placate her, and when Philippa and I moved the trolley down to the next few rows, the three women were giggling among themselves.

With the absence of a third girl, Philippa had to keep running back to the galley to replenish ice, lemon and minerals, so despite some passengers already having fallen asleep, the drinks service took much longer than usual. When we reached the last few rows, I told Philippa she could return to the galley to prepare teas and coffees for the snack service while I collected empties.

Two-thirds of the way up the cabin, I felt something tug on the trolley. The woman in 9C had grabbed one of the legs, stopping me from moving forward. "Give us more of those miniatures, will you?" she asked, handing me another ten-pound note.

"Er …okay," I replied. Purchasing so many miniatures was a little unusual. If passengers wanted to get blotto, they would normally get their duty-free bottles out and sneak the spirits into their glasses of Coke, but all three of them were still laughing and didn't appear inebriated, so I dished out the bottles she asked for.

Back in the galley with the cabin curtain closed, and in consideration of the people sleeping in the first few rows, Philippa and I dismantled the drinks cart as quietly as we could.

Then we heard singing.

"Oh, when the saints come marching in. O-o-o-h when the saints come m-a-a-arching in."

I pulled the galley curtain back and surveyed the cabin. Most peoples' heads were lolling to the side, mouths agape, some snoring, some drooling. But the three women in row 9 were clutching their drinks, their heads thrown back and belting out the song, "Oh, when the saints come marching in." As if she was Andre Previn conducting the London Philharmonic Orchestra, Cockpit Woman was waving her glass in the air, a lit cigarette squeezed between her fingers as she held tight to her drink. Passengers in the rows in front and behind them were fidgeting in their seats, glaring at row 9 with the unspoken words written on their faces, *Shut up!*

Groaning inwardly, I approached the three amigas.

Cockpit Woman was now sitting in the aisle seat. All three women were clutching their still-full plastic glasses, two sheets to the wind. How had they become so drunk so quickly?

Dealing with plastered passengers was a common occurrence, but with this one, for the first time I felt a tad unnerved, as if I didn't quite have control.

While anxious passengers believe it is just technical failures that bring planes down, I knew that it is often passengers—drunk or temporarily insane—who are the real threat. And this woman was a loose cannon in a tight space—unpredictable and potentially dangerous.

Could you please shut up? was what I wanted to say as I leaned over their seat. Instead, I smiled my hostess smile. "Ladies, I'm glad you're having a good time. And your singing is lovely, but I'm afraid you are keeping the other passengers awake."

The hard, flinty look in Cockpit Woman's eyes became even steelier. "Oh," she scoffed, raising a hand in the air, the lit cigarette between her fingers spilling ash on her pink sweater. "Thoshe peeeple are jusht no fun. Tell them they schould have more f-u-u-un. Wake up, pe-e-eple," she shouted, bending around her seat and addressing a middle-aged man sitting behind her. He merely gave her a look dripping with disdain, closed his eyes and probably hoped he would wake up in another reality.

Oh God. I'm not in the mood for this.

"I think," I said ever-so-gently, "that these people do want to have fun once they get to Tenerife, but right now they're trying to—"

"Well, I ...," she raised her hand again to emphasize the point that she didn't care as this was all about her, "*I* need to go up to the cocktail. My hushjband told me if I'm afraid of flyeeeeng, I sjhould go and sheeee the captain."

"Okay," I soothed. "Tell you what. If you keep quiet, I will go and ask the captain when would be a good time. Okay?"

"Oh-ka-a-ay." Her combativeness melted a little.

"I'll be right back."

As I entered the darkened flight deck, with just the lights of the dashboard reflecting on the captain's face, I felt the relief of being away from that woman. I waited until he had finished his conversation with air traffic control.

"Captain Wilson?"

"Yes, Natasha?" he said without turning his attention away from the panels in front of him.

"I have a situation. There's a very drunk female passenger who is adamant that she come up to the flight deck. She and her two friends insist on singing loudly and waking the other passengers. I kind of bribed her with a visit up here. I think she's really afraid of flying and it might calm her down if she can ask you some questions."

"Oh, God." The captain's shoulders slumped as he considered my unattractive proposition. "Well, you have to come up here with her, Natasha. I don't want to be accused of any improper behavior."

Wha-a-a-t? Where did that come from? The image of Captain Wilson even being capable of improper behavior brought a smile to my face. And how would he manage anything improper in this cramped space while flying a plane, and with a first officer sitting right beside him. Maybe I had two looney-tunes on my flight tonight?

"But we're only two cabin crew and—" I was about to remind him that Philippa was new, and we still had a lot of work to do.

"Either you come with her or she doesn't come up," he snapped.

Oops. Maybe he didn't get any sleep today either. "Okay. Thank you." I turned and left the flight deck.

Back in the cabin, my nemesis watched me coming down the aisle. Half- excited and half-terrified, she got up out of her seat. "Am I goingk up to jhe cockta-a-a-il?" she slurred, reverting to four-year-old childlike behaviour.

"The cockpit. Yes, but first you have to leave your drink and your cigarette here. In the flight deck, there is a center consul between the captain and first officer. If you drop any liquid on that, the electrics will blow a fuse and we'll all be in big trouble."

"Oh-ka-a-a-y." She giggled as she clumsily pushed her half-smoked cigarette into the armrest ashtray. Then she flipped her lap table down and placed her drink on it.

Once she was safe to enter the flight deck, I beckoned. "Come with me."

I opened the flight deck door. As she peered into the darkened space and saw the silhouettes of the two men flying the plane, her face filled with awe. She let out a huge gasp. "Oh-er."

I pointed. "Captain Wilson is on the left and First Officer Ryan is on the right."

"O-o-o-h, Shank you," she said, sounding pleasant for the first time.

She stepped forward, and in the darkness, immediately fell on her knees before the center consul and between the two men. She slung one arm around the captain's shoulders and the other around the first officer's. Her lips were almost on the captain's ear as she said, "My husjband told me I ha-a-a-d to come up to the cockta-a-ail cuz I'm sho schared of flying."

Ron pulled his head away and studied the woman for a moment, and then glanced over at me standing just inside the door.

"It's okay, Natasha. You can go."

"I'll come and get her in ten minutes? Thank you." Relieved, I left my nemesis in the hands of the captain so Philippa and I could begin the snack service. When I reentered the galley, I was delighted to see that she had already loaded up the cart with stacks of plastic-encased sandwiches. Steaming pots of tea and coffee waited on the galley's metal counter.

"You're so efficient, Philippa. Thank God!"

She beamed.

"Com'on. Let's get this done."

I pulled the trolley into the cabin and dished out snacks while Philippa followed with the beverages. Instead of waking the sleepers, I unlatched their lap tables and left a snack for them. Perhaps by the time they wake up and eat them, the sandwiches might have defrosted, I thought. When I arrived at row nine, the other two drunken amigas were drifting into a soporific haze. I left a snack on each of their tables.

"Philippa," I called. She was just two rows ahead of me and pouring hot liquid into a cup. She came up to the cart. "Can you go and get the woman out of the flight deck? I think she's been in there long enough. Check with the captain though," I smiled. "Maybe he likes her."

She grinned, turned and disappeared into the flight deck. After a few minutes, she re-emerged, followed by Cockpit Woman who seemed elated as she came back down the aisle. She climbed back into her seat, picked up her drink, lit another cigarette and gesticulated wildly as she related her exciting experience to her two sleepy friends.

Philippa resumed pouring teas and coffees.

We had only moved another four rows when I looked up and saw that Cockpit Woman was getting up out of her seat again, drink in one hand and lit cigarette in the other. She was heading for the cockpit.

"Philippa!" I pointed up the cabin. "Go and grab her! Don't let her go into the flight deck!"

My colleague marched up the cabin and intercepted the woman just before the woman reached for the door handle. Instead of marching her back down the aisle, Philippa began chatting with her, perhaps in an effort to placate her. They looked as if they were talking about the weather.

There was a tap on my shoulder. I turned. A tall woman with concern written all over her face pleaded, "Could you please come? My friend can't breathe."

Wha-a-at? Oh, God!

Against my ingrained instincts, I left the trolley unattended in the middle of the aisle and followed the tall woman back to 15A. Her fifty-something friend was sitting in a window seat, gasping for breath. *Oh, God. Oh, God, Oh God.* The next worst scenario to an out-of-control drunken passenger is a dying one.

Going instantly into emergency drill mode, I knew that to offer oxygen, the captain would need to turn on the therapeutic oxygen on the flight deck and unless we wanted to blow ourselves up, Philippa who was at the front, would have to do a "No smoking" PA.

I returned to the cart and stabbed at the stewardess button in the overhead hat rack, pulling it up and down, trying to get Philippa's attention. On the galley panel, behind Philippa's head, I could see the red light flashing, but as she was still engrossed in a conversation with Cockpit Woman, she wasn't hearing or seeing it. I wanted to yell, "Philippa!" but didn't want to alarm passengers. The hostess button dinged again in the galley as I urgently pressed again and again, willing Philippa to look up and see my distress.

I began waving.

Finally, she turned and peered down the cabin. Once she saw me gesticulating, I put a pretend oxygen mask over my face, hoping that she would understand that I needed the captain to turn on the oxygen.

But she just squinted down the aisle at me and frowned.

"Oxygen!" I mouthed. "Oxygen!"

Still not understanding, she shook her head and began walking down the aisle. Behind me the woman's gasps were raspier, more desperate. I groaned as Philippa took an eternity to arrive at the trolley.

"Ask the captain to turn on the therapeutic oxygen and do a no smoking PA!" I called out as soon as she was within earshot.

She glimpsed the woman behind me making rasping noises, nodded understanding and hurried back up the aisle.

I rushed to the rear port cupboard where the oxygen masks were stowed. Grabbing one of the yellow plastic masks contained in a see-through plastic bag, I hurried back to 15A. I pushed the end into the overhead panel. It didn't connect. Oh, no! The woman clutched the armrests, gasping and searching for oxygen, any oxygen. Don't die! Don't die!

I tried again. Push in and twist. It was supposed to be a bayonet fitting, like a light bulb, but it wasn't working. I inspected the metal end. It was the wrong attachment!

As Philippa's voice came over the PA, I rushed back to the cupboard and emptied the bag, frantically studying each of the thirteen attachments. The twelfth metal end appeared to be different from the others.

Back at 15A, the woman was bending forward, one hand on her chest, the other clawing the fabric of the seat back in front of her. I inserted the fitting, twisted it and ...heard a hissing sound! Thank God! I quickly put the yellow plastic over the woman's nose and mouth, gently pulling the elastic over the top of her head and letting it rest in her grey curls. She slumped back in her seat, dragging in large gulps of air. Her friend, relieved, sat on the armrest on the other side of the aisle. I waited until the poor woman's breathing calmed and levelled into a steady rhythm.

"Do you have a respiratory problem?" I asked the now-breathing woman. She nodded, clutching the yellow plastic mask to her face, obviously still focused on reaching for her next breath.

"Yes," her friend replied on her behalf. "She just had a lung operation." *Wha-a-a-at?* "When?"

"Yesterday," the woman mumbled through her mask.

Oh, my God. "Did your doctor tell you that you could fly so soon?"

She shook her head. "No ...he told me ...not to." She waved a hand at me impatiently, between short breaths. "I just ...wanted ...to get home to Tenerife."

Alive or dead? With the relief of her not dying on this flight, my anger now bubbled up. "This is one of the worst aircraft for people with respiratory problems, you know? You should have waited at least a month."

She removed the oxygen mask for a second while she gasped, "I ...know. I'm sorry ...to cause you ...trouble."

I relented then, feeling badly that I had snapped at her, aware that I was trembling from her near-death experience. "I'm just glad you didn't die." I'm not sure though that the ground engineers will live after I get back to Gatwick and give them hell for putting the wrong masks on the plane.

After another five minutes of calm breathing, the woman removed the yellow plastic from her face. "I think I'll be okay now."

"I'll tell the captain he can turn off the oxygen but keep the mask just in case."

She nodded. "Thank you."

The friend, still obviously shaken, moved tentatively back into her seat.

"Let me know if she needs oxygen again," I instructed.

Relieved, I returned to the trolley which thankfully, without any of the usual turbulence, hadn't barreled down the aisle into the galley or back toward the rear. Before continuing to hand out snacks to the last few rows of fast-asleep passengers, I looked up the cabin to see how far Philippa had come with teas and coffees. She was just emerging from the galley and coming down the cabin with refilled pots. I glanced up at 9A. Where was Cocktail woman?

Philippa came right to the trolley, resting the heavy beverage pots atop the plastic trays. "How's that woman? Do you want me to—"?

"She's breathing. Where's the drunk?"

Philippa turned and saw the empty seat. "Oh no!" she groaned. She turned to me again. "Could she be in the loo?"

"No, she hasn't come down the back."

"Flight deck!" we said in unison.

Philippa started up the aisle. I called after her. "Tell Captain Wilson he can turn off the oxygen. And then do a PA. They can smoke again."

With eyes peeled on the flight deck door, and still holding onto the hot beverage pots balanced precariously on top of the trolley, I waited. The potential disaster of a drunken woman with a drink and a cigarette on the flight deck did not bear thinking about. Minutes later, the woman stumbled out of the cockpit ushered by Philippa. Cocktail Woman's body language was belligerent, resisting Philippa who was impatiently goading her back towards her seat. Maybe a passenger would die tonight after all ...and Philippa and I would be charged with manslaughter.

I looked at my watch. *Ugh.* There was still one hour and ten minutes before beginning descent.

While Philippa finished serving beverages, I collected empties and offered duty free goods to a few still-awake passengers. As I arrived at 9A, I held my breath. The woman's head had fallen to the side, her cigarette dangling dangerously from her fingers. Very, very gently, I removed the cigarette. The butt hissed as I threw it into an almost empty coke can on my tray. The woman didn't stir. Perhaps she's descended into an alcoholic coma, I thought, envisioning her leaving the aircraft on a stretcher. And I realized it wasn't just her alcoholic behavior—reminiscent of my mother—that I found unsettling. It was also how she brought out my dark side.

At almost 1:00 am, except for the odd restless person, all our passengers were in a deep sleep. I asked Philippa—a nurse after all—to go and check on the breathless woman in 15A. If she was still alive, we could sit down and enjoy a hot beverage and a snack out of the hostie pack. Not that I was hungry. I was too mad to eat. I was mad at crewing, at the drunken woman, the breathless woman, the airline and especially the ground engineers. Being punchy with tiredness and frustration was probably not the right time to write my flight report. I'll do it on the return sector.

Impatient for this flight to be over, I made the pre-landing PA a little early so that passengers could also slowly wake up, go to the loos and fill out their landing cards in preparation for disembarking. From behind the galley curtain, I watched as the three amigas came to, looked around and began sorting their belongings. To my amazement, they suddenly looked like three sober, respectable grandmothers, going on holiday.

"Do you think the woman in 15A needs an ambulance?" I asked Philippa, deferring to her medical expertise. "Or a wheelchair?"

"Wheelchair would be a good idea."

"And maybe a straightjacket for 9A?" I smiled as I entered the flight deck to inform the captain to request a wheelchair.

While Philippa ensured that everything was stowed safely in the galley, I checked in the cabin that seat belts were fastened. My nemesis barely acknowledged me as she handed over copious empty miniature bottles.

Once we had safely landed on the tarmac at Tenerife, I relished the thought of our four-hour return sector on an empty plane. The thought of getting some sleep also improved my mood. As I cheerily wished our disembarking passengers a good evening, Cockpit Woman approached.

"You know," she said almost nicely, "you remind me of my daughter."

"Really?" I said, instantly empathizing with the poor girl. "And you remind me of my mother."

"Well, I know I caused you a bit of trouble," she said, laughing as though she had provided entertainment for the flight, "but we were just having a bit of fun. At least you don't have to see me again."

God, I hope not. "How long are you in Tenerife?" I enquired.

"Two weeks. Why?"

"Oh nothing."

She turned to exit the aircraft.

"Have a good time," I called out cheerily as she clambered unsteadily down the stairs. happy to see the back of her—literally.

Once we had taken off for Gatwick and the *No Smoking* sign was off, I told Philippa, "You go and rest first. I have a helluva flight report to write. And I want to get it down while I'm still mad."

"Oh?" Philippa frowned. "I'm sorry if I ..."

"God, no. Not *you*, Philippa. You did a *great* job. I'll be writing you a rave review," I reassured her. "Everyone else, though; crewing, catering, ground engineers and the office is going to hear about this nightmare. The airline's dam lucky no one died tonight."

Relieved, she retreated to the overwing, lay down across three seats, covered herself with a blanket and promptly fell asleep. I made sure the flight deck crew were fed and watered before I settled in on the front seat and began writing.

About fifty per cent of my flight reports consisted of two words. "Uneventful flight." But tonight, I vented. Over an hour later, I was just about to sign off when I remembered my words to Philippa before the flight. "Nothing can go wrong." Like the captain of the Titanic, had my over-confidence in positive outcomes tempted fate? Or had tonight's combined potential disasters just been part of that eventful fifty percent? As I stuck all four pages of my report into the brown envelope, I promised myself never again to say, "Nothing can go wrong."

And another note to self: If rostered for a Tenerife in two weeks, have a credible "sick" story ready.

14

AND NOW FOR
SOMETHING DIFFERENT

March 1976 – March 1977

They say that the way a relationship begins is usually how it continues—and sometimes ends. And when I first met Emma in March of 1976, so it was with her.

"Are you my number one on the Split tomorrow?" Her voice on the phone sounded delicate but not afraid.

"Yes," I responded warily.

"My name is Emma Blinkensop. I'm awfully sorry to have to ask you this but would you be able to pick me up? You see, I live in Horley, and I can't *possibly* get to the airport at 5:00 in the morning."

How about a taxi? I thought.

"I can't even book a taxi," she added, reading my mind.

This was a tad audacious and highly unusual for a new junior crew member to ask her senior hostess for a lift to work. Though part of me rebelled, I sighed and acquiesced. "Yes, I could pick you up. Where do you live exactly?"

And so began the pattern of my relationship with Emma.

In the early morning dark of a cold March drizzle, I saw that I had been right. Emma did possess a certain fragility. Her fine auburn hair framed a pretty, pale face while her startling blue eyes bore the expression of simultaneous delightful mischief, deer-caught-in-the-headlights surprise and deep sadness, almost as if she was confused about whether life was a hoot or an unbearable tragedy.

"Thank you for picking me up," she said as she placed her plastic Dan Air crew bag into the passenger side of my mini and clambered in.

"Not a problem," I lied. Collecting Emma had caused me to miss out on another thirty minutes of precious early morning sleep.

Once the 89 tourists had been served inedible light snacks, copious teas and coffees, and duty-free goods, we still had ten minutes before preparing for landing. Emma and I sat down on the jump seat, each with a hot beverage.

I asked her the perennial question. "How long have you been flying?"

"Three months," Emma answered, sipping tentatively on her hot coffee.

"Are they keeping you on, do you know?"

If, after the initial six-month contract, the new hostesses proved to be competent and willing slaves to the airline, they were then made permanent staff. Sometimes the higher-ups gave an indication of their decision early on, and sometimes they didn't let the girls know until the last moment.

"God, I hope so," she said, looking desperately into her coffee, perhaps remembering something awful. She shook her fine hair as if shaking off a fly. "You don't happen to know of anyone needing a flat mate, do you? I have to be out of my place at the end of this month and there's just *nothing* available!"

No wonder she was frantic. It was already March 15th and new air and ground crew were flocking into the Gatwick area in preparation for a busy summer season. "Actually, I do," I said. The timing would work. Joan and Paul, my current flat mates would have to approve, of course. "I'm leaving for a year to go around Europe at the end of the month with my boyfriend. You could take my place."

"Really?" her blue eyes grew large and watery. "Where do you live?" Emma's face had suddenly brightened, breaking out into a huge grin. Doing a Monty Python imitation and elbowing me, she added, "What's it loike then, eh, eh?"

I smiled. "Actually, it's lovely and the rent's good. It's a three-bedroom neo-Georgian house in Three Bridges with a small garden. Why don't you come and take a look on your day off? Then you can meet my flatmates. See if you like each other."

"Of course. That would be *such* a relief. Thank you."

Something in Emma's voice hinted at her utter and impenetrable loneliness. I felt compelled to help her. Did she have this effect on everyone?

"Europe!" she sighed wistfully, getting up from the jump seat. "Lucky you!"

Although I was an avid student of metaphysics, I hadn't yet decided about luck or fate. Didn't we just make things happen?

On my days off, as well as introduce the hapless Emma to my flat mates, Julian and I were furiously completing preparations for our imminent departure. Gifted at woodwork and other inventions, he had installed a herb rack on the inside of one door of our 1965 blue and white VW van, and a bookcase on the other. Underneath the seats, which—with the addition of a board—doubled as a bed, were two large storage areas. We filled them both to the brim with our food supply —dried peas and carrots, pasta, rice, cans and cans of spam, corned beef, ham, soups, dried fruits, digestive biscuits, chutney, marmite and raisins.

The first month of our trip would be spent exploring Belgium and Holland and then driving through Eastern Germany to the walled-in city of Berlin to visit our friend, Franz, a student of journalism. We were not due to arrive at the Norwegian cauliflower farm in southern Norway where we were contracted to work until May 15. On the farm we would be provided with lodging and meals and a 100 kroner or £10 sterling per week, so our money and our stash of dehydrated food were meant to last a long time.

After growing and planting cauliflowers on the farm from May to July, our plans were then to drive up the Norwegian coast all the way through the artic circle to the northernmost point of Norway. *Nordkapp* as it was locally known was where we would experience the midnight sun. By early August, we would be driving back down through Finland, visit southern Sweden as well as Denmark, and by September we would be entering the communist countries.

To journey behind the Iron Curtain, through communist Poland, Rumania, Bulgaria and Czechoslovakia, we were required to detail our exact route, the addresses of the hostels, the times we would arrive and leave, as well as explain our reasons for being there.

Julian and I spent many evenings completing the hard-to-read forms, but the Rumanian Embassy demanded that we deliver our documents in person. As we stood before the black wrought iron gates guarding the white stately home and saw the blood-red carpet leading to the front door, I shivered. Nasty memories of Boris Karloff's *Curse of the Vampire* film popped into my head. Did those blood-sucking beasts really exist? When a Lurch look-alike opened the front door, I expected him to intone, "You rang." Instead, he looked us up and down, sniffed, then ushered us into a regally furnished drawing room that felt like a waiting area for vampire victims. After he took our passports and applications, without speaking, he left the room.

"Do we really want to go to Rumania?" I asked Julian who appeared to be equally uneasy.

"We can always change our minds later," he said, frowning as he stared up at the elaborate chandelier hanging from an ornately decorated ceiling, perhaps wondering if it was bugged.

"It'll be winter by the time we get there," I reminded him. Having flown into Berlin many times and seen the greyness of East Berlin from the plane, even in summertime, I knew that the communist countries would not be cheery places. But they would be fascinating.

Then Lurch re-entered the room, handed our passports and documents to Julian and announced. "Your visas."

After my early morning Charles de Gaulle flight the following day and in the driveway of his parent's home in Horsham, Julian and I added the final touches to our van and home for the next year. When I brought items out of the house to be packed, he looked at me, shook his head and smiled. "Only the essentials," he intoned, or "we don't have room for that." I did insist on taking my Scrabble, though.

That night, Emma rang me, effusive in her gratitude. "Oh, *thank* you, Natasha. Both your flatmates have agreed that I can move in. I'm so happy!"

"That's great." I was also gratified that my leaving had opened up a home for Emma. "Well, if it's okay with them, you could move in tomorrow. I'm staying at Julian's until we leave on Tuesday."

"Even better ...but why don't you come over on Monday for a final cuppa. Around 4:00? I'm sure Joan and Paul want to say goodbye."

When Emma opened the door to the living room at #1 on that Monday, Julian and I were ambushed with a group of smiling people hollering, "Surprise!" Twelve of our friends and neighbours had gathered and were now laughing at our shocked and delighted faces.

"I just wanted to say thank you and wish you *Bon Voyage,*" Emma cooed, proud of her ruse.

"And I thought you just all wanted to make sure we actually left," I teased and smiled back at my neighbours, Brian Hodges, Samantha and Jennie, and my friend and ex-flatmate, Felicity. Just months earlier, she had moved out of #1 to purchase her own home. Julia had come without her boyfriend, Adrian, with my other Dan Air buddies Pauline and Alicia who were themselves due to leave for their trip around Australia the following month.

"Don't let those Norwegian trolls eat you," Pauline teased.

"And you, watch out for the dingoes," I told her and Alicia.

I wondered who had invited my new neighbour, Stewart, a handsome pilot who lived on the opposite side of the courtyard. When Emma interacted with him, I noticed, her translucent blue eyes became even bigger and a shameless coyness emerged. *Hmmm?*

After waving goodbye to everyone, and before climbing into the van, I thanked Emma for our farewell party.

"No, thank *you,* Natasha," she responded, her blue eyes watering. "You picked me up in more ways than one. You found me my new home and a new set of friends. And maybe," she smiled and nodded toward Stewart who was striding across the lawn back to his home, "a new romance."

Uh-oh. I hoped that while I was gone, luck or fate, that this *was* all for the greater good.

In March 1977 one year later, despite my urging Julian to continue our travels through Turkey, Greece, Yugoslavia and then North Africa, he had balked. Although he hadn't verbalized it, I sensed that he might also be afraid that he couldn't protect me, a blonde, in those unfamiliar cultures. Instead, he wanted to leave our temporary home in southern Germany—where we had worked in restaurants, dabbled in skiing and regularly sampled our landlords' home-made schnapps—to return to the UK.

Maybe I was postponing the inevitable—going home and what that might mean. But during our year-long adventure, our plans had often changed—usually for the better.

Six months ago, shortly after getting off an old boat in Helsinki while returning from an unscheduled four days in Leningrad, we had learned from the farm that three French student workers had not turned up for the harvest. To save their crop, they were in urgent need of help.

The decision whether to continue with our plans to tour the Iron Curtain countries or to help our new friends at the farm was not difficult. Having driven through East Germany at the beginning of our trip and then experiencing the tension of our recent Russian visit, neither Julian nor I had relished spending our winter in cold, grey communist countries, being shadowed by secret police and enduring the curiosity and ominous stares of restricted citizens.

Without dilly-dallying, we had driven straight across Sweden and back to Hobol. For another month—while I had improved my Norwegian vocabulary—we picked the cauliflowers we had sown earlier in the spring. We also befriended a German couple who promised us winter employment in Stuttgart.

When the harvest was in and we had left the farm, Julian and I had decided—en route to Germany—that we still wanted to explore southern Sweden. In the six months we had been travelling together, even in cramped quarters, we had become even closer. I had assumed that on our return, as part of the natural evolution of our relationship, we would continue living together and eventually get married.

We were parked in a tree-lined side street of Stockholm, sipping on tea and savoring the last of our digestive biscuits when I began pondering our future. "When we get back, where do you think we should live?" I asked Julian.

He gave me a strange look. "We won't be living together."

"Wh-what do you mean?"

"I'm going back to live at home." Then to add insult to injury, he mumbled, "It's much cheaper."

I sat there, stunned, a half-eaten digestive biscuit poised in mid-air.

Plunge a knife into my heart, why don't you?

"Must be nice," I snapped, "to have a home to go to." My own family had disintegrated, and I had no home. My parents' numerous dramatic separations had finally ended in a vicious divorce. My father had gone AWOL and my mother had descended into some kind of raging alcoholic schizophrenia. With my two favourite brothers in Canada, and my other two siblings having disowned the family altogether, I was essentially an orphan. And now I was being abandoned ...again.

As I snivelled over my tea and biscuits, he pretended to be fascinated by the trees on the street.

In the days and weeks that followed, while we explored the gentle scenery of southern Sweden, the beaches of Denmark and before entering Germany—like many women before me—I made the fatal mistake of thinking, "Maybe he'll change."

But exactly one year after leaving England, nothing had changed and he had said, "Let's go home."

So here we were, back in jolly olde England.

And it wasn't just our adventure that had come to an end.

When we arrived back in Horsham, although we were still officially a couple, and I was welcomed into his parent's home with open arms, through silent agreement, we settled back into mostly separate lives.

My first week at Julian's parents, I snuck out to a red phone box and rang Emma. "Hello! We're back! How are you?"

"Ooh, lots has happened," she answered, gleeful mischief in her voice. "When can you come over?"

"Well, first I have to find a place to live. I can't stay with Julian's parents too long. And no, before you ask, Julian and I are *not* getting married."

"Oh, I'm sorry." As if reading my thoughts, she added, "No one's leaving #1 at the moment ...but why don't you give Brian Hodges a call? He's moved out of Halland Close and bought his own three-bedroomed house in Crawley."

Brian, my old neighbour, and I had long been friends and he had always made me giggle. "Thanks. I'll give him a ring. I'm also going for airline interviews."

"Me, too!"

"I've booked an interview with Dan Dare, but they would just be a last resort. I *really* want to fly long haul."

"Really? I just *can't* imagine why you're not *dying* to go back to Dan Air!" she snickered, her voice loaded with sarcasm.

"Dying being the operative word."

We both chuckled.

"Of course, you can move in!" Brian exclaimed over the phone the next day. "That would be great. I hope you can get on with my flat mate, Honor. She's a bit of a one, if you know what I mean. She's been around, wink, wink. Some say they've been on 'er and off 'er all night!" He chuckled at his own joke. "But Natasha," he added as if this was her most unforgiveable trait, "she works for BA."

"Well, then!" I exclaimed, feigning disgust, "The deal's awff!"

We agreed that I would move in within days. The relief of now getting out from under the dark shadow of my failing relationship with

Julian allowed me to finally exhale. Contrary to Brian's version of Honor, she reminded me of the virginal Hayley Mills.

In the following weeks, between me moving and Julian also going for airline interviews, he and I barely saw each other. As it turned out, my BA appointment wasn't for two months. British Caledonian were also taking their time to respond. Meanwhile my Dan Air interview the following week "was just a formality" they said.

When I sat before my former airline's panel, I realized I had flown with all five of these women before I had left and in just one year, most of them had been promoted to management. They all greeted me with smiles and asked me about my trip around Europe.

"How's your Norwegian?" One of my interviewers asked.

"Actually, it's pretty good," I told her, surprised at her question. Our time in Norway had been one of the highlights of our trip and I had taken to the Norwegians and their sing-songy language very easily.

"We have a big Scandinavian contract now, so Norwegian will come in very handy," Marion commented. "We also fly to Sweden and Denmark and as the languages are so similar, you will be classed as a Scandinavian speaker. We'll have to test you, of course."

"Of course."

"The good news is that we pay for languages now." Sylvia grinned. The women knew that I was already qualified as a French, German and Italian speaker.

That is good news, I thought. The airline had extracted their pound of flesh from me and my unpaid linguistic ability on so many European flights, not to mention all the Zurich-Geneva and Le Bourget-Rome doubles.

"Per flight," she added. "£3 per language." She watched for my reaction. "With Scandinavian added to your list, you'll make a fortune."

"Great." I sat up and did the math. With my goal to buy my own home within the next year, getting extra pay on most flights would come in mighty handy.

I had initially questioned my sanity in learning Norwegian, a language that wasn't spoken anywhere else in the world except by 10 million Norwegians and in some parts of Minnesota. I had wondered, where would I ever use it again after leaving Norway? Only the Danes and the Swedes spoke vaguely similar languages, and many people of those three countries could not only understand each other, but they could also speak good English. Who knew that absorbing a new language by picking cauliflowers on a Norwegian farm, watching copious TV fjord-fishing programs and Norwegian-subtitled Frank Sinatra movies would pay off?

"The bad news is that you will have to start at the bottom," the red-haired Marion continued, referring to my being demoted to junior status. "How do you feel about that?"

I shrugged, not wanting them to see my delight. The paltry £2 per week difference in salary for the extra responsibility of being a number one—totally culpable for one hundred plus passengers' safety in-flight, managing two to three cabin crew, accounting of monies, customs issues, in-flight paperwork and dealing with idiosyncratic captains—was not worth it. Despite the slightly lower pay, flying as a junior would be much more enjoyable.

"I understand," I said with downcast eyes.

"You could start training next week," Marion stated, scooping up her papers and beaming. "Welcome back!"

And that was it. Before I knew it, I was once again wearing a Dan Air uniform, although this time I would be donning a smart, new red-trimmed navy-blue outfit with a red blouse and bowler-type hat.

But would I be doomed to the hard labor of short haul forever? Even though I loved my Dan Air friends, I knew how the airline could swallow us up into their slave-driving machinery. No, I thought, I must not give up. As soon as I could get my interviews with those long-haul airlines, I would also be winging my way to exotic corners of the earth. In the meantime, my knowledge of Norwegian would prove to be more lucrative than I could have imagined.

"So how have you liked living in Halland Close?" I asked Emma a few weeks later as we sat inside the cozy Lamb's Inn.

"Oh, it's been wonderful. I suppose I owe you one."

"You don't owe me anything. I'm just happy it worked out." I took a sip of my homemade blackberry wine. It was good to be home. "Did you get on okay with Joan? She can be a bit dramatic when she's PMS-ing?"

"She's fine." Emma's eyes twinkled. "When she's like that, I just tell her, 'Oh, shut up!' and she's good again."

"And isn't Paul a cutie?" I had half-wondered if my new friend might make a play for the male flat mate, but he was too devoted to his aloof girlfriend, Sheena.

"Yes, he's very sweet," Emma said, twiddling her glass on the table. "But..." she paused, looking dreamily out of the window at the budding spring countryside.

"But what?" I asked, feeling dread and not sure why. "It's Stewart, isn't it?"

"How did you know?" she said blushing, hardly able to contain her joy.

She grinned from ear to ear, shaking her hair and peering down into her drink. "Yes."

Uh-oh.

"But doesn't he have a girlfriend at the moment?" I was sure, Samantha, my other friend and Stewart's flatmate had brought me up to date correctly.

"Oh, *her*!" Emma said, a little too vindictively. "He's not in love with *her*. *That* won't last long."

Did Emma believe that Stewart was in love with her while still seeing someone else? Living opposite each other they'd had a year to find out if there was any passion. I knew Stewart was emotionally reserved but, in my mind if a man fell in love with a woman, he would move mountains to be with her. And he hadn't.

I could empathize with Emma's hope, though. After all, I was still hoping that Julian would come to his senses and beg me to marry him *and* that I would get a job on a long-haul airline.

Miracles happen, I reminded myself. Even Dan Air was paying for my languages the second time around.

One month later, after being retrained on the same old aircraft, the Comet and BAC 1-11, I slipped back into the same old uniform and the same old routine. Or so I thought. But while I had been away, I soon found out that the uniform wasn't the only thing that had changed.

15

NAUGHTY IN NORWAY

April 1977

"You 'ave been away for a while, yes?"

I nodded. "Yes, one year."

"Zere is somessing I 'ave to tell you," the French, Angeline said in hushed tones.

On my first flight to Kristiansand, she was the number one. While I was carrying out one of the pre-flight duties and "doing seat-pockets," she had hissed at me, "I must speak wis you," and then beckoned me to follow her into the galley.

The other hostess was down the back and we were alone at the front. Still, I had to step closer to Angeline to hear what she had to say.

"On zese Norwegian flights, we now 'ave a leetle ...agreement ...wis zee Norwegians."

"Okay." I waited. She was searching for the right words as if slightly embarrassed.

"Well, you know 'ow zese people lerve to drink and smoke cigarettes?"

Having lived with a family of Norwegians for three months and then driven all the way up to the north of Norway, I was familiar with their social habits, especially above the arctic circle when they lived in three months of twenty-four-hour daylight followed by nine months of continual darkness. Who could blame them? I nodded.

"And in Norway, zee cigarettes and alcohol are so-o-o expensiff." She raised her hands in the French way, as if horrified. "So ...we 'elp zem a leetle."

"Yes?"

"When we get to Kristiansand, zee cleaners come on with garbage bags and zey buy cigarettes and whisky from us. Zey pay us a leeetle more than we would sell them on board, but zey are so-o 'appy.'"

Though Angeline made it sound as if we were about to embark on a humanitarian mission, I frowned, wondering what the legalities were.

"And zese passengers lerve to buy all ze miniatures so zen we are forced to tot." She shrugged the French way as if there was nothing else to be done.

Totting, I knew meant more money for us. While people enjoyed the same quantity of alcohol as in a miniature bottle for the same price, one half-bottle of whiskey contained eight tots. By totting, we made an extra £1.40p over and above the duty-free cost of the bottle. Cabin crew then divided the profit between themselves.

Angeline was staring at me, searching for my reaction—and my agreement—or was it approval? "We make a lot of monee," she said encouragingly. "Sometaimes one 'undred pounds!"

Hmmm? Visions of the house I wanted to buy popped into my head.

"But I need you to agree to do zis, or we cannot do eet."

I faltered, thinking of all the angles. The airline was getting paid for their goods. No theft was actually taking place, except maybe depriving the Norwegian government of their outrageous duty on cigarettes and alcohol. But did I have a choice in the matter?

"Everybodee is doing eet," Angeline added, as if to tip me over the edge of my indecision. The pervasive attitude amongst cabin crew was that Dan Air treated us like cattle fodder. With no union to protect us, we retaliated by always trying to get one up on management. And we weren't stealing from anyone, I told myself. We were even promoting duty-free sales and that's how the airline made its profits.

"As you are ze speakair, we will need you," Angeline added for good measure.

In other words, if I refused, I would be the villain. "Okay," I said, not completely comfortable.

"Eh bien." Angeline exhaled. "Don't worree. You will be 'appee."

"Passengers!" Felicity called from mid-cabin. Over Angeline's shoulder, I saw the first of 89 happy Norwegians begin to ascend the stairs. I took my position at the door and greeted them with a *Morn, Morn* or *God Dag.*

As Angeline predicted, on the one hour forty-five-minute flight to Kristiansand in southern Norway, we sold out of all miniatures. Passengers smuggled the small bottles into various corners of their clothing and baggage. We then had no choice but to tot the *jin o jus*— gin and juice—or *whisky* from the bigger bottles.

After passengers—some very inebriated—had disembarked at Kristiansand, cleaners came on board. I was so engrossed in the routine of replenishing seat pockets that, at first, I didn't notice the man lingering in the galley, looking hopeful, his empty black garbage bag hanging from his right hand.

"*Har du cigarretter og whisky?*" he almost whispered.

So this is how it works. "*Ja,*" I replied, nodding. "*Men et oyeblikk,*" Just a moment, I added, signalling he should wait while I found the number one to do the deed.

Angeline emerged out of the flight deck, saw the man standing there expectantly and immediately understood what he wanted. "Can you ask eem 'ow many 'e would like?" she addressed me.

"*Vhor mange skal du har?*" I asked him.

"*Ja, vi skal har tvve stange cigarette og ti whisky, vhis de er mulig.*" We would like twenty cartons of cigarettes and ten whisky if possible, he asked humbly as if this was indeed a humanitarian mission and he was begging for food.

I translated to Angeline who immediately began pulling cartons of Rothmans, Dunhills and Benson & Hedges from galley bar boxes. "Sometimes," she told me as she gathered the rest of the contraband, "we leave ze bar boxes in the 'old and zey just 'elp zemselves."

My God. This was quite the operation. "Do the flight deck know?" I asked Angeline as she pulled the tenth bottle from the bar box and placed it carefully in the man's thin plastic bag.

"Oui, some of zem, but zey choose to ...er ...turn a blind ear?"

"Eye," I corrected, smiling. "Turn a blind eye."

The man then handed Angeline a wad of kroner bills which she counted.

"*Oui, c'est correcte.*" She smiled at the man, letting him know the deal was done.

"*Tusen, tusen tak.*" Thank you very much, he said earnestly as if we had just saved his life. Smiling, he retreated down the forward stairs, hauling his hoard behind him, bottles clanking against each other as he disappeared into the dark night.

While taxiing to our stand at Gatwick and enjoying our landing drink in the galley, Angeline divvied up the spoils. She handed Felicity and me our cash. I put the money directly into my handbag without looking to see how much our enterprise had made, still feeling uneasy about the whole thing.

However, when I got home and counted my earnings—seventy-eight pounds and change—I was beginning to see the wisdom of this system. Everyone was winning, I told myself—the airline through extra duty-free sales, the Norwegians with cheaper relaxation tools, and the crew who so deserved these perks.

On my second flight to Norway, this time to Stavanger, we arrived again at night. After the money was paid, the number one asked me to direct the cleaners with the two empty garbage bags to go and empty the five bar boxes in the hold. While we, the cabin crew, prepared the plane for our inbound passengers to Gatwick, we heard the scraping of metal on metal from below as bar boxes were emptied followed by the clinking of bottles as they dragged them back across the tarmac into the night.

Four months passed with me doing more than one flight a week to Norway. Despite some of them having a propensity for getting blotto, I had always found the Norwegians to be charming. The passengers and ground personnel's curiosity about how I, a thoroughly English person, could speak Norwegian was also amusing.

"*Er du Norsk?*" Are you Norwegian, they would ask, hearing my accent.

"*Nei, jeg er Engelsk.*" No, I'm English.

They would frown. "*Men vhordan snakker du Norsk?*" How come you speak Norwegian?

"*For tre maneder, har jeg pfluckte blomkohlen i Norge,*" I picked cauliflowers in Norway for three months, I informed them.

They would nod and say, "*Ja, vel,*" sitting back frowning, still mystified as to why an English girl would bother to learn any language, let alone Norwegian. They all beamed at me, flattered as if I had learned it just so I could communicate specifically with them.

The Norwegian bongo drums worked well at every single airport —Trondheim in the Arctic Circle and towns further south—Bergen, Stavanger, Kristiansand and Oslo—where all the cleaners had the same system. Everyone seemed happy. Even though I had my occasional qualms about "the agreement," thanks to the extra income, and my language payments, I was well on my way to reaching my goal of saving the twelve hundred pounds I needed as a down payment on my first house.

Perhaps things were going *too* well.

Angeline, Felicity and I were yet again on a Kristiansand together. We were sitting on the ground at Gatwick at the front of the 1-11, waiting for engineers to fix a main door that wasn't closing properly. We knew the repair would take a while.

"Natasha, you know zat we are not doing anyssing with ze Norwegians now?"

There had been a rumor that the gig was up, but I had hoped it was just a rumor.

"Why? What happened?" The loss to my income would be tragic.

"Oh, it was *terr-eeeble*!" She exclaimed. "And it was *all* my fault." She hung her head, remembering. "We were night-stopping in Kristiansand, so I decided to take some bottles to sell to ze taxi drivair. Just four bottles, so I put zem in my crew bag."

Uh-oh. Dan Air was a cheap airline, and our crew bags were made of horrible cheap imitation leather. The bags were definitely not built for longevity or smuggling. They were barely strong enough to hold our cabin shoes, in-flight bar kit, toothbrush and spare knickers. The whisky bottles, I imagined, would have been crammed into the top.

"I was just walkeeng through Kristiansand Airport, minding my own beesiness," Angeline told us, shaking her head, "when I was passing zee Customs officairs and, *quelle horreure,* ze strap on my bag broke. Puff, just like zat."

"*Mon Dieu,*" I exclaimed, unconsciously falling into French mode.

"You know 'ow small zis airport is?" she said raising her shoulders in the inimitable French shrug.

"*Oui, d'accords.*" Kristiansand's terminal was more like a large living room where passengers arrived on one side and departing passengers squeezed by—going in the opposite direction—on the other. Customs were relegated to a small table in the corner. It was cozy but always crowded.

Felicity and I both sat with mouths open, imagining the scene.

"Of cour-rse, ze bottles fell out of my bag and made a *beeeeg* crash! Zen they broke into pieces all across ze floor. Ze smell of whisky filled ze airport. Everybodee stopped and stared including, of courrrse, ze customs men."

Just then an engineer in a green coverall poked his head around the bulkhead. "All clear, ladies. Shall I tell ramp to send passengers?"

Angeline nodded despondently.

"Quick." I urged. "Finish the story!"

"One of ze customs men went like zis to me." Angeline beckoned with her forefinger. "Well, zen ze 'ole crew was taken to an office including ze captain and ze first officair."

"Who was the captain?" I asked. Depending on who he was, would have determined Angeline's fate. Some would have a sense of humor and defend "the girls," while some would be very nasty and could just have had her fired.

"Oh, ssank God!" Angeline visibly exhaled. "It was Bob Wilson."

Yes, Bob Wilson was one of the good ones. "So, then what happened?"

"At first, zey threatened us with jail, but zen Bob talked to them. 'E told them zat we were just trying to 'elp ze Norwegians. In ze end, zey impounded ze aircraft. We could not leave until we paid £200! But Bob paid. I offeraired to pay 'im back, but 'e refused. He is my 'ero!"

Yes, Bob Wilson was one of the good ones.

Before we had time to comment, a Norwegian loaded down with plastic duty-free bags—goods bought legally—stood in the galley entrance wondering where to go next. "*God Dag*," he greeted us cheerfully.

God Dag, I replied automatically and showed him to his seat.

But actually, I thought, it's not such a good day.

16

NOT WITHOUT MY BOOT POLISH

April 1977

As I entered the crew room in Concorde House at 2.30 p.m. on a grey rainy Saturday in April, I observed a crowd of hosties, some appearing haggard–obviously inbound, and some outbound, looking as fresh as daisies–sitting or standing in clusters and chatting. If only, I thought, I could muster some enthusiasm for this flight.

Things had changed since I had returned to the airline. Pauline and Alicia were still on their Australian adventure that had made my trip around Europe with Julian sound as mundane as a night Palma. My friend, the ever-so sophisticated Julia had been promoted to a check stewardess and we barely crossed paths now. My other friend, Felicity Farmsworth had left Dan Air, or as rumor had it, been fired for smuggling bottles of Ballantines down her knickers. Now she was a croupier on the QE2 sailing to New York and Barbados. My relationship with Julian was barely hanging by a thread. Flying for Dan Air the second time around was definitely ...different, and definitely not as much fun.

"Is that you, you old tart?" I recognized the familiar blonde bobbed hairdo of one of my favorite hosties. Laurie Borling—or Boring as she was lovingly known—was standing by the pigeonholes reading her roster. Anything but boring, Laurie was a mischief-maker. My kind of friend. She looked up and beamed.

"Ratbag! I heard you were back!" She came closer to speak to me.

"I thought you were in Bahrain!" I said. Like me, she had abandoned her senior position with Dan Air a year earlier and had been so excited about her two-year contract with Gulf Air. So why was she here, standing in front of me in a Dan Air uniform? "When did you get back?" I had so many questions. "And *why* are you back? Anyone who willingly returned to this airline must be quite mad, I thought. I knew because here I was.

"Oh. It's quite the story!" She giggled her inimitable laugh. Her "hee, hee, hee, hee," sound was infectious, and I couldn't help but laugh, too. I felt a wave of gratitude for her funny quirkiness. "I'll tell you later," she muttered as Marion Albright, our number one, approached.

"Well, this should be an easy flight!" Marion exclaimed. "Two ex-number ones, on a Kristiansand? Thank God, cos I've got a wicked sore throat and I'm not in the mood for new girls or drunken Norwegians." Her Welsh accent sounded even more dour with her nasal intonation. "C'mon. Transport's here."

As the three of us sat at the front of the concertina bus that took us to our BAC 1-11, in between loud sneezes, Marion gave us the flight briefing. "As you're the speaker, Natasha, you're in the cabin. Laurie, galley. Flight time, one hour fifty. Only 65 plus 2 pax outbound, so not a full load, thank God. We'll do drinks, snacks, two teas and coffees and duty-frees. You can tot," Marion addressed me "but nothing else. Understood?"

"As if I would!" I responded in mock indignation.

"Totting" wasn't as lucrative as our other way of earning a little extra cash had been on the Scandinavian flights–but at least it was legal, and the extra cash supplemented our flight pay. No harm, no foul.

On the other hand, supplying Norwegian airport handlers with cigarettes and alcohol through our recent but now defunct contraband scheme *was* naughty. Though I hadn't been the ring-leader, I had been tarred with that brush—perhaps because I spoke the language.

"And Captain Willie," Marion continued, sounding more thick with cold by the minute, "is our intrepid leader ..."

No! Not Captain Willie. While he was one of my favorite pilots, I always had difficulty announcing his name over the PA, especially when one of the girls made me giggle.

"…and the first officer is, oh Natasha, your favourite, Christopher Wolsesley."

Oh God! Marion had rescued me from Christopher's amorous attempts once before—that time in Brussels—but I was sure she still blamed me for inciting his ardour. "And Natasha," she added, "if you're the speaker, can you do *all* the PAs, Norwegian and English, if you don't mind, flower."

"You speak Norwegian now, too!" Laurie asked, impressed. "Herdy, herdy, herdy, herdy," she chimed, bobbing her head from side to side and imitating the Swedish chef on the Muppets. "But why?"

"Cos I was bored picking cauliflowers on a Norwegian farm? And …why not?" I asked. "Actually, it's paying off."

Marion threw me a disapproving look as if I might be tempted to start up another contraband plot.

I mouthed to Laurie, *Tell you later.*

Once on board, Marion flopped into a front row seat and proceeded to fill out her paperwork. While Laurie organized the catering and set about preparing the galley, I began the routine of checking emergency equipment, refreshing the seat pockets with brochures, sick bags and duty free price lists and then replenishing the two rear loos with paper goods.

"Cabin's ready," I reported to Marion who was still sitting in the front row blowing her nose ferociously and looking paler by the minute. "You don't look so good, Marion. And you shouldn't be flying with a cold. Why don't you go home?"

She grimaced. "I'd love to, but that'll mean delaying the flight while they find another number one and everyone will be pissed off."

I turned to Laurie who was ripping the tops from cardboard mineral boxes. "We can probably handle these Vikings, at least on the outbound, couldn't we?"

"Nod's as good as a wink to a blind Norse," Laurie replied and tittered. Tee, hee, hee.

"Thank you, girls," Marion rasped. "At least if I'm on board, we're legal, even though the two of you are highly qualified." She pulled herself up and handed me her brown envelope of paperwork. "You'll need that." She picked up her purse and crew bag and retreated to the last row of seats where she instantly lay her head back and closed her eyes.

I joined Laurie in the galley where she was now slicing an apple and orange and placing the fruit in one of the stainless-steel coffee pots.

"What on earth are you doing?" I asked, mystified. "Is this some special Bahraini tea you learned while you were away?"

Laurie giggled. "You haven't had my famous new landing drink yet, have you? Instead of boring old scotch and coke, we can now all enjoy a real cocktail."

"Is this your way of making up for a year as a teetotaller in Bahrain?"

"Who says we were teetotallers?" she responded. Tee, hee, hee, hee.

I watched in fascination as she emptied a bottle of thick orange concentrate into the pot, followed by a half bottle of brandy, a miniature Glayva liqueur and one miniature Johnny Walker. As she stirred the concoction, she explained as if she were teaching a cooking class, "It needs to brew for a good six hours. Then just before landing, we add two cans of soda water and lots of ice. *Et voila.*"

"Sounds lethal. Does Marion know about this? "

"Oh yes. She *asked* me to make it."

I watched as Laurie carefully placed the precious coffee pot into one of the galleys' stowages. "I'm so-o-o-o happy you're back," I told her.

"'Allo, 'allo, 'allo." Captain Willie's jovial voice reached us as he came up the front stairs. Behind him was my nemesis, the tall and gangly Christopher Wolsesley "I see we've got the troublemakers today," the captain said as he stepped into the galley. "Good job that Marion the Sensible is the official number one."

"Actually, Marion's not feeling well," I told him, "so she's put us in charge."

"Well, I can guess what kind of a flight this is going to be then?" He grinned and disappeared into the flight deck.

Christopher lingered in the galley, leering at me as he always did. "Good to see you back. Natasha, maybe you can help me later?'

"Oh, he needs a lot of help," Laurie whispered behind me.

"What with?" I said, immediately regretting that I had asked.

"My knobs and switches," he said lasciviously.

"Maybe we can switch *you* off," Laurie said.

A little wounded, Christopher opened the flight deck door and went inside.

Once the mixture of 65 Norwegians and English passengers were belted in, and we started taxiing, I began the pre-take-off announcements. Marion and Laurie positioned themselves in the cabin, ready to do the safety demo. Without my friend Pauline here to make me laugh when I pronounced Captain Willie's name, maybe I could get through the PAs without stuttering. "*Mine Dame og Herrer*," I began. "Ladies and Gentlemen, on behalf of Captain W-willie and his crew ..." *Phew*!

Marion took her position on the rear jump seat while Laurie and I sat in the galley. After take-off and we heard the *thunk* of the undercarriage coming up, I asked her, "So, when did you get back from Bahrain?"

"Oh ...about a month ago," she said. This time she was not laughing. She shook her hair, a habit that reminded me of my friend, Emma, and what she did when she was agitated.

"I thought you were meant to be there for two years? Didn't you like it?" I persisted.

"Oh, I loved it, but–"

The *No Smoking* light extinguished, which was my cue to do the announcements. I stood up and grabbed the black handset while Laurie went to the rear to retrieve the trolley. Then, like well-oiled machines, Laurie and I worked seamlessly together to load the drinks. As she placed a jug of ice and sliced lemons on the top of the trolley, she said, "Hey, Natasha, do you wanna have some fun?"

"Of course, but, er, what do you mean exactly?" Laura's antics were often over-the-top. Although I was still dreaming of abandoning Dan Air, I still needed my job for the present.

She cocked her head to one side. "Do you think the passengers really notice us, you know, what we *actually* look like?"

Where was she going with this? I frowned. "Yes, I think so."

"Wanna bet?" She shook her head and pointed to the cabin beyond the closed curtain. "Those plonkers wouldn't notice us if we suddenly sprouted proboscises on our foreheads. I'll prove it to you."

"How?" I asked.

"You'll see." Hee, hee, hee, hee. "You start the drinks service and then I'll come and join you when I'm ready," she said as she helped me manoeuvre the cart into the cabin.

"*Whisky med is, takk,*" the woman in 5A requested. I handed the Norwegian her totted scotch and ice. What was Laurie doing?

Then the galley curtain was thrust aside and stone-faced, she entered the cabin. Her blonde hair was tucked behind massive pointy Dr. Spock-like ears, and on her feet, she was wearing yellow Big Bird hairy socks, complete with googly plastic eyes. But it was when she grinned at me, that I got the full effect. Some of her lovely white teeth had disappeared and she gave me what appeared to be a partially toothless grin. She took her position at the other end of the cart and leaned over to speak to the man in the aisle seat.

I watched.

"Would you like a drink, sir?" She beamed at him, revealing the toothless smile and adjusting her fine hair behind the plastic ears.

"*Ja, takk*" the Norwegian replied, not batting an eyelid at her strange appearance. "*Gin og jus, vaer sa god.*" Gin and juice, please.

Maybe she was right. Passengers didn't see us.

We carried on down the cabin. The lighting was subdued but whether English or Norwegian, none of the passengers laughed, snickered or even commented on Laurie's strange get-up. Their obliviousness to her impish appearance made it even funnier. Even Marion, who squeezed by our trolley on her way up to the flight deck, didn't seem to notice.

"Told you," Laurie said. After we had served up the last row of seats, she slipped into the portside loo and removed the ears and cleaned the black make-up off her teeth.

"Well, you're right," I said, as we pulled the drinks trolley back into the galley and began to unload in preparation for the next service. "We're faceless wonders."

"Not always." She looked down at the spooky plastic ears, now lying limp on the metal galley surface. "Being *un*noticed in Bahrain would have saved me *a lot of* trouble," she said ruefully.

"Maybe you should have had a disguise?"

"Oh, I did as it happened. It was black boot polish and a scarf."

"Boot polish! What–"

A red passenger light dinged on the forward panel. I groaned and peeked through the curtain into the cabin, looking for where the "Hostess" button was illuminated in the passenger's overhead panel. "I suppose I better go and see what she wants, just in case she can't breathe."

"Oh make 'er wait." Laurie smiled. It wouldn't have been the first time a non-breathing passenger had been kept waiting, and nearly died.

"What did she want?" Laurie asked when I returned.

"Do you haff a Charlie?" I mimicked the Norwegian lilt of the passenger who had asked me for the newest Dan Air duty-free perfume.

Laurie grinned. "Yes, we haff a right bunch of Charlies here. Herdy herdy herdy."

"What about a noice bottle o' channel?" I asked mimicking our Cockney passengers' mispronunciation of Chanel Number Five.

"Nah, darlin'," Laurie caught onto the accent. "'Ow about a bottle o' Reevy Gowchy?"

I giggled and put on my ever-so-snooty voice, "Oh, dahling, do you mean *Rive Gauche*?"

"Well, awroight then, gimme foive lair doo temps." Laurie played along

"Oh, Madame, I think you mean *L'Air du Temps*."

The flight deck door opened, and Marion stepped out. "Nothing changes, does it?" she said, seeing us chuckling. Her voice was now thick with cold, but her eyes glistened in humor. "Maybe it's a good thing you two are not number ones anymore?"

Laurie suddenly spread her arms wide and to the tune of *Who Wants to be a Millionaire* sang, "Who wants to be a number one?"

"I don't!" I responded in the same tune.

"Can't say I blame you." Marion sighed. "See you two reprobates after landing," she said, pulling back the curtain and disappearing into the cabin.

When the service was finally done, and many passengers had put their heads back and dozed while others read or chatted with their co-travellers, we still had fifteen minutes to relax before beginning the descent. Laurie made us both a cup of tea, and we sat on the jump seat.

"Laurie, tell me. So, what *did* happen in Bahrain?"

"Oh, it was awful," she said, staring down into her beverage, more miserable than I had ever seen her. "I had been there about ten months when we went to a party."

"They have parties in Bahrain? But I thought they didn't–?"

"Drink? Oh, you wouldn't believe what they are not allowed to do and still do," she scoffed.

"So, what happened at this party?"

"I was introduced to this sheikh ...he was very important, like a prince."

"How exciting!"

"Not really. Well, he took a shine to me. Being blue-eyed and blonde an' all. I thought, I was just a novelty and my appeal would wear off but..."

"It didn't?"

"No. I mean it was okay at first. I liked him, and the luxury of the way they live, but I knew it wouldn't go anywhere. I thought it was a bit of a lark."

She would. Everything was a lark to Laurie.

"He started buying me gold jewelry, lots of it."

"Lucky you."

"Well, at first, I thought so, too. But then I realized he was becoming very serious." She shook her head as if trying to shake off a fly. "So then, I tried to cool it, and I told him not to give me any more gifts. Well, you never refuse a gift from an Arab, you know, especially a sheikh. It's a serious insult."

"Uh-oh."

"Uh-oh is right. He told me he wanted to marry me so that I would become his third wife."

"N-o-o-o-! What did you do?"

"Well, when he wouldn't take "no" for an answer, I went to the airline and asked them for advice. When I told them who he was, a sheikh, they told me I had no choice. And they wouldn't let me out of my contract, anyway. I had to stay and marry him."

"Wha-a-a-t?" And I thought I was a femme fatale—or femme fattle as Felicity called me—with the wrong man always falling for me and me falling for the wrong man.

"Well, of course, I knew then that I *had* to leave Bahrain," Laurie continued. "But I couldn't just jump on a Gulf Air flight and land back at Heathrow. The airline wouldn't allow it for one, and by then the sheikh was having me followed. I was trapped. Then one of the girls told me about this man who is a professional at getting western women out of the country. It's quite a business." She took a large sip of her tea, remembering.

I waited.

"So ...I met with Mr. X— secretly, of course—and he told me how he could smuggle me out. He put the fear of God into me, warning me that it could be dangerous ...and expensive."

Laurie's eyes became watery, and she exhaled. "But it wasn't just me I was worried about. He was, after all, risking his life to save mine. If he had been found out, he might have, at the very least, been thrown in jail.

They would have considered it a crime of treason." She looked at me, imploring me to understand the severity of her situation. "But I had to get out!"

"Of course, you did! Oh, my God, Laurie. You never do things by halves, do you?"

"So, for the escape, he brought me a scarf, and a tin of black boot polish." She grimaced. "He made me promise not to leave without my boot polish."

"And that was for...?" I asked, feeling a little dense.

"My face and hands!" She looked at me as if to say, *Keep up with the plot.*

Of course! Laurie's complexion was whiter than white, and her fair hair only accentuated her contrast with the colouring of middle Eastern women.

"On the night," she continued, "I blackened my face with the boot polish and put a hijab over my head. First, he smuggled me onto a cargo ship to Saudi. In Damman, somebody else met me and put me on a bus. I travelled all the way up through Iran, then Syria. Once I got into Turkey, I had a guide who walked me through the mountains. We trekked for days, stopping at some villages. Finally, I got on another bus to Istanbul. From there, I got a flight back to Heathrow." She took another gulp of tea.

"My God!"

She blew out a puff of air. "It was like the incredible journey."

"That's a lot of cloak and dagger to get away. How much did it cost?"

"Everything I had, all my savings ...but it was worth it!" Her eyes suddenly lit up. "I was so happy to land on English soil."

"I'm so glad you got out, Laurie." But I *was* unhappy to see my funny friend so sad. Something told me she was still traumatized. Facing death can change a person. In Dan Air, we knew all about that but in a different context.

"Are you safe now? I mean, he won't come after you, will he?"

"I don't think so. I think his ego and his pride were more hurt than anything. They are not used to being refused." She got up to throw her empty cup in the garbage. "So, I'm living at home now and I'm starting from the bottom again."

"You'll soon be back on your feet," I reassured her. "Look at me. I plan to buy my own house by next spring."

"I thought Norwegian customs put the kibosh on that." She smiled at me, her old smile.

"Oh, so you know about that, do you?"

"Word gets around. And if I've learned anything, it's to pay attention."

On our return sector, the flight was full. Laurie was in a more reflective mood and Marion insisted—despite feeling groggy—on counting the bar herself before landing back at Gatwick. After I had checked seatbelts and given the "Cabin secure" signal to Captain Willie, I stood in the galley. Laurie took out the "cocktail" pot and added the final touches to the brew.

"Can't wait to try it," I said.

"It'll melt the knickers off a nun," Marion warned.

"Well, I've been drinking scotch and coke for landings for years, so I'm sure I can handle a little brandy and orange."

Marion gave me a strange look. "I hope so."

As soon as all passengers were off, and the customs officer had sealed the bar boxes, Laurie emerged from the galley clutching two glasses of the orange cocktail. Marion plonked herself down in the front row window seat while I sat in the aisle seat.

"Bottoms up," Laurie chimed, as she handed them to us.

The flight deck door opened, and the captain emerged with an already empty glass. "God, that's good," he said. "Any chance of another one?" He sank down on the other side of the aisle. Laurie immediately obliged and refilled his glass.

"Where's Christopher?" I asked, always needing to know where he was lurking.

"Why?" Marion asked, as she took her first sip. "Are you missing him?"

I gave her my *Oh please*! look.

Whether it was because of hearing Laurie's traumatic story or because post-flight, we always had an unquenchable thirst that water just didn't slake, I chugged the sweet mixture quickly. "It's just like drinking orange juice!" I exclaimed.

"Slides down easily, doesn't it?" Laurie said. Tee, hee, hee.

Then I picked out a piece of apple and ate it. *Whoa*. That definitely had a kick!

The flight deck door opened, and Christopher emerged with jacket buttoned-up, hat on head and clutching his black flight deck bag. His eyes, I thought, looked a little unfocused.

"Aren't you going-k to have a drink?" Marion asked sounding even more plugged with cold.

"Already had one," he announced.

"Well, have another one, man," the captain urged. "We're celebrating the prodigal hosties return."

Christopher shrugged and sat down between Marion and me. "Okay. Fill me up," he said.

As Laurie brought the coffee pot into the cabin and gave Christopher another glass, I was already beginning to feel warm and fuzzy.

Christopher, I noticed, was giving me the cold shoulder. Was he still pouting because Laurie and I had mocked him? "Ssso, Chrishtopher, how have you bee-e-e-n?" I asked, aware of slurring my words.

"Good." His face lit up as if I'd just given him back his Meccano set. "Are you still with that boyfriend of yours?"

Uh-oh. "Ye-e-esss," I told him, not willing to divulge the truth of our dwindling connection. "And are you shtill married?"

"Ooh. Touché," he said, pretending to swipe a sword in mid-air.

Once Laurie had topped up all our drinks and the pot was empty, she sat down in the window seat on the other side of Captain Willie.

When I looked over at the middle-aged portly man, he suddenly reminded me of a warm, cuddly bear.

"Yer know...," I began, becoming aware of a buzzing beginning in my head. "Captain W-w-willie, when I do my PAsh, I jush can't–"

"Drrrink up, pe-e-e-ople," Marion interjected, dragging out her words. "Cleaners will be here sch-o-o-o-on." She knocked back the last of her drink.

As if on cue, the clanking we heard coming up the front stairs heralded the imminent arrival of the cleaning crew carting their buckets of disinfectants and vacuum cleaners.

"Evenin' all," the first cleaner said, and gave us a knowing look as he saw us slouched in the first row, still clutching our landing drinks. He and his crew moved on down the cabin.

"We gotta get o-o-off." I started to stand and teetered. "Oopsh!"

Christopher grabbed my arm, steadying me. "Whoa, careful there, little lady." He stood up but banged his head on the hat-rack.

While Marion laughed at us, Laurie was saying something about getting to the "crew room" but her words sounded garbled and when I looked at her, she had doubled into two blurry images.

"But I don't wanna mo-o-o-ve," Marion moaned as she snuggled down into her seat.

The crew room! It seemed so-o-o far away. "Oh, I don't shink I can walk," I said, then felt something touch my right foot. When I looked down, Christopher was taking off my shoe. "What are you do-o-oing?" I asked, trying to sound as indignant as I could.

"Jush helping you with your shoos," he muttered to the floor. "You have to get dressed."

"But I am dreshed," Then I realized that, yes, I still had to change into my uniform high-heel shoes and don my uniform jacket, hat and gloves. *Ugh!*

Captain Willie started muttering something about aliens on the flight deck and chuckled. The sound reminded me of Harry Secombe's infectious laugh, so I giggled too and couldn't stop. Then Christopher fell back into his seat and roared with laughter, his mouth wide open revealing yellowed teeth. Then we were all laughing at God knows what.

"I don't know what the he-e-e-ll you put in thish drink," Marion said, hugging her glass, "but thish ish the bescht I've felt a-a-all day."

"Do you want me to call for transport, luv?" The cleaner had reappeared and addressed me, as if I was in charge, and sober. "You'll never make it to the crew room like this. God knows 'ow you're all goin' to drive 'ome."

"Ho-o-ome!" Marion moaned. "I jush wanna go ho-o-o-o-o-me!"

Captain Willie was the first to stumble out of the transport and into the crew room. When I walked in, our pilot was for some reason on the floor, on his back, kicking his legs and waving his arms in the air, still giggling and muttering about aliens. Christopher had sunk into one of the red plastic seats along the wall and was staring at Captain Willie, confused. With a "harrumph" Marion collapsed onto one of the chairs at the center table, slumped forward and rested her head on her arms. I sat down next to her. Laurie was still standing.

"La-au-rie," I asked, "Why have you got black teeth?"

She clasped both hands to her cheeks and exclaimed. "Oh my God, Natasha? What have I done? I think I've given you all alcoholic poisoning. I'm so-o-o sorry." Distraught, she surveyed her crew and the brain damage she had inflicted. "How will you get home, Natasha? You can't drive like that?"

"I can take her ho-o-ome," Christopher said, getting up and unsteadily approaching the table. "I know where sh-she lives." He leaned over me, leering and grinning.

Even in my drunken state, I knew that something was terribly wrong about his offer. "No-o-o-o-o!" I clutched Laurie's arm. "Don't let him take me! Not without my boot polish."

"Can Julian come and pick you up?" she asked.

Oh, do I have to ask him? Laurie was unaware of the fragile state of my relationship with my almost ex-boyfriend. "Ring him," she commanded.

"O-o-o-k-a-y." Precariously, I stood up and staggered the five feet to where the black public phone was attached to the wall. The numbers and letters on the rotary dial were blurry and on my first attempt, I heard a disgruntled woman's voice. Oops, wrong number. The next time I dialled, I heard Julian's deep tones.

"Oh, Ju-u-ulian!" I breathed with relief. "I'm sho shorry to ashk you but can you pleeeshe come and get me."

After a long, stony silence, he said, "You're *drunk!*" his words, dripping with disgust.

"Yesh, I am," I said, and burst into giggles. The captain was still lying on the floor, talking to himself. Would he have to be taken away in a straightjacket?

"Where are you?" Julian asked, icicles in his voice.

"Gatwick ...Crew room. I'm shorry ..." I started. I still loved Julian and had always had his respect, so part of me cringed at his disapproval, and part of me thought it was hilarious. I giggled again.

"Ugh. I'll be there in twenty minutes." He snapped. "Wait for me by the gate."

"Aye, aye, cap'ain. Shank you!" Even though he couldn't see me, I saluted.

When I turned around, Christopher and Laurie were picking the captain up off the floor, dusting him off and placing him carefully on one of the seats. Marion, still slumped over the table, was snoring like a stuck pig.

"Natasha, I can drive Marion home, but can you order taxis for these two?"

"Oh, okay." I must be sobering up as she was asking me to be responsible. Above the phone set, there was a number for a taxi service. I supposed I could manage that.

As we waited for our lifts home, Laurie completed Marion's flight report, omitting the alcoholic poisoning part. I sat at the table, watching her and wondering why Laurie always attracted drama. Maybe ordinary life was too boring for her, and she needed to feel more alive?

The buzzing in my head had lessened now and I wasn't seeing double anymore. The captain was seated on one of the red plastic chairs, his head lolling on Christopher's shoulder. Over Marion's loud snoring, I asked Laurie, "How come we're all so drunk and you're not?"

"Oh, God," Laurie moaned. "I should have warned you. It's the fruit. I didn't eat the fruit." Then her face crumpled, and tears spilled down her cheeks. "What have I done, Natasha? Why does everything I do seem to hurt people?" Her frail shoulders began to shake as she sobbed. "I'm just a terrible person."

"No, No, No," I exclaimed, patting her on the arm, her sadness instantly sobering me up. "We lo-o-ove you, but ...maybe you live a little *too-oo far* out there on the edge." Hell, who was I to talk? I flew for Dan Air, didn't I? "Perhaps you need to live a bit more in the middle. You know," I said, holding thumb and forefinger half an inch apart, "balance your exciting times with a teensy-weensy bit of boring."

Laurie stopped crying and looked up at me. "You're right, Natasha" she said, wiping her eyes. Then something dawned on her. "Maybe I'm trying to prove too hard to people that I'm *not* boring. You know? Like my nickname?"

"Oh, that's just a play on words." I waved it away dismissively. "And you don't have to prove *anything* to *anyone*. You could afford to be a *lot more* boring and still be lo-o-oads of fun."

"You *want* me to be boring?" she asked, shocked.

"Well, not too-oo much. I still want you to be my funny friend, but maybe just not go to over-the-top, nail-biting, near-death levels of drama."

Laurie seemed to absorb this concept and nodded.

"But whatever you do, Laurie," I added, wagging a finger at her.

"What's that?" she asked, smiling at me.

"Do *not* leave without your boot polish."

17

THE UGLY, THE NOT-SO BAD AND THE GOOD

May 1977

"Ooh, lucky you! You're flying with Liz Good!" my flat mate, Ellen cooed as we met in the crowded crew room. She had just returned from a night Athens, and I was about to check in for my early morning Faro.

"Oh, no." I moaned. "Not Liz Good." I said, inspecting the flight sheet for myself. Flying with hosties who had been junior when I left and had since been promoted to number one could provide some interesting dynamics. Liz Good was one of those. More than that, I was shocked to hear that Liz was still with the airline, let alone a senior.

The corners of Ellen's mouth, I noticed, were curled up in a suppressed grin as she donned her gloves, ready to leave. "You know what they say," she taunted, "sometimes she's good, sometimes she's bad and sometimes she's downright ugly!"

I sighed, remembering the first time I had met the lovely Liz Good. After seeing her surname on her uniform tag, I had asked her if passengers ever made wisecracks.

She had sighed and responded wearily, "Men mainly ask, "Are you?"

But I remembered even when Liz was brand new, how her bad reputation had preceded her.

Just a month before Julian and I were due to leave for Europe, I was in the crew room checking in for a Palma. Remembering that there was probably a pay cheque in my pigeon-hole, I had moved over to the left wall where the mail slots hung. As I sifted through airline bulletins and friends' messages, the crew room door flew open and a pretty brunette burst in.

She strode over, loomed in front of me and stared into my eyes. "Are you the number one on my Palma?"

Though I had not yet checked the flight sheet to see who my cohorts for the Palma were, it suddenly dawned on me that this might be the infamous Liz Good.

"Er ...I still have to ..." I pointed to the table in the center of the room where the flight sheet lay. Despite the early hour of the day, the large white paper already appeared grubby with its curled corners. "Well ...there are a few Palma flights today ...," I told her.

"Oh, good! I'm Liz Good and I'm sure I'm on your flight. I must tell you I'm so-o-o-o-o relieved that you're my number one ..." Her face was only inches from mine, and she was blocking my path to the table.

Oh God, I groaned inwardly. It was going to be one of those days. I inched forward hoping she would get the hint and step out of the way. "Please, just let me ..."

"Oh, yes, of course," she responded, flustered. "I'm so-o-o-o sorry." She stepped aside, but then followed me to the table, still talking to my back.

The flight sheet confirmed that, yes, indeed, Liz Good was on my flight. The other hostess was my friend, the Scottish Maddy. Praise the Lord. Maddy and her wicked sense of humor would provide comic relief.

"Yes," I told Liz, with my back still to her and attempting to keep dismay out of my voice. "That's right. You are on my Palma."

"I'm very new," she informed me as I turned to face her. "I hope I won't be too much of a nuisance ..."

Her nose was inches from mine—and being a person who likes a little physical space—I was forced to arch back over the table to get away from this close encounter.

"Och, Natasha. It's you. Thank God."

The novelty of Maddy's strong Glaswegian accent, and presence, in the crew room caused Liz to back away from me in order to survey her new prey.

"I'm just not in the mood for all these silly holiday punters today." Maddy added and plonked her crew bag on the floor, as yet blissfully unaware of the real threat. The punters or bucket and spaders—and other derogatory terms we used for our passengers—would probably be the least of our problems. Liz, the Good, on the other hand ....

Liz strode over to poor Maddy who, without warning, was instantly assaulted by a monologue from the new girl. Maddy's eyes went wide with astonishment, and she glanced over to me, silently pleading for help.

I shrugged, relieved that for the moment, I was not the victim.

Maddy then found her sense of humor and responded "Och, is that right?" and "Well, I never," to whatever the new girl was spouting at her.

"Liz," I said, trying to intercept her monologue. "Liz!"

She finally turned to me, and Maddy's shoulders slumped with relief.

"Liz, how many flights have you actually done?"

She strode back over to me and stood close enough that I could feel her breath. "Well, just three but ..."

She blathered on, but I wasn't listening. I envisioned the next eight hours with this boundary-challenged, close-talking young woman, talking not to me, but at me. There was no way, I decided, that she was going to work with me in the cabin. "I think it's time you mastered the galley ..."

"Oh, no!" Her face fell in horror. "But I'm not ready, Natasha. I've only done three flights and ..." More white noise.

She was correct, of course. She was very new and not really ready for the demanding galley position, but short of stuffing her into the hat rack with a sock in her mouth, the galley was the only place where she could go. Otherwise, after eight hours in a confined metal tube with Miss Good, I might do something very bad.

"And Maddy, you can work in the cabin with me."

Maddy gave me a knowing look and smiled.

"You'll be fine, Liz," I told her. "We'll guide you through it, won't we Maddy? Com' on. Transport's waiting."

Halfway to Palma I had decided that just maybe putting Liz in the galley hadn't been such a good idea after all. Despite my guidance on every step of every service and making sure she understood what was required, she still came into the cabin repeatedly, butted into my conversations with passengers and demanded immediate answers to her constant questions. God bless her, I kept reminding myself, she just wants to get it right.

In the crew room back at Gatwick eight hours later, Maddy and I watched Liz leave. Then we slumped into two battered chairs. "Och," Maddy exclaimed, "I'm going to tell those plonkers in crewing if they even think of rostering me with her again, they can stick it up their wee kilt!"

I laughed. "It doesn't take much for you to tell crewing to stick it up their kilt, and I don't know how, but you always get away with it, Maddy."

She grinned, proud of her antics. "So, Natasha, what will you write about Liz her in your wee fright report?" Maddy asked. Reporting on the performance of "new girls" on flights during their six-month probationary contract was required of number ones. And though we joked about calling the flight report a fright report—a one-pager giving details of any aberrations, emergency situations, disruptive events, people dying, coffins on board, rude passengers before, during or after the flight—the term was much closer to the truth than we admitted.

"Liz means well ...and she's bright. She's just so intense!" I faltered, my pen hovering over the lined page. I began to write. *Liz Good is bright, conscientious and a hard worker. Once she gains confidence in her work, her interaction with other crew members and passengers will, I am sure, be more relaxed.*

"Is that fair?" I asked as I showed it to Maddy. I had to tell the truth without ruining the poor girl's chances at a flying career.

"Och, you're too nice, Natasha. I would ha' written that she's a pain in the arrrrse and she needs to take a pill. What's she gonna be like in an emergency, for Gawd's sake? A bluddy liability, if you ask me."

As I drove home that night, I wondered if Maddy was right about Liz Good. With that kind of intense perfectionist energy, how would she handle an emergency?

Fifteen months later, I was flying with Liz again, she now a senior to my junior position. As the number one, she would now be telling *me* what to do. *Oh joy!* Maybe I should have been a bit more specific in my flight report when I had had the chance.

When Liz appeared in the crew room, it was soon evident that, even after one more year of flying and her promotion, Liz had not changed. She still had not yet learned to give people breathing space, literally. While she was a nice person and I could not help feeling a little sorry for her, did she know that everyone groaned when they heard her name? Demanding up-close and personal attention when she talked *at* us, we were like deer, not only caught in the headlights, but also pinned to the wall, the airline seat or the bulkhead. In the cramped space of an aircraft, there was no escape from Liz the Good. So I was happy when on this particular flight to Faro, Liz designated me to the galley position.

All went well—on the outbound.

Once on the ground in Lisbon and passengers had disembarked, Liz came rushing down the aisle from the rear.

"Oh my God!" she cried. "Have you seen my paperwork? I've lost my paperwork!" Her hysteria was motivated by the manila A4 envelope containing forms; a blank flight report, bar counting documentation and catering information. The envelope was usually delivered to the aircraft prior to the flight and left somewhere at the front for the number one who, to save time post-flight, would complete most of the forms before landing back at base.

Liz then came flouncing into the galley where I was in the process of accepting catering for the return sector; large cardboard boxes filled with one hundred and nineteen ham sandwiches.

"Oh my God! What shall I *do*?" She pushed the surprised Portuguese caterers out of the way and began opening and scouring all the galley cupboards. I was not amused. She was making a mess of my neatly organized workspace.

"Liz? What are you doing?" I used my serene voice I usually reserved for hysterical passengers. "It's okay. Calm down."

She turned on me, her already large eyes now nearly popping out of her head. "But I've lost my paperwork!" she screamed.

"I understand that but, Liz, don't worry! I'll help you find it." To prevent her from having a seizure, I was tempted to slap her face just as I had seen done in countless movies. But Liz probably would have burst into loud sobs and accused me of assault. Instead I gently turned her around. "You go and search in the cabin," I said, urging her to leave my galley before she caused an international Anglo-Portuguese incident, "and I will look in here and the flight deck."

Huffing, she returned to the cabin and began climbing on seats and peering into the overhead hat rack.

"It's only paperwork," I called after her. "You can get another set of documents back at Gatwick. I'll help you fill them out." The process might take another hour post-flight but perhaps the offer would prevent her from going catatonic.

I watched as she worked her way up the aisle, frantically pulling at the seat pockets while repeatedly moaning. "Oh, my God! They're going to fire me!"

At that moment something told me to look in the hat rack above the first row of seats portside. I stood on the seat frame, pushed myself up and groped underneath a blanket. I felt the familiar edges of the envelope.

"Here it is!" I called to her back, waving the envelope in the air. She was now almost at the rear of the empty cabin.

She gasped, turned and strode back down the aisle, a mixed expression of anger, relief and gratitude on her face. For one horrific moment, I thought she might gather me into a ferocious bear hug.

Instead, she reached out and snatched the envelope from me. "The cleaners probably hid it," she muttered.

Trying to tell her that the cleaners didn't know or care about the envelope's contents and that she had probably left it there herself was a waste of breath.

I returned to my galley and gushed an uber-friendly thank you and goodbye to the Portuguese caterers and cleaners as they eagerly left the aircraft. Once I had finally restored order in my galley, I exhaled. But the thought came again. My God. If Liz is hysterical over lost paperwork, how will she react in an emergency?

Two months later, we would discover that there was a little more to Liz Good than any of us could have guessed.

After one late evening Malaga, my colleagues and I wearily traipsed into an empty crew room, laughing at a shared joke. As soon as we saw the lone figure sitting at the table in the center, our laughter quickly died.

At first, I didn't recognize her. Then something about her body language made me stop in my tracks. The head was down, the shoulders slumped, and the hands were clasped together in a defeated gesture. And the fact that she didn't even look up when we noisily entered the room made it clear that something was terribly wrong.

"Liz?"

She didn't move. Her head sank even lower. She shook her head.

"Liz?" I asked again, approaching. "Are you okay?"

"I've got to write this flight report and ...I don't know what to say," she muttered tearfully.

All three of us moved over to the table and sat. Liz the Good looked white, devastated. Tears trickled down her cheeks.

"What's happened?" Sarah, my number one asked her, compassion in her voice.

"O-h-h." Liz banged the table with a flat palm. "I could have saved him!" she made a hiccupping noise which I realized were sobs with pangs of angry frustration in her voice.

We waited for her crying to subside. Sarah retrieved a box of Kleenex from the top of the pigeon-holes and offered them to Liz who took a wad of tissues and blew her nose loudly.

"I just came off a Corfu." Liz waved an arm as if dismissing a horrible memory. "There was a little boy, about ten, Downs syndrome, with his older parents."

Sarah moved her chair closer to Liz and put a hand on her arm. Diana, my other colleague sat frozen on the other side of the table, perhaps sensing what was coming. I remained standing, holding my breath.

Liz swiped a tear with her tissue from her cheek. "I *told* them that he needed oxygen! But they wouldn't listen!" She looked up at Sarah, pleading for what...? Validation? Forgiveness?

"Tell us from the beginning," Sarah urged.

"Well ...," Liz took a deep gulp of air. "We took off from Corfu and everything was fine. The little boy seemed happy but then when we were about one hour out, I noticed that he'd begun to look really pale. I don't know anything about Downs, but I knew that he wasn't looking good. So I said to the elderly parents, 'If your boy's not feeling well, I could give him some oxygen.' But they said, 'No, he doesn't need oxygen. He always looks like that.'

Well, you can't argue with parents, can you?" Liz looked at Sarah, seeking confirmation. "So I said okay and let it be. But it didn't feel right."

"That was the correct thing to do," Sarah, the veteran number one, assured her quietly.

Liz shook her head. "Twenty minutes later, the boy looked even worse. I thought he was ill. Again, I suggested to the parents that he needed oxygen. I mean you can tell when someone is not getting enough oxygen, can't you?" This time, Liz looked at me.

I nodded and whispered, "Yes." A few passengers had almost nearly died on me a few times, too. That ever-so-white look was scary.

"Still the parents said, 'Oh, he's all right. He'll be okay once we get him home.' But on the descent, he was becoming really ill and that's when they finally began to worry. But because we were almost on the ground, we couldn't get the oxygen to him on time ..."

We all inhaled.

"When we landed ..., he was ...dead."

The three of us gasped simultaneously.

"Oh, no," Sarah moaned.

Liz sobbed again and put her face in her hands. "I *told* them he was ill. If they had just let me give him oxygen."

It occurred to me that in this terrible moment, Liz was the sanest and most normal I had ever seen her. Strange.

Sarah got up and put an arm around Liz's shoulders. "You did everything right. It's not your fault that he died. Like you said, you can't override the parents' authority. There's nothing more that you could have done."

The sobs quietened, and Liz stared up at Sarah with mascara-streaked cheeks. "Oh! Do you really think so?"

"Of course! And," she continued on her mission to comfort Liz, "you don't know for certain that the oxygen would have saved him, do you?"

"No. No, I suppose not," Liz nodded and exhaled as if a huge weight had been removed from her shoulders. "It was just hard when the ambulance came to meet the aircraft and the paramedic asked me if the boy had been offered oxygen ...," her voice wavered, "as if it *would* have saved him."

More tears trickled down her cheeks.

"Well, you *did* offer, but the parents refused," Sarah insisted. "If anyone is at fault here, I would say it's the parents. But certainly not you!"

We all sat in silence, our own tears spilling for the boy, for the parents and for Liz the Good who, despite her best intentions, and staying calm in an emergency, had been prevented from saving her young passenger and from perhaps needlessly stopping the awful inevitable finality of death.

Only three months after losing that passenger and suffering the added trauma of punishing inquests and interrogations, Liz surprised us yet again.

"Would you like to go for a wee bevvy?" Maddy's unmistakable accent came down the phone line. "This bluddy miserable weather, hen! Pauline and I are here poolling our hair out."

"Is it your day off, Maddy, or are you evading standby yet again?"

"Och, how could you accuse me of such a thing, Natasha?" Maddy laughed, but she knew exactly what I was talking about because Adrian in crewing had relayed the story.

In the first few months of her flying career, while we were all still on "probation," Maddy had been scheduled on a day standby, which meant from 7:00 in the morning to 7:00 in the evening, she was supposed to be at home and available to do a flight. Not being at the end of a phone line was a serious infraction of company rules and could mean, especially on a temporary contract, being fired.

She also happened to share a house, with among others, Julia, the girlfriend of Adrian in crewing.

Adrian had called from crewing. "Good morning," his voice had droned.

When Maddy had answered, she had instantly recognized Adrian's familiar tones and sighed.

"Dan Air crewing here," he said. "Can we speak to Maddy Macdonald?

"Och, I'm tairrribly sorry," she said ever-so-politely. "But Maddy's nawt here."

"Where is she?" Adrian asked, fully aware that there was only one girl with a Scottish accent at that contact number.

"Waill, I do believe she's gawn shopping for a few wee things."

"Is that right?" Adrian responded. "So Maddy, when do you expect to be back?"

"Och, I might be a wee while."

"Well, Maddy, when you get back, can you give crewing a call. You're needed for a flight in two hours."

"Och, yes. I'll tell her. Nawt a problem. But mebbee give 'er half an hour."

Now three years later, it was amazing to me, that after this and other similar antics, Maddy still had her job.

"No, Natasha. It really is ma day off." Maddy assured me. "Let's meet at the Lamb, say at twelve?"

"Great. I'll see you there."

I was the first to arrive. With a glass of white wine in hand and a lunch of ham and cheese quiche on order, I stepped over the landlord's two large rescue dogs sprawled in front of the fireplace and parked myself on the floral-cushioned bench behind the corner table.

The pub was, as usual, crowded with airport people, off-duty flyers, office workers and ground staff. Behind the bar, John, the gregarious landlord, was in fine form joking with patrons. One of his eccentricities was to—as one way to empty the pub at last call—play earsplitting renditions of "Land of Hope and Glory" or "Willie is a Wanker." Both worked.

Behind him on the shelves above copious bottles of spirits, several penises carved out of wood and silver were still on display, a sight that had taken me three years to notice. But once I knew they were there, I could never quite ignore them.

The door opened and Pauline and Maddy walked in, shaking off the winter drizzle like dogs coming out of a pond. I waved them over. Pauline sat down next to me on the bench with her usual Carlsberg beer. Maddy came over with a scotch and coke and sat opposite us, her back to the fire.

"So, Natasha, have you heard about the new 1-11 Dan's got? Bravo Echo's the registration?" Maddy asked as she took a large gulp of her drink. "It's a 200 series."

I knew that the airline had acquired a few second-hand aircraft as a debt payment from British Caledonian the previous year. This must be a more recent acquisition. "What about it?" I asked. Pauline and Maddy were flat mates, so this was probably old news to them.

"Well," Maddy huffed. "It makes you really sick."

"Doesn't all flying make you sick?" I grinned.

"No, I mean the aircraft has a wee problem. Somethin' to do wi' them missing a part on the autopilot," Maddy continued, serious for once. "And Dan Air is too tight-arrsed to fix it. When it's flying along, it jerks through the air. After a wee while, all the pax are doing technicolour yawns, showing us what they had for breakfast, lunch *and* dinner. It's so bad, now the aircraft smells o' puke so when you get on it, you want to puke, too!"

"So Bravo Echo is appropriate?" Pauline added, smiling. "You know, echo, repeat, throwing up?"

Maddy and I groaned.

John appeared and presented us with our lunches. "Here you go, girls."

I surveyed my quiche, not quite so hungry now. "Sounds lovely!"

At that moment, the door of the pub burst open and all three of us looked up ...and stared. The strait-laced teetotaller, Liz the Good, was standing there, looking as if she had been in a fight with her hairdresser.

We all frowned, exchanged puzzled glances, and then surveyed her again. The usually oh-so-neat long brown hair was hanging down in a dishevelled mess over her shoulders. A raggedy navy sweater hung loosely on her small frame over what seemed to be her uniform. Even more incongruous to her usual fastidious appearance, was a large brown stain splayed across the front of her navy skirt.

Many turned to stare and snicker. She wasn't fooling any airport workers in the pub as to the fact she was a Dan Air hostie. She materialized as if, like many before her, she had just come off a flight, badly needed a drink and had done little to disguise the uniform and give herself a "civvie" look. And if there was any doubt as to her identity, her airport pass was dangling from the strap of her Dan Air handbag.

But it wasn't even her messy attire that held our gaze. Her complexion was deathly white. Her large eyes frantically scanned the pub, apparently looking for someone she knew. Finally, her eyes rested on us. She strode over to our table.

Without preamble she asked, "Have you seen Jane Higgins? We were supposed to be meeting here?" Liz's energy was much edgier than usual. Perhaps another passenger had died on her? She turned and scanned the pub again, frowning.

"No ...what's up Liz?" I asked. "You look like you've seen a ghost?"

"You could say that!" She snorted. "My ghost!"

"What do ya mean, hen?" Maddy frowned up at Liz, intrigued.

"I just came off a flight. Oh my God!" She put a hand over her eyes. "We thought we were going to die!" She hiccupped. I remembered that was her version of a sob.

"Why don't you sit down and join us until Jane gets here," Pauline suggested gently. Even though the three of us would never normally socialize with Liz the Good, we were dying to hear the story, and the poor girl seemed distraught.

"Well," Liz hesitated, "normally I don't drink but ..."

"Och, pull up a pew." Maddy dragged a chair over for Liz to sit in. "I'll get you a wee brandy. You look like ya need one, hen!"

Gratefully, Liz slumped into the chair. Once the brandy was handed to her, she shocked us all when she threw her head back and tossed the hot liquid down her throat. She then unceremoniously wiped her mouth on the sleeve of her raggedy jumper. We waited patiently until she was ready to tell her story. Our lunches remained untouched on the table.

"We were on a return flight from Tenerife to Gatwick," she began with a large exhale. "Full load. You know what *they're* like, drinkers, rowdy holidaymakers. The plane had just reached cruising altitude at 35,000 so most of them had lit up cigarettes and unbuckled their seat belts." Liz's voice was uncharacteristically low, so we all had to lean in to hear. "Flight time was three-and-a-half-hours." As the alcohol began to take effect, she blew out the tension in her body and we all got a whiff of her brandy fumes.

"As usual, we had the drinks cart filled to the gills. Bottles of spirits, miniatures, minerals galore, two large buckets of ice. We were at row nine when it happened." Liz suddenly turned to Maddy. "Would you mind getting me another drink? I can pay you ..." she reached down for her handbag.

"Nawt a problem." Maddy got up and went over to the bar.

"Are you hungry?" I asked Liz and offered her my quiche.

"No, no." She shook her head. "I still feel *so-o-o-o-o* sick at the thought of it all."

Had she been flying on Bravo Echo?

Maddy returned, careful not to step on the dogs as she resumed her seat and handed Liz her drink. "Jane called and left a message for you. She's terribly sorry, but she said she had to gaw straight home. She's a wreck."

Liz nodded understanding. This time, she just sipped on the brandy.

"For God's sake, what happened?" Pauline urged, sitting forward again.

"As the number one, you know, I was serving from the back end of the cart and Jane, poor girl," Liz shook her head again, "was on the forward end. My number two, Allison Higginbottom was in the galley getting tea and coffees prepared for the meal service. The curtain was open between the cabin and the galley so she could see if any replenishments were required."

Yes. Yes. Get on with it, I wanted to say. We knew the routine, but we were all aware of how punctilious Liz was.

"Then suddenly," Liz continued, splaying her hands up in the air as if trying to stop an invisible assault, "we heard this really loud, shrill, pulsing alarm on the flight deck." Her eyes grew large with fright.

Maddy, Pauline and I exchanged looks of *Uh-oh*. We knew what that meant!

"It was so--o-o-o loud in the cabin, too." Liz let out another hiccup of a sob. "I just froze. At first, Jane and I frowned at each other and then it dawned on us what was about to happen!"

"Oh, ma Gawd!" Maddy sat forward, holding her breath.

"I dropped a rum and coke all over me," she whimpered, pointing at the stain on her skirt, as if that was the trauma of the day. "I crouched down on the cabin floor and grabbed the chrome leg of the drinks trolley with one hand and the metal seat strut with the other." She held out her arms demonstrating. "Then the floor just fell away from under our feet! The whole plane tipped forward and went down into a dive." Another sob. "I didn't know if it was a rapid decompression or whether the pilots had gone nuts or were sick or whether we were crashing. So many scenarios go through your head, don't they?" She searched all of our faces.

We nodded, but in reality, not having experienced a rapid descent, none of us had a clue.

"Jane had also crouched down. She had her back against the cart with her feet wedged against seat struts. Poor girl! All the bottles, ice and cans fell on top of her, but she still clung to the seats on either side of the aisle. I kept shouting, "Hang on, Jane! Hang on, Jane!" We both knew that if the drinks trolley flew into the flight deck, we could all end up dead. It was *so-o-o* noisy, what with the sirens blaring on the flight deck, the oxygen masks hissing, passengers screaming, crying ...and farting. From my position on the floor, I yelled as loudly as I could 'Fasten seat belts!' 'Put out cigarettes!' I was terrified that with everyone smoking and all the oxygen coming out of the masks we would just blow up!"

"Did the cabin fill with a blue mist like they say in training?" Pauline's eyes were huge.

Liz nodded. "Yes, that scared passengers even more. People cried and prayed and clung to each other. The cabin started to smell really bad ...because people were ...you know..."

"Shittin' their troosers?" Maddy supplied.

"I bet you didn't tell them to go into the brace position, then?" Pauline snickered. "And kiss their asses goodbye?"

Liz gave Pauline "the look" that we all gave passengers who made inane comments.

"Sorry, Liz." Pauline sat back. "Carry on."

"I knew that if it was a rapid decompression, the flight deck had four minutes to get down to breathing altitude ...and they didn't have time to tell us what was happening. But four minutes is a bloody long time when you don't know whether you're going to live or die." Liz covered her face again, shook her head and let tears fall. "I didn't think I would see my family or my boyfriend ever again," she sniffled.

"Boyfriend!" we all exclaimed in disbelief.

Probably a nerdy accountant, I thought.

"And I'm only twenty-three, I'm too young to die." She added, still with a hand over her face.

Maddy put an arm around Liz's shoulders. "But hinny, you *did* live to tell the tale, didn't you?" I had never seen the normally abrasive Scot be so ...compassionate. Had she changed her mind about Liz the Good?

Buoyed by Maddy's unusually kind words, Liz wiped her eyes and carried on.

"Allison was in the galley. I saw that she was thrown back against the forward bulkhead. A pot of coffee crashed to the floor and spilled. I was so-o-o worried that she was scalded. And with the aircraft in such a steep dive, and fighting G-forces, she couldn't possibly get onto her jump seat."

"Is she okay?" I had flown with Allison a few times.

Liz nodded. "Shaken, but okay."

"Did all the oxygen masks come down?" Pauline wanted to know.

"Not sure. From where I was crouching, I could see some masks still dangling from the hat rack. Some passengers weren't putting them on. So I yelled again, 'Put on oxygen masks!' I didn't know if they could hear me over the noise. Because I was holding onto the trolley, I couldn't get oxygen for myself and I worried that I might pass out. But I couldn't move. A man and a woman on either side of me were also hanging onto the trolley but ...I told them, 'Whatever happens, don't let go!' The woman was sobbing with terror, but they both held on."

Liz continued, calmer now, "I knew that if the pilot levelled out at 10,000 feet, most people would survive without getting brain damage, but I was so scared that ...you know ...heart attacks ...I didn't want to lose another ...." She glanced at me.

"I know ..." I said, softly remembering the downs syndrome incident. We all went quiet, thinking of the boy who had died.

Liz stared forlornly into her brandy.

"I kept praying," she finally continued, "that no one would try do anything heroic like get up and help us. I just kept yelling instructions. 'Everyone listen up! We will level out in four minutes! Keep seat belts fastened! Oxygen masks on!' I kept yelling even though I had no idea if we would make it." Another hiccup came out of her mouth.

Pauline leaned forward. "How did the passengers react?"

"Aye. That's what I want to knaw." Maddy huffed. "There's always one bluddy nutter, right?"

"Oh, I know!" Liz turned to Maddy, now her new best girlfriend "Well, thank god, they all did as they were told. But you know, after a while, they all went really quiet. It was a little eerie. Funny. You just never know how people will behave in an emergency, do you?"

All three of us stared at Liz gobsmacked and said in unison, "No ...you don't...."

"Finally, finally, finally, the engines shifted tone and the pressure gradually eased up on my arm. That awful siren stopped and the blue mist quickly cleared." Liz exhaled as all the tension left her body and we were hit with more fumes. "Then thank the lord, the plane levelled out!"

"So, everyone was okay?" Maddy asked finally.

"Yes." Another long exhalation of brandy-breath came out of Liz. "Thank God!"

"Och, those passengers must ha' been cheerin'!" Maddy threw back the last slug of her own drink.

"Yes, they did." Liz beamed at her. "When we finally got up off the floor, people were taking off their oxygen masks, crying, laughing and hugging each other." She paused, more tears threatening to fall down her cheeks. "Then a clapping began at the rear of the cabin and spread forward. I-I don't know why but they were clapping at *us*."

"Well, no wonder. You were amazing!" Pauline said, deep respect in her tone. "If that'd been me, I would have jumped into a passenger's lap, sucked my thumb and prayed for my Mummy. They were lucky to have you on that flight ...and not any of us."

"Speak for yourself," I quipped. But maybe Pauline was right.

For the first time, a small smile lit up Liz's face. She put her shoulders back and raised her chin. Suddenly she didn't look so dishevelled. "But this is the real miracle," she said, leaning forward.

"What's that?" Maddy was getting up to get herself another drink.

"No one died and ...Captain Willie offered *free* drinks to the passengers."

"What? Na-a-w!" Maddy sat back down. "Too right, that *is* a bluddy miracle. Och, what a passenger has to go through to get a free drink on Dan Air!"

"Yes!" Liz was grinning now. "When the captain made the announcement, the passengers clapped again. I wasn't sure if it was because they were getting a free drink, or that they would be getting off that deathtrap of an aircraft very quickly."

We all laughed. Who knew? Liz Good actually had a sense of humor.

"Did Captain Willie tell you why they had to do an emergency descent?"

"Air system failure. We had to get down to breathing altitude ...fast."

"I hope you didn't fly all the way back to Gatwick on one air system?" Pauline enquired indignantly, knowing that Dan Air considered us to be like robots, replaceable.

"Yes, of course we did!" Liz smiled again, now more relaxed. She was either slightly inebriated, or the shock was wearing off, but I could see that sharing her trauma with us had also helped calm her. "You know,

Dan Air. And Captain Willie said we'd be safe if we stayed at 10,000 feet."

"You did an amazing job, Liz," I told her with awe. "Constantly giving commands like that was a good strategy. Keeping them in the know. Showing them that you knew what was happening and that you knew what to do ...even if you didn't."

"Aye. Fake it till you make it, eh, hen?" Maddy gently nudged Liz in the arm. "You poor wee girrall. What a rough time you've had. But what doesn't kill you makes you stronger, eh?"

"I'm strong enough now," Liz added sardonically and looked sadly into her empty glass.

"Do you want another drink?" Pauline offered.

Oh no. Would she now become an alcoholic like the rest of us?

"No, thanks," she said suddenly peering behind me out of the window at something that had caught her eye. She reached for her handbag and stood up. "I need to go home and sleep."

"Are you okay to drive?" I asked. "We can take you home. After all, we'd hate for you to survive a near plane crash and then get schmucked in a car accident."

The pub door opened and a tall, dark handsome man in a pinstriped suit entered. The three of us watched with an *ooh-who's-he?* look in our eyes. He was walking in our direction.

"No, thank you, though," Liz responded. "My boyfriend's here to pick me up." Just then Mr. Handsome appeared by Liz's side and put a protective arm around her. Accountant maybe, but definitely not nerd, I surmised.

"Thank God!" he breathed, giving her a cherishing squeeze and searching her eyes. "Are you okay, darling?"

Liz smiled up at him. "Better now." She turned back to us. "This is David, by the way. Thank you for listening, girls. Maddy, what do I owe you for the drink?"

"Och, nothing, hen. Ma wee treat."

After the couple had left, the three of us sat in silence. "We better eat up." I said. "It'll soon be last call." As if on cue, "Land of Hope and Glory" blared deafeningly throughout the lounge and saloon.

"Och, thank gawd, he didn't play that "Willie is a Wanker" song," Maddy muttered through a mouthful of bread and cheese.

"I know one thing," Pauline murmured, soberly. "Captain Willie is not a wanker. He probably saved a lot of lives today."

"And who knew about Liz?" I said, when the music had died down. "It just goes to show. You can never predict how any of us will react in an emergency."

"Aye, right enough." Maddy delicately touched the corners of her mouth with her serviette. "Och, she's still a pain in the arrse, but she's like her name, she's also vairry, vairry good!"

18

THE GHOST OF MIKE BRAVO

November 1977

"Oh, no!"

"What is it?" the small, dark-haired girl standing behind me in the crew room enquired as she peered over my shoulder, both of us inspecting the flight sheet for our imminent duty. Her soft Irish lilt was charming.

"Harriet Coulsdon is my number one!" I muttered.

"Are you on de Trondheim, too?"

"Yes, I am." Then I also noted the registration of our aircraft. My heart sank. This day was just getting better and better. "*And* we're on Mike Bravo!"

"What's de matter with Mike Bravo?" she asked.

I turned to her. "You must be new."

"I am, to be sure. By the way, I'm Trish."

"I'm Natasha ...Mike Bravo is one of the oldest planes on the Comet fleet—and it's haunted."

"Jesus, Mary and Joseph," Trish whispered, crossing herself. "And who's de poor soul that's doin' de hauntin'?"

"We think it's an angry engineer who makes fire bells go off without a fire, and messes with the lights on the flight deck panel so the captain declares emergencies that aren't emergencies. There's always some kind of a problem." And that means a delay. I thought, and I won't make my party.

Then Ellen, my former-and-now-married roommate rushed into the crew room, somewhat flustered. "Got called out for the Trondheim," she said, still panting. "Somebody went sick."

"Well, I'm sorry you got called out, Ellen, but I'm *so* glad you're on this flight! Guess who our number one is?

As if she had heard me, Harriet Coulsdon's bulky frame suddenly appeared in the doorway, her large energy already emitting a dark cloud. She stomped over to the table and looked at the flight sheet. "Ugh," she groaned, "we don't have a Scandinavian speaker."

"Yes, we do." I piped up. "It's me."

"You? Since when do *you* speak Norwegian?"

"Since spending three months in Norway and travelling the country," I responded, proud of my linguistic idiosyncrasy.

"So, you can work as number four, Natasha," Harriet commanded. "Ellen, you go in the galley. And Trish, you're number three." Working alongside Harriet was going to make for a long flight. And although the Irish Trish seemed as if she might have a sense of humor, I still felt an air of doom.

As number four, I sat next to Harriet during take-off on the double jump seat at the rear of the aircraft. Thankfully, with her paperwork attached to her clip board and the headset covering her ears—connecting her to the flight deck—there was no need for conversation. As we ascended through the wintry clouds, I peered out of the small round window in the rear port door and thought about what I would wear to the London party I was going to that night—if we made it back in time. With Dan Air, anything was possible. I never believed the scheduled arrival time until we had actually landed, and I was out of crewing's reach *and* the fat lady was singing.

Except for intrepid adventurers, Trondheim or *Tronhjem* as the locals pronounced it, was not a holiday destination. Our passengers were mostly Norwegians flying home from vacation or Scottish and Englishmen returning to oil rigs in the North Sea. To my amazement, the outbound flight was uneventful. Maybe I would make it to the party after all.

Two and a half hours later, after we had come to rest on the snowy Trondheim tarmac and intoned "Goodbye and *Har det bra*" to the departing passengers, Trish and I immediately set about replenishing seat pockets.

Then I heard a loud groan come from the galley. It was Harriet. What had happened?

She shoved aside the galley curtain and appeared in the cabin. With a thunderous look on her face, she stomped down the aisle.

"What's the matter, Harriet?" I enquired from where I was at mid-cabin.

"Ugh," she groaned, waving a hand at me as though I was an annoying fly. She carried on walking.

I trotted up to the galley. Ellen was just signing off for the catering. "Why's Harriet got her knickers in a knot?"

"We have a stiff. "Ellen shuddered. "And they're putting the coffin in the rear hold on top of the suitcases." Having lived with Ellen in my own haunted home, I knew how dead people gave her the heebie-jeebies.

"Why is that a problem?" I shrugged. "Where else can they put a dead body?"

"Harriet wants him to go in the hold below. But down there, he would be frozen. It might interrupt rigor mortis or something, He just died today, and they didn't have time to ...you know ...prepare him. He might get stinky, so ...." Ellen shuddered again. "Oh, I don't know."

Obviously, she did not want to talk about the dead body, so I returned to helping Trish in the cabin.

"I tink it's disgustin'," Trish commented from the overwing. "De poor blighter. He should be treated with a little more respect than just bein' tossed on a heap of dirty suitcases like a pile o' rubbish." Evidently Trish was a good Catholic girl.

"I'm sure it's...." I was going to say *the best they can do under the circumstances*, but just then Harriet came stomping came back down the aisle from the rear. Trish and I stepped aside to avoid being mowed down.

"Passengers!" she barked.

Trish and I quickly took up our positions with me at the back of the plane where I was acutely aware of the rear vestibule behind me, the two toilets, six stowed bar boxes, our jump seat flipped upwards against the bulkhead, the rear luggage hold with its pile of suitcases—and the makeshift coffin with the dead man in it.

Passengers settled into their seats. We assisted the strugglers with large bags, heavy coats and other paraphernalia ready for their flight to Gatwick. After doing safety demonstrations, I sat next to Harriet at the rear. Her permanent frown and grumpy energy often reminded me of a ready-to-charge bull.

On the ascent, and as the undercarriage clunked into its recess, Harriet suddenly clasped both sides of the headset tighter to her ears.

Uh-oh. Something was wrong.

She leaned into the aisle—as if the noise of the engines was quieter toward starboard—straining to hear something she couldn't quite make out. Then she groaned, rolled her eyes, tut-tutted and exclaimed, "Bloody hell!"

I stared at her. What was happening?

Her cheeks twitched as she put her head down, listening more intently. "Oh, bl-l-ludddy hell!" she repeated, hissing into her lap.

What? Were we going down? What?

She roughly pulled her headset off her head, causing fine strands of her short, brown hair to stand on end and turned to me. "One of the hold doors is showing unlocked," she snapped, as if it was me and not a ground worker who had neglected to close it properly.

"Oh?" I instantly remembered the DC10 plane crashing just out of Orly a few years prior because a cargo door hadn't been properly latched. Everyone on board had died, including a former work colleague of mine.

Mistaking my shock for confusion, she explained oh-so-patiently as if to a four-year-old, "It means that if it's not closed, it's not fully pressurized and the aircraft could implode."

I know that! I wanted to say but thought better of it. Harriet liked to be superior.

"Sso-o," she continued in her school-marmish tone, "he's going to fly at 10,000 feet all the way back to Gatwick!"

"Well, that's not so bad, is it?" Maybe the ghost was just messing with us.

Harriet huffed impatiently. "Yes, it is bad. Flying at that low altitude will take us twice as long. Instead of two and a half hours, it's going to take at least four. Bloody Mike Bravo!"

Four hours. Oh, darn! The party was due to start at 9:00 and the earliest I would get there would be 10.30. now. Oh well, I would be making yet another late entrance. But maybe I should be worrying about more important things like, would we survive?

On the crashed DC10, the unsecured hold door had opened outwards, causing a decompression and destroying essential aircraft operating systems. "It's still safe, though, isn't it?" I asked, Harriet. "I mean, the plane won't implode."

"Oh, who knows on Mike Bravo. One of these days, I swear..." Harriet shook her head, stood, hung up her headset and disappeared into the back to peer into the rear hold, presumably to check on the coffin.

"He hasn't escaped, has he?" I enquired grinning when she returned, forgetting momentarily that Harriet's sense of humor had never been oxygenated.

She gave me her oh-grow-up look and opened one of the bar boxes. "We may as well begin the drinks service." Then she added, "The captain did warn us that at the lower altitude, we might experience severe turbulence."

As we maneuvered the trolley up the still steep incline of the aisle, I asked Harriet, "Is the deceased man travelling with a wife or a family?" The toughest part of returning with a dead body was dealing with grieving relatives.

"No. Poor bugger was visiting friends in Trondheim. Family in England have been informed though," she announced, blithely.

Once the captain had addressed the passengers about the extended flight time—which he blamed on air traffic rather than a potential implosion—and the collective groans were done with, passengers settled back in acceptance of their epic flight and we began serving drinks.

The "oilies" returning home to England guzzled alcohol as if they were men coming out of a hot desert while the Norwegians just wanted to drink—and get drunk. Instead of spacing out the service, Harriet wisely planned to feed the passengers immediately after the drinks service and let them soak up some of that alcohol. "Then," she declared, "perhaps they'll all sleep for the rest of the flight."

We were half-way down the cabin serving our gourmet snack of cold sliced turkey, a dollop of potato salad and a frozen bread roll when the turbulence began. "Uh-oh," Harriet muttered. "Here we go."

"Ladies and Gentleman," Ron's tenser-than-normal voice came over the PA. "For the next twenty minutes or so we will be experiencing a period of mild turbulence. We would ask you to remain seated with belts fastened until I extinguish the *Fasten Seat Belt* sign. Stewardesses, prepare to sit down."

Harriet peered over my shoulder towards the flight deck and frowned. We both knew it was unusual for the captain to tell us to return to our jump seats. Maybe "mild" wasn't quite the word for the turbulence we were about to endure.

"You unload the trolley," Harriet instructed. "I'll check the cabin."

Behind me, Trish, who had been serving teas and coffees at row ten, disappeared back into the galley to dispose of the hot liquid.

As the plane began to jostle and jerk through the sky, I hung onto the hat rack with one hand and pulled the trolley back into the galley with the other. Trish went into the cabin again to collect snack debris. In the galley, Ellen was unusually quiet as she helped me stow the untouched trays back into their cardboard boxes. "I don't like this," she muttered. "Something's up. Ron's normally nice, but tonight he's so snappy."

"Flying this low probably makes it a lot harder—and more work," I offered. "Ach, he's probably just tired. Or maybe ...he now has to forego a tryst with a sex goddess."

Ellen laughed. Ron was hardly Mr. Sexy. "Yeah, that's it," she said, chuckling.

Harriet barged into the galley, pushing us out of the way and carried on through to the flight deck. Beyond the curtain, we heard her say, "Cabin secure," and then there was more muttering as if Ron was issuing instructions. Was this more serious than I'd thought?

"Take your seats, ladies," Harriet ordered as she reemerged.

By the time the two of us reached our positions on the rear jump seat and put our seat belts on, the plane was violently jumping and jerking through the sky. It's always worse down the back, I reassured myself. Harriet donned her headset and listened intently to the flight deck exchanges. She looked concerned. I gulped. Maybe I wouldn't make it to this party ...or any other party.

For what seemed like an eternity, the plane bumped, lifted, fell, jerked, rolled and shuddered. Occasionally we hit bigger air pockets, lifting and then suddenly sinking again. Small gasps and yelps came from passengers.

A loud thud sounded behind us. I jumped. Then there was a banging, I looked at Harriet and frowned, but with her headset on, she hadn't heard it. The noises had come from the rear hold. Perhaps it was just the suitcases rearranging themselves, I told myself. I hoped the man in the coffin was *really* dead and he wasn't banging on the lid, trying to get out, or unhappy with his "seat" and this was his way of complaining. I shuddered. Or the ghost was taunting us.

Then the banging stopped.

Harriet was nodding again and muttering something into her headset microphone that I couldn't hear. "Roger," she finally said to the flight deck, nodding.

I looked at her enquiringly.

"We can get up. Turbulence is over."

Thank God for that.

"You and Trish finish the snacks service. I'm going to the flight deck."

"Okay." Without looking back to the hold, I hurried up to the galley.

We still had another two hours on this eternity of a flight so there was no big rush to get the service done. Hungry passengers at the rear of the plane, though, were happy to see us handing out their long-awaited food. Many of them were now asking for more drinks. I didn't blame them. I needed one myself.

On our second drinks service, from 15A, a tall, athletic young man grinned at me as I handed him his "*jin og jus*" Gin and orange juice. Then he asked, "*Er du Norsk?*" Are you Norwegian? I was flattered but puzzled when passengers even asked me with that question. Although I had mastered the sing-songy intonation of their language, there was still a strong English-tinge to my pronunciation.

"*Nei, Jeg er Engelsk.* No, I'm English," I replied, smiling.

"*Ja vel.*" The man nodded, incredulous, and studied me as if he was trying to understand the insanity of an English person learning Norwegian.

"*Vhordan snakker du Norsk?*" How do you come to speak Norwegian? he persisted.

"*Jeg har arbeidet pa en Gard i Hobol og der har jeg pfluckte Blomkohl og laerte a snakke Norsk,*" I worked on a farm in Hobol, picked cauliflowers and learned to speak Norwegian.

"*Ja, vel!*" He pondered this idea and finally commented. Then in English with a strong Norwegian accent, he added, "Dat's impresssiff."

"Well, you speak English!" When travelling around Norway, I had also been impressed with how many Norwegians spoke my language so fluently.

"I haff to. I am a helicopter pilot. But very few English people bother to learn anosser language, let alone Norwegian." He grinned, his boyish face lighting up. "You must *really* like the Norwegian people."

"I do." Out of all the countries we had visited, my memories of living and working on the Norwegian farm were my favourite. The farmers had taken us in like family and then paid us double for our labour.

From the other end of the trolley, Harriet tut-tutted at me. Her irritation with similar conversations that had transpired several times on our way down the cabin was growing.

"But Harriet," I asked her, "don't you think it's nice to have time to actually *talk* to passengers for a change?"

She huffed. Apparently, treating our in-flight guests as if they were actual human beings was not in *her* airline manual.

When the whole cabin had been fed and watered, we pulled the trolley back up the aisle into the galley for unloading. Harriet deposited her large frame on the front jump seat and began to fill out her paperwork. "Let's hope they sleep," she muttered.

Ellen, Trish and I huddled closer to the ovens in the small, shadowy space. While we foraged in the "hostie pack" with the same old unhealthy cheddar cheese, sliced ham, white bread, branston pickle, ritz crackers and chocolate bars to snack on, we also kept an eye on passengers through the partially open galley curtain.

"Did yer really learn Norwegian pickin' cauliflowers," Trish asked, as she chomped on cheese and biscuits.

"To be sure." I smiled, teasing her. "As well as travelling and meeting people all the way up to the top of Norway, including Trondheim."

"Yes, the lucky bugger," Ellen piped up. "She travelled around Europe for a whole year."

While I was sending her postcards from Amsterdam, Berlin, Oslo and Copenhagen, Ellen had been dealing with the stress of her mother organizing the perfect wedding. On our return, when I had showed Ellen our photographs, the new bride had been a little jealous.

"Isn't it bloody freeezin' there?" Trish said. "Bein' in the arctic circle, an' all."

"In the winter, yes, but we were there in summer. At that time, and for three months, these people are living in twenty-four-hour daylight followed by absolute darkness for the rest of the year. I don't know how they do it, but they survive on a diet of fish, dried fish, reindeer meat, dried reindeer meat and a few mangy week-old vegetables. Fresh fruit and veggies are a luxury."

"No wonder they like a drop of de hard stuff," Trish commented. "Were you hitchhiking or ....?"

"No, we drove and lived in our VW camper. It was—"

"Ellen!" Harriet suddenly barked, making us all jump. For a brief moment, we had forgotten she was there, engrossed in her paperwork. "Go down to the rear hold, will you?" she commanded. "I forgot to check on the coffin after the turbulence."

I glanced at my friend. She stared at me, her large eyes pleading for help.

"I can go," I offered, not feeling brave at all.

"For God's sake, Ellen can go," Harriet snapped. "Just do it."

I watched Ellen's back through the curtain opening as, shoulders hunched and clutching the hat-rack for support, she made her way to the rear. Passengers who were getting up to go the loo obscured my view of her. I let the curtain go and Trish and I continued snacking.

"*Aaagh!*" A muffled scream came from somewhere near the rear of the plane.

All three of us in the galley frowned. I yanked back the curtain and peered down the cabin. Passengers were also staring toward the rear of the plane. Something was amiss.

Harriet barged past me into the cabin and rudely pushed gawking passengers out of the way as she marched down the aisle. Trish and I stared from behind the curtain, waiting.

"What do you tink's de matter?" Trish whispered.

I shook my head. I had a very bad feeling and didn't want to acknowledge that I might be right. Finally, passengers stepped back, and a very pale Ellen emerged followed by Harriet who was supporting her by the elbow.

"Sit down." Harriet told Ellen as they arrived in the galley. "Natasha, give the poor girl a glass of water."

"What de hell happened?" Trish asked.

"I ...I ...fainted." Ellen covered her face in her hands. "I'm so sorry, Harriet." Even in the shadowy galley, I could see that my friend's normally pale complexion was even whiter, her brown freckles more pronounced.

"Well, it was a shock." Harriet the Gruff had suddenly morphed into Miss Compassion. Now *I* was shocked.

"What de hell shocked yer?" Trish persisted.

We waited while Ellen regained some poise. "The man ...the dead man ...in the hold ...w-w-wasn't in the coffin."

"Jesus, Mary and Joseph!" Trish shrank back against the galley counter clutching the metal sides for support with one hand and crossing herself with the other.

"Well," Ellen stammered, "he was there ...in the hold ..., but he's fallen out." She shuddered again.

"I told *those* handlers to put him downstairs," Harriet huffed ever-so-self-righteously. "The baggage hold is no place for a coffin. Now we're going to have to put him back." She looked directly at Trish and me.

"Wh-wh-a-a—a-t?" I stared right back at her. "You mean ...I ...the coffin ...I ..."

"Yes," Harriet said briskly. She could see my eyes were bugging out of their sockets. Oh, how I wished I was still a number one and could delegate this one right back to her. "Well," she stated, "Ellen can't do it, can she? She's still in shock."

"N-n-n-o, you're right, I suppose ...but...." I glanced at Trish who was studying the galley's padded ceiling and muttering what sounded like a prayer.

"Go on ...you two. Go and put the poor bugger back where he belongs."

Trish and I exchanged God-help-us glances as we turned and made our way down the aisle to the rear hold. The wooden door with Keep Closed During Flight was opened just wide enough to poke a head through and to see total blackness. I gulped.

I turned to Trish whose previously pink complexion was now a deathly white. Maybe before the night was done, we would also be in coffins, frightened to death. "Ready?" I asked her.

She crossed herself. "Je-e-seus, Mary and Joseph," she repeated as if she had invoked them and they were all standing right behind her now. "Do it," she breathed. "Open de door."

I yanked on the sliding door. It moved slightly and then caught. The build-up of oily dust often made it stick. Now it was lodged open, but not more than a foot. I pushed again and suddenly it gave way, opening a little wider. When Trish and I stood peering into the darkness, it took a minute or so for our eyes to adjust to the shadowy outlines of suitcases piled high. Then we saw the bleached white wood of the makeshift coffin. It had slipped down the pile of luggage, so the narrower end was closest to us. The lid was askew, half on, half off ...as if the dead person inside had wanted out. I shuddered. The top half of the corpse was indeed out of the coffin, having toppled to our right, his legs still draped over the narrow end of the pine box. He was lying on his side resting on the mound of suitcases, but somehow, his face was turned toward us. Instead of eyes closed and a having nice peaceful demeanor, the eyes were half-open, as if he was watching us. I shuddered. Was it my imagination or was his white clawed hand reaching out, pleading to us? Had he seen the ghost of Mike Bravo?

Trish and I gasped in unison.

"God in heaven," I heard her mutter beside me.

I turned my back on the scene, struggling for breath. Memories of watching Saturday night horror stories on BBC all flashed through my mind. "Oh God. I can't do this," I muttered, my mouth dry.

"But we can't leave the poor soul," Trish whispered as if she was afraid of waking the corpse.

"No. I-I can't do it." I turned away. "Let the handlers at Gatwick put him back in the box."

Trish grabbed my arm. "Ach, Natasha, do yer tink I want to do dis. But the poor man can't be left like dat. He'll be turning in his grave

...well, once he has one. And Harriet will have another fit." She took a deep breath in. "No, we have to do it, Natasha." For a new girl, I thought, she had a lot of guts.

I gulped and peered in the hold again. The deathly white face and hand were taunting me. "You, first." I nudged Trish forward.

She hesitated. "But how are we goin' to do dis? We need a plan. I tink he'll be heavy, so he will."

"*Kann jeg jhelper deg?* Can I help you? A man's voice came from behind us. We both jumped. "Isss something wrong?" It was Mr. Helicopter speaking in his sing-songy accent.

"Oh ...uh..." I contemplated whether it was correct procedure— when putting a dead man back in his coffin—to enlist the assistance of a passenger. To hell with it, I thought. "*Ja, tak.* Yes, please."

Trish and I stood aside to let him assess the problem. Frowning, Mr. Helicopter stepped forward and, after adjusting his eyes to the scene, also gasped. "*Ja, Vel. Ja, Vel,*" he muttered. "We haff a problem."

No kidding.

Finally, he seemed to make a decision. "He vill be very heffy so I think all three of usss will need to go in."

This was not the resolution I had hoped for. "Oh, okay."

Suddenly he stuck out his hand to shake, and beaming, said "By the way, I am Peter. Nice to meet you both." He shook our hands as if we had just met—not over a spread-eagled dead corpse—but in an elegant Knightsbridge wine bar. "You ..." he peered at my colleague's name tag. "Trish ...should go in first ..."

She blanched and appeared as if she might throw up the snack she had just eaten,

"...and hold the coffin so it doesn't move. You and I ...Natasha . . vill take his torso and lift hiss body back in. *Ja?*"

We nodded, grateful for Peter's dynamic presence.

Trish stepped into the abyss and scrambled on all fours over the luggage until she got to the other side of the coffin. I heard her groan as she went. Peter stepped over the threshold next and lithely climbed around the corpse and got down onto his haunches near the man's head, with his back against the hold bulkhead. He slid the lid off the coffin and out of the way.

I gulped.

"Come on, Natasha," Peter urged, sensing my cowardice.

As I entered the shadowy space, something stinky met my nostrils. "Oooh." Had the man's bodily secretions let loose? As I found a suitcase to crouch on, I tried not to breathe. Somehow, the man's arm had now gone limp, the clawed white hand now resting inert on a bag. How I hated my flying job today.

"Let's do thiss," Peter whispered, as if not to wake the dead man. "When I count to three, Trish, you hold the coffin upright and guide him in. Natasha you lift his middle and I will lift his shoulders."

I knelt and precariously balancing on the soft suitcase under my feet, slid my arms under his torso. "Oh, God," I moaned. The closer we got to his body, the more unbearable the stench became.

"One ...two ...three," Peter muttered.

I closed my eyes to concentrate and strained forward. Peter grunted as he lifted the man up and toward the coffin. Trish, holding the box upright, reached forward and pulled on his other arm, ensuring the torso was aligned with the box.

"Now let him go," Peter said, obvious strain in his voice.

I pulled away and the stinky man landed with a soft thud, his torso crumpling, back into his righted box.

"*A Gud*, he ssstinks!" Peter put an arm over his mouth and nose. "Let's get out of here."

Gasping for cleaner air, we all clambered back towards the opening and into the shadowy yellow light of the rear vestibule.

As I emerged and inhaled large gulps of air, I was aware that strands of my hair had fallen from my top knot and my navy uniform bore white patches of pine sawdust. Behind me, Peter and Trish looked equally dishevelled. When a woman passenger, who was just entering the port toilet, saw the three of us burst out of the hold gasping for air and looking unkempt, she appeared shocked. From the disapproval in her eyes, we knew what she was thinking. "Well, really!" she exclaimed before she disappeared into the toilet.

Suddenly Harriet loomed in the vestibule. "What the hell are you two doing?" She glared at Peter.

"Peter here was just helping us get the man back into—," I began.

"Thank you, sir," she snapped, "but it is against airline regulations, unless it's an emergency, for crew to engage passengers in our duties. Please return to your seat. Thank you."

Before he moved away, Peter turned to me and rolled his eyes as if to say, *Who's this stiff?*

"Is the man back in his coffin?" Harriet demanded as she pushed Trish and I out of the way and squinted into the hold. "Oh, for God's sake!" she barked at me. "You didn't put the lid back on and his left arm is still hanging out."

But I was sure the whole body had landed, albeit unceremoniously, into the coffin?

"Deal with it, Natasha," Harriet commanded. "Trish, I need you down the front."

The rear vestibule was now empty. Even the judgmental woman from the loo had returned to her seat. I was alone. Holding my nose, I peered once more into the darkness. Harriet was right. Although his torso was stuffed back into the coffin, his arm attached to that long-fingered hand was still hanging loosely over the side.

"Jesus, Mary and Joseph," I said, mimicking Trish. "Help me." Once more I scrambled over the mound of luggage. Holding my nose with one hand, I shuddered as I picked up the man's arm by the fabric of his suit and lifted it into the box.

A light buzzing began in my head. Was I imagining it or, like a horror-story of old, was the hand reaching for me, the long, clawed fingers wrapping themselves around my wrist and pulling me down ...down ...into the coffin ...? I felt faint. Everything went black.

The voices seemed to be coming from far away. "Natasha! Natasha! ...Are you all right?" When I opened my eyes, I realized I was sitting on the rear jump seat. A semi-pleasant pungent smell was assaulting my nostrils. I looked up. Trish removed the bottle of smelling salts from under my nose. In her eyes, I saw concern and ...something like bemused curiosity. Harriet was standing behind her, arms across her chest, a look of disgust on her face, as if I had committed some heinous crime. What had I done? Peter was standing on my right, a comforting hand on my back, an intrigued onlooker.

"What happened?" I asked. Then I remembered. The dead man, the coffin, the hand!

Peter explained. "You were in there alone and for sssuch a long time ..." He gave Harriet a scathing glance. "...sso I came back to check on you. You must haff fallen into the coffin." He tried hard not to grin. "You know, you had your head ...in the man's ...lap."

Harriet glowered at me and nodded. Both she and Trish were giving me the who-are you-really look.

What? "No, no ..." I protested. "I ...he ...pulled me in!"

"Of course, he did!" Harriet scoffed. "Dead men come on to us all the time." She moved away.

"Well, if you're all right, den," Trish said in a whatever-turns-you-on tone as she put the top on the smelling salts and added "I'm sure de poor man is *really* at peace now." She also turned and disappeared up the aisle.

Peter sat down beside me on the jump seat.

"Do they really think...?" I waved a hand at my two shocked colleagues.

He grinned. "There are *other* ways to haff fun, you know."

I exhaled. "Yes, you're right. I really must stop attacking dead men. Actually, I'm supposed to be going to a party in London after this flight with some very lively people—if we make it in time."

"Where in London?" he enquired.

"Kensington. Why?"

"Funny. That's where my hotel iss. In Kensington." He grinned.

"You're so subtle. Okay," I smiled. "I'll play. Would you like to come to the party with me?"

"Only if you promise to attack me, too."

"No, sorry," I smiled. "I only like dead people."

Later that night, in the shadowy living room of my friend's Kensington flat, Peter and I discussed our deadly experience.

"I probably shouldn't tell you this, Peter, but there was more happening on that flight today than the dead body."

"Oh, ja. I know," he said, suddenly somber.

"Wh-wh-what do you know?"

"*Ja, vel.* I am a pilot, remember. And I know there are only a couple of reasonsss to fly at a lower altitude.

"What do you mean?"

"Either an air system failure or somessing wass unlocked. But that wass very dangerous. The captain should have landed and checked. We could haff all died." He paused. "Maybe the ghost of Mike Bravo was just messing—"

"You *know* about Mike Bravo's ghost?"

"Ah, hiss story iss famous in the RAF, and I haff good English friends, pilots who told me. Somehow the poor man got trapped in a cargo hold and suffocated, *ikke sant?*"

"Yes, that's the story." I shuddered. "Poor soul. What a horrible way to die, trapped, alone, freezing and without air." We both fell silent. "Maybe," I said after a while, "the ghost of Mike Bravo doesn't like to see anyone trapped and wanted to help the spirit of the dead man escape from the coffin and fly free?"

"But he'd already paid for his ticket, *Ja?* Peter grinned.

"Very funny. But perhaps the ghost gave the captain a false red light that the hold was unlocked which necessitated us flying through lower altitude turbulence which then tossed him out of the coffin." I shuddered as goosebumps travelled down my arms, always a sign of truth. "Come to think of it," I continued, "I *did* hear banging coming from that hold during the turbulence, almost as if someone was trapped and was dying to get out."

Peter took a slug of his beer, considering my whacky theory. He smiled. "Or it wasn't anyssing to do with a ghost. Just physics."

"Yes, that too." Pilots are always so pragmatic, I thought. "But then why did he pull me into that coffin...?"

"Did he?" Peter chuckled.

I feigned hurt. "Now *you* don't believe me?"

"Ach, maybe he just didn't vont to be alone and cold anymore."

"Thank you, Peter, but I do prefer warm, live boyfriends."

"*Ja, vel,* that's good," he said as he put an arm around my shoulder. "So let's dance."

19

THE GREAT ESCAPES

January 1978

On January 16, 1978, the BBC Radio newscaster was dramatic in his delivery of the news. "The Shah of Iran has been deposed. Chaos has broken out in the streets of Tehran, the capital. The Ayatollah Khomeini will now soon be reinstated as the religious and political leader of Iran."

Oh my God! Emma was there, in Tehran training for Iran Air! But wasn't she due to come home ...when was it ...in two days? So where was she in all this chaos?

A partial answer came the next morning, again via the BBC. "British Airways crews are being held hostage in Tehran," the radio voice announced. "There is no information on when they will be released or where they are being held."

Hostage! But what about the other English crews, including Emma? Oh God. Did that mean she, as a western stewardess, was also unable to get out of the country? What were the Iranians planning to do with them? So many questions, so few answers.

After the fifth day and still with no more information, I was getting antsier and antsier. Morning, noon and night, when I wasn't flying, I was glued to the radio, and then also hounded our pilot friend, Stewart for any news of her. "The Iran Air office in London has closed down," he told me. But what was happening to her? Was she still alive? What could we do? He didn't know any more than I did. The silence of no news was deafening. Recent memories of my times with Emma resurfaced…

It was a dark and stormy night in December when the phone rang.

"Can you come over?" Emma's tearful voice on the phone had sounded desperate. Sleepily, I grappled for the light switch. Outside, rain spattered in the blackness against my window. The clock read 12.10 a.m. I groaned.

"What's the matter?" Maybe I could resolve this without having to get out of my warm, cozy bed and navigate the wet, murky countryside and a twelve-minute drive to Emma's place.

"It's Stewart!" she exclaimed, before collapsing into sobs.

"Is he okay?" I asked, imagining the worst, wondering if he had died in a plane crash or driven to his death racing in his MGB.

"Ugh! Just come over," she moaned. "I'll show you."

Though tired, I remembered that I had the following day off—unless Dan Dare hunted me down at the pub or found me at a friend's dinner party. Crewing and their penchant for always being able to find us hosties was somehow creepy. Were they psychic or did the airline employ crewing spies?

"Okay. I'll be right over," I told the now-calmer Emma.

"Thank you!" She exhaled and hung up.

Even before knocking on the door of #1 Halland Close, my old home, Emma called out. "Come in!"

In the shadows of the half-lit living room, she was sitting on the floor by the settee, surrounded by opened wrapping paper, her shoulders sagging in despair. As I took off my jacket, she exclaimed, "Look!" while thrusting a flat green box at me, disgusted. It was a game of Scrabble.

I frowned. What was so offensive about Scrabble?

"That's what Stewart gave me for my birthday!" she spat the words out as if she had swallowed a bunch of razor blades and each one was slashing her throat.

"Oh." I paused, trying to figure out the crime.

"Well!" She huffed at my dense reaction. "It's hardly romantic, is it?"

"Oh." Now I was getting the picture. Emma had been expecting jewelry, perhaps even a proposal. Stewart was all she could talk about. "One day, he'll realize ..." she would intone.

I didn't know what to say. None of our group of friends could even determine what the status of their relationship was. They spent a lot of time together, but were they lovers or just platonic buddies? On the outside of their bond, I could see that Stewart was fond of Emma and enjoyed her company, but I didn't feel that he was in love with her. Endearing as Stewart was, he was also emotionally reserved.

Emma's situation reminded me of my dilemma with my friend and landlord, Brian, but in reverse. Ever since I had begun renting a room from him the previous April, he had been adamant that I was in love with him. Apparently, I "just didn't realize it." Then when Julian and I finally had split up later in the summer, that had only fuelled Brian's hopes of a relationship with me. He now refused to believe that I was buying my own home and planning to leave his house in March.

"I'm sorry, Emma," was all I could muster. "You know men can be idiots about these things sometimes. But you do love to play Scrabble together, don't you? Maybe he thought it was a special romantic thing between you?"

Emma collapsed into more sobbing, both hands covering her face. Obviously, I had said completely the wrong thing. Helpless to console her, I just sat on the couch and let her cry.

The hopelessness of Emma's unrequited love reminded me of how much I missed Julian and it suddenly made me want to imbibe alcohol. When her sobs subsided, I asked, "Want a drink?"

"Ooh, yes." She said, recovering and dabbing her eyes. "There's all kinds of miniatures in the cupboard." She waved a hand toward the kitchen. As I dropped ice into our brandy and cokes, she called through the glass doors. "Guess what? I got into trouble with crewing again!"

"Surprise, surprise," I called back.

Back in her living room, I handed her the strong concoction and sank into the soft cushions on the settee. "What d'you do this time?"

"I was on a night standby and I was just about to go to bed at around eight when they called. I mean, how dare they!"

I frowned. "Well, you do know that night standby is from 7:00 pm to 7:00 am the next morning so they were allowed."

"'Miss Blinkensop,' she said, ignoring my comment and mimicking the usual crewing tone, "we would like you to do an Athens departing at twenty-two hundred hours, flight number 5255. Can you confirm that you will be at the airport by twenty thirty hours?' he said. So I told him, 'I'm awfully sorry but I'm sick.' 'Oh, really,' he said—I think it was Adrian, he's always so snarky—'And Miss Blinkensop, when did you go sick exactly?' 'When you told me that I had to do a night Athens,' I told him.'" She giggled.

Emma was incorrigible. "So, did you do the flight?"

"Of course not. I told them to stick it!"

"But ...didn't you get called in to the office?"

"Of course. I got Jane Philoughby, no less." Normally minor infractions were delegated to her deputies to hand out penalties, not the chief stewardess, but this wasn't Emma's first reprimand.

"And...?"

"I told her I was genuinely sick, but I had forgotten to report it as I was on night standby and I didn't think they'd call." Emma flicked hair out of her eyes and chuckled at her own cheekiness. "She couldn't dispute it. And anyway, they can fire me if they want."

As she sipped on her brandy and coke, serious again, she said. "You know, I really hate Dan Air. I can't stand it. Sometimes, I have this thought..."

"Yes. What?" I asked absently, the brandy and my sombre mood were having a soporific effect.

"Sometimes, when I'm driving home from work, I have this thought of just driving into a tree. You know, making it look like an accident." She sat up. "That would show the bastards." Emma was grinning, but her eyes were off somewhere else. Which bastards was she referring to? The airline, her parents who had moved to America and abandoned her, Stewart? Or all of the above.

Would she? I wondered. "Oh, I kno-ow, I kno-ow," I touted, doing my Sybil imitation, and trying to lighten the mood. I was fighting my own downward spiral. In my first summer and then winter back at Dan Air, and due to all my languages, my flying schedule had been relentless. Both my dream of flying long haul and living happily ever after with Julian had disappeared over some distant horizon.

"But wouldn't driving into a tree hurt?" I asked, realizing that I also had thoughts sometimes of just going to sleep and never waking up.

Emma shrugged. She was eerily calm now.

"And too messy," I continued. "I'd take sleeping pills."

"But then they would know it's suicide." Emma pointed out.

"Would you care, though, if you were dead?"

"S'pose not," she said, shaking her fringe over her eyes. A silence fell between us, the only sound was the spatter of rain on windows. "You don't have to stay, you know," she said. "I'm okay, now."

"Are you sure? Promise me you won't get in your car and go and find some poor unsuspecting tree?"

"Promise," she said.

On day six of Emma's absence, I wondered if I should try and track down her parents but what would I tell them? When I called the BBC the following day, with Western reporters no longer welcome in Iran, there was only scant new information. The Shah had escaped, and his nephew had been assassinated outside his own palace. Unable to concentrate on the rug I was creating for my new home, I replayed my very last visits with Emma.

"It's so good to see you," I told her as she presented me with a mug of tea, and I sat at her kitchen table. "How long's it been?"

"Feels like six months!" she said, sitting down opposite me.

"You're right. My winters are almost as busy as my summers," I moaned. "I tell you, speaking four languages is a curse!"

"Bloody Dan Dare!" Emma blurted. "Even if you were dead, they'd just give you adrenaline and slip a roster into your coffin."

"You're right. Did you hear about Sheila Stanwick? She was on a Munich when they hit an air pocket and dropped 400 feet. One of the bar boxes landed on her foot and broke it. Two days later, Crewing asked her if she would operate a Malaga. 'But my foot is broken. I'm on crutches!' she told them, gobsmacked. 'Oh, you don't have to do anything,' they reassured her. 'We just need you to sit there. By law, we just need a number one to be present on the flight.'"

Emma shook her head. "Bloody typical!"

"But what if there had been an emergency?" I wondered out loud. "The pax would have had to help her out of a burning aircraft."

"I hope she told them to stuff it!" Emma's blue eyes were fiery with indignation.

"No. She caved."

"Ugh!" Emma groaned. "We have to tell them to shove it where the sun don't shine or nothing will improve."

I glanced outside. In the late November afternoon, beyond the French doors, trees–now devoid of leaves–gently weaved from side to side under darkening skies. Was this heaviness a foreboding of things to come or was it just my fatigue dragging me down?

"Of course, there are other airlines." I offered.

"Well..." Emma grinned, sheepishly. "I've actually been meaning to tell you..." She looked down into her teacup until her fringe almost fell over her eyes.

"What?"

"Well, you'll probably think I'm crazy, but I'm going to do it anyway..."

Uh-oh. "Tell me."

"I've applied to Iran Air." She looked up and a secretive smile appeared on her lips, as if pleased with my shocked reaction. "And ..., I've been accepted."

"What? Iran Air!" I put my cup down. "So, you'd be based in Tehran?"

"No, Heathrow, but we would go to Tehran for training."

"But Emma...?" There had already been murmurings about political unrest in Tehran. The Ayatollah Khomeini was gaining power and the Shah's days were numbered, or that's what the news implied. "Is that a wise choice?"

"I know, I know," she said, waving a dismissive hand, acknowledging the folly of it. "But you should see their uniforms ...and they have such lovely suitcases. Real leather!"

"Well, then," I huffed. "If the suitcases are real leather, then everything should be just fine."

As I drove home that afternoon, I thought, what's the point of talking to Emma? She has a death wish and I am powerless to change it.

A week later, after an early morning Le Bourget, I dropped by Emma's for a coffee. She was in the middle of decorating a large Christmas tree in her living room.

"Are you okay?" she asked me as I shed my high heels, threw off my uniform hat, gloves and jacket and sunk into her sofa.

"Brian's still not getting it." I sighed. "Although I've told him repeatedly, 'I'm sorry, Brian. It's never going to happen between us,' he responds with this puppy-dog hopefulness and says, 'Natasha, your lips say no, but your eyes say yes.' I would suggest that he get his eyes tested, but as you know, he already wears spectacles for the almost-blind."

"What are you going to do about it?" Emma asked, adding more tinsel to her decoration-laden tree.

"I think if I can just last until the middle of March when I take possession of my house, it will be fine. But then we have these heated discussions and I offer to move out, cos I know he's in love with me. Then he accuses me of being an egomaniac and denies it. Then I say,

'Well, that's good, then.' I relax, we resume our friendship and then it starts all over again."

"Hang in there, Natasha. It's only a couple of months away," Emma said as she picked up stray tinsel off the carpet.

"How about you? Has Iran Air called and cancelled yet?"

"No," She turned to face me, her watery blue eyes were ablaze with excitement. "We've already begun training!" she exclaimed. "And I love it! It's nothing like Dan Dare! Oh God, I'm so happy to be out of there."

"What? Where are you training?"

"We're doing some psychology classes in London first. It's so interesting! You can't imagine Dan Dare even thinking of giving us courses about how to deal with white knucklers or psychos."

"Dan barely knows how to keep the planes in the air," I pointed out, "so the white knucklers have good reason to be terrified. Three plane crashes in eight years is something to be afraid of."

Envious, I was also relieved that Emma had finally managed to escape the slavery of Dan Air. Maybe she could be happy now.

"Then we go to Tehran in January for the rest of the training." Emma beamed. "I'm so-o-o-o excited!"

"How long will you be there?" I asked, suddenly apprehensive. The atmosphere in Iran was becoming more intense, according to the news. The number and ferocity of demonstrations for the return of the Ayatollah were increasing daily.

"Oh, just a week, I think. We've already been issued our suitcases. They're so lovely!"

"Good," I responded, absently, hoping that Emma–despite her naiveté or her death wish–would return safely, leather suitcases and all.

On the Monday evening, and the tenth day without news, Brian had gone to bed. Unable to sleep, I sat in a silent living room and busied myself with hooking a new rug for my first home. I envisioned the autumn colors of brown, orange and yellow adorning the bedroom floor. In just weeks, I would be the proud owner of a three-bedroomed maisonette, never again to be vulnerable to the whims of amorous landlords.

When the phone rang, I jumped, the trill sounding extra loud in the quiet house. Who could it be? The clock showed 1:11 a.m. Oh my God! Whoever it was, late calls were always ominous. Good news could usually wait until morning.

"Natasha! Natasha!" Emma's hysterical voice on the other end sounded disembodied. "Can you come and get me?" Was it really her?

"Where are you?" I asked, having visions of flying to Iran to pick her up.

"Heathrow! Oh my God, I'm at Heathrow!" She sounded as if Scottie from Star Trek had just beamed her into the airport and she couldn't believe her luck.

Surprised at myself, I burst into tears. "Are you all right?" I sobbed.

"I just want to come home!" Her voice sounded so frail. "Can you come and get me?"

"Of course!" Even though it was one in the morning, and dark and rainy outside, I was now wide awake. "It'll take me just over an hour, if I drive really fast."

"Okay," she breathed. "Thank you." She exhaled with so much gratitude and relief that I probably *would* have gone to Tehran to collect her.

As I raced through the darkness of the familiar narrow Sussex country lanes, with only yellow cats' eyes for company, so many questions flooded my mind. Emma had sounded so traumatized on the phone, as if she couldn't believe she had made it back to England. Had she been assaulted, beaten, tortured and/or starved?

One hour and ten minutes later, I pulled into an unusually deserted Heathrow car park. Once inside Terminal Three, I found a ground stewardess who was able to direct me to the correct gate for this ad hoc flight.

The click of my heels echoed eerily in the empty arrivals' hall. Where was everybody? The Heathrow I was accustomed to usually seethed night and day with masses of people of all colours and races. Now gates were locked and there was just one lone male figure ahead of me, pacing up and down, obviously waiting for the same flight. As I got closer, I recognized his profile.

"Stewart!" I groaned at the futility of us both being there. "Did she call you, too?"

While I was ecstatic that I was about to see Emma again—and that she was safe—I was not impressed that she had dragged us all this way to collect her in the middle of the night. There was no doubt in my mind who she would travel back with.

"Bloody hell!" was all I could come up with.

"I'm so sorry, Natasha." Stewart said, removing his pipe from his mouth. "I didn't know she'd called you, too."

I should have known, I thought.

"No point in waiting around," he said, his eyes, twinkling. "If you like, I can bring her home and we can meet up at #1," he said, gesturing with his unlit pipe towards the closed doors. "They might be a while apparently. Debriefing or something like that. I'm sure it's all very top secret, you know." He winked at me and grinned.

He must be relieved that she's home, I thought, but all I could say was "Yes," and stand there, stunned. Was I relieved, angry, happy? I knew Emma wouldn't want me to be around to spoil a dramatic and potentially romantic reunion with Stewart. She was probably ecstatic that her knight in shining armour had rushed here to take her home in his blue steed, or at least his MGB.

I cast a glance at the door open a sliver between customs and arrivals, hoping to, at least. catch sight of Emma. "Okay," I said. "I'll see you back at the ranch."

"Jolly good." He nodded, sucking on the dead pipe. "I'll tell her you came."

"So will I!" I muttered.

An hour and a half later, the three of us were sitting in the living room of #1, each nursing a stiff drink. I was perched on the edge of the settee at one end while Emma curled up at the other end, close to the big comfy armchair in the shadowy corner where Stewart sat.

"I couldn't get hold of Stewart," Emma explained apologetically, "so I left a message with Samantha but ...I wasn't sure that he'd come."

"Oh, okay," I said, softening. That made sense. And why was I being so testy with her, anyway? Maybe it was just relief. I remembered my mother's reaction when my brother was returned after being missing for twelve hours. She had burst into tears. Being just six years old, I had wondered why she was so sad that George had come home. Later I understood that hers were tears of relief.

"I'm just glad you're back home safe." I muttered.

"Oh, yes. It's so-o good to be home," Emma sighed, looking around the dimly-lit living room and letting her eyes rest on Stewart.

He smiled, relaxing back into the armchair, puffing on his now-lit pipe. The three of us sat in silence, Stewart and I waiting for Emma to tell her story. But she remained still, drinking in the details of her living room, and him.

I couldn't wait any longer. "So where were you held hostage?"

Emma shook her hair, that endearing mannerism I had forgotten. "Well, we weren't exactly kept hostage," she began. Once she spoke, her story spilled out picking up speed like a runaway train.

"That day, we had all gathered in one hotel room, about seventeen of us. There were some crews from other airlines as well as Iran Air. We had been told that something big, the revolution was about to happen, and that to be safe, we should stay out of sight. After all, one of the reasons they wanted to get rid of the Shah was because of his western ways. And we were western women, obviously not muslims, Although I found the Persians to be very sophisticated.

"Go on." Stewart took his pipe out of his mouth long enough to speak and then puffed on it again.

"Well, we were stuck in that hotel about a day and a half when there was a knock on the door. When we opened it, an Iranian man in a cream suit was standing there. He looked quite dapper, but I could see that underneath his cream hat, he was sweating.

'You must come with me–all of you,' he said. 'You are not safe here!'

"Well, of course," Emma continued, her voice tremulous. "We thought it might be a trick. We didn't know who he was. So, we hesitated. Then he just stepped right into the room. 'I can't be seen with you,' he explained. 'The situation is very dangerous.' Then one of the girls asked him, 'Who are you?'

'It's better that you don't know,' he said, 'for your own safety and mine. You must split up into pairs or small groups. I will show you where to go.'"

Emma's eyes dilated as she continued breathlessly. "My friend, Allison and I decided to pair off together. I wondered if she knew Cream Suit, but she didn't say anything. She'd been dating the nephew of the Shah for about six months and seemed to think that this man was okay. As soon as we had figured out our groups, Cream Suit said 'Come' and opened the door. We were on the seventeenth floor. Allison and I were with the first group that got into the lift. Cream Suit took us down to the third floor. When the doors opened..." Emma shook her hair and stared at some point on the opposite wall. "I'll never forget this scene for as long as I live. We stepped out of the lift into this huge mezzanine. The floor was really shiny marble and the massive arched glass windows almost filled the whole wall. You know how exotic those hotels are..." She glanced over at me.

How would I know? I shook my head.

"Quite, quite," Stewart muttered.

"Well, it was magnificent. But through the window we could see all the way down this main street and ..." she shook her hair again. "There was this sea of men, all of them yelling and shouting, moving en masse, like a tidal wave coming toward the hotel. Even though they were still about a hundred yards away, we could hear their shouts. They were destroying everything in their path, turning cars over with their bare hands, smashing plate glass windows. It was amazing to watch. And they were all bearing down on our hotel! The massive ornate wrought iron gates at the front of the property were closed, but I knew that wouldn't stop them. Their rage was terrifying. Cream Suit just stood staring at them and said something in Farsi."

"Good Lord!" Stewart muttered.

"Actually, it was probably more like 'Oh, fuck!'" Emma snickered and took another gulp of her drink before she continued. "'You and you,' Cream Suit said, pointing at Allison and me. 'Go through that door, down the stairs, and out the back door. Cross over the street. There is an empty building. I know the owner. You must hide there. Wait for me to come and get you. Whatever you do, don't leave that building without me, you understand? It is very, very dangerous.' Allison and I nodded and ran to the stairwell. Behind us we heard Cream Suit giving instructions to the other girls who had just arrived off the lift. We found the building and went inside, locked the door and waited. No one was there and it was so quiet in that back street. No one came, thank god. We didn't hear any noise."

"What was it? A hotel, a home?" I wanted every detail.

"It was like an office and so there was a small bathroom and some food. We were okay for a while. But after a day and a half, there was still no sign of Cream Suit. We didn't know if he had been shot. When we poked our head out the door, it seemed everything had gone quiet. We were so-o-o-o bored so Allison decided we should go to her boyfriend's place."

"You mean the nephew of the *Shah*?" I asked, incredulous. Only Emma would be crazy enough to affiliate herself with a family member of a despised ruler in the process of being deposed. "Was that a smart move?" I asked. Stewart's cheek, I noticed, had begun to twitch.

"Oh yes, it was *fine.*" Another shake of the hair. "His palace was like a fort with barbed wire and dogs and tanks and things. So we were well protected."

"But I thought the nephew was gunned down right outside his home about a week into the revolution?"

"Oh, yes, he was," Emma said quietly, "Poor Allison. So, when that happened, we thought it best to leave."

No kidding.

Stewart was making strange sucking noises on his pipe and studying Emma. Was he wondering about her sanity as well?

"We went into downtown Tehran and roamed the streets for a while. We put scarves over our heads and boot polish on our cheeks, so we didn't stand out as western women. There was so much destruction everywhere. Places on fire, shops destroyed. But it was eerily quiet. Finally, we found the Iran Air office. Their place had been ransacked, but there were two people still there and we asked them if they could get us back to England."

"And?" Stewart finally spoke.

"Oh," Emma huffed. "They just told us there were no planes flying into or out of Tehran. 'You are lucky to be in such a beautiful city!' she mimicked the Iran Air staff member. "Please enjoy your stay while you are in Tehran, Miss Blinkensop.' Talk about denial!" Emma added.

"Crazy," I muttered, not too sure who I was referring to, Emma or the Iran Air staff member.

"Then we decided to go and find a hotel. We walked into this beautiful building downtown. From the outside it appeared untouched, all white and huge glass windows. But when we walked into the lobby, we saw that all the elegant furniture had been piled into the center of this marble floor and set alight! It was still burning!"

"Huh," Stewart muttered. He was usually full of jokes but tonight he was silent. Who knew what he was thinking?

"The place looked empty," Emma went on. "This tall Iranian man was standing behind the front desk, dressed in his suit working as if it was business as usual, and as if it was perfectly normal for the hotel lobby furniture to be on fire right in front of him! We asked him if we could have a room for a few days. He just shook his head and said, 'I am very sorry, but I'm afraid we are full.'"

Emma was quite good at copying the Iranian accent, I noticed.

"'Full?' Allison asked. 'So where is everybody then?' 'Full! Full!' he snapped. Then he said, 'Have a nice day. Please enjoy your stay in our wonderful city of Tehran.'"

"So where did you go?" Stewart sounded concerned.

"We wandered back to the Iran Air office and met another trainee. She was bunking down with some other hosties in a ransacked home nearby. We stayed there until we got the call."

"Did Iran Air fly you home?"

"No, it was a British Airways jumbo. We think Cream Suit organized it. We heard he had been going around Tehran, rounding up all the western crews and making sure everyone was safe. Everything was so chaotic." She let her eyes rest on Stewart. "What a relief to be home!"

"How many of you got out?" he enquired.

"Not sure. Not everyone, I don't think. There were only about fifty of us on this massive plane, and we all sat huddled together. It was amazing We kept bursting into song, singing *Jerusalem*. You know, the hymn?" Emma began singing. "And did those feet in ancient time walk upon England's mountain...?'" Her words trailed off as her eyes began to water. She stifled a sniffle and shook her hair.

"Well, jolly good, then." Stewart suddenly sat forward. "We're very happy you're home safe and sound. But I have to fly tomorrow and it's..." He glanced at his pilot's watch, "Goodness ...it's almost four o'clock."

Emma stared at Stewart, then at me. Her sudden panicked expression of joy mixed with hopefulness and disappointment told me that she wanted me to leave now, so Stewart, if he was going to express his relief at their reuniting, would be less inhibited if I was not there.

"I have to go," I said, standing up and stretching. "I'm so happy you're okay, Emma. And that you won't be going back!"

I moved toward the door. Behind me, Stewart stood and then hesitated. I hoped he would at least stay and comfort Emma tonight.

"I'll ring you in a couple of days," I told her. "Get some rest. And remember, there are other airlines."

I gave Emma a week to recover before I rang her.

"How are you doing?" I asked, wondering if the reality of her near miss with death had sunk in and scared her into sanity.

"Better," she answered tentatively. "But don't ask me whether I have nightmares about tanks driving through my room at night."

"I'm sure you do." I paused, contemplating that image. "Have Iran Air been in touch? What's happening?"

I fully expected her to say that they had sent her a letter saying Thank you very much for flying with Iran Air and please return the leather suitcases. So how she responded took my breath away.

"They want us to go back for a uniform fitting."

"But ...why? Isn't the airline defunct now?"

"You would think so," she responded, "but they want us to go on Tuesday." It had only been seven days since we collected her at Heathrow, a neurotic mess.

"But you won't go, will you?"

Well ...te-ch-nically," she drawled, "I'm still an employee."

"So?"

"I have to go," she said, as if there was no argument.

No, you don't, I thought. "If you go Emma, be it on your own head." I heard the anger in my own voice. "But next time, don't call me in the middle of the night expecting me to come and pick you up."

"Point taken," she responded, understanding my complete frustration with her and my powerlessness to change her mind.

The following week, while Emma was in Tehran, I busied myself with preparations for the purchase of my house and tried not think about her.

I'm ba-a-a-ack!" she cooed on the phone a week later. "Let's go to The Lamb," she urged. "I can tell you all about it."

When we were settled in our favorite spot, I asked, "So how was it this time?"

She shrugged. "Nothing happened really. We had to disguise ourselves as Muslims again. Just in case."

"You mean with boot polish and hijabs?"

"But everything was much calmer," she added, ignoring my question.

"Did you get your uniform?"

"No." She grinned and shook her hair. "They'd burned the uniform store down."

"Oh." Our ploughman's lunches appeared on the table in front of us. I was hungry and cut a generous slice of the port-soaked stilton. "Did you ever find out who your saviour was? The man in the cream suit?"

"No. Apparently he saved a lot of us by arranging that flight on BA."

"Do you think he's okay? I mean, can he stay in Iran and be safe if he was helping all the nasty westerners?"

"Don't know," Emma shrugged. "I hope he's okay. He was like an angel appearing out of nowhere and then disappearing again."

"Maybe he *was* an angel," I offered.

"Maybe."

"So, what will you do now?"

"Ugh! Dan Air have said they'd take me back." She twizzled her almost empty glass in her hand thinking. "It's a job!" Emma sighed and then added, as if in defiance of her fate. "But I am going to keep looking."

"Me, too!" She was darn lucky, I thought, that the airline would take her back after all her infractions.

"By the way," she enquired, "is your amorous landlord behaving himself?"

"Brian? Well..., he's okay but something's building. Just another six weeks and then I'll be out of there."

What I didn't know then was that Emma wasn't the only one who needed to make the great escape.

"Oh, thank God, Stewart! You're home." I had never been so happy to hear my friend's dulcet tones on the line.

"Ah, Natasha! Is everything alright?"

"Well, actually no." It was 6:20 p.m. on a February evening, pitch black and as usual raining outside. "The thing is Brian and I have fallen out. I can't live here anymore. I was wondering if... I could move in ...with you?"

I knew Emma would hate me for even asking Stewart if I could take up residence in his home at #36. She had often threatened to tamper with the brakes of any female who came within six feet of him as she considered Stewart to be hers, all hers. But right now, he was my friend and my only option.

"Oh?" Stewart chortled. "Is he being a cad?"

I laughed. Brian was no cad. He was just, like Emma about Stewart, disillusioned about love.

"No, but he's refusing to accept my imminent move and it's getting nasty. The situation is untenable," I told Stewart. "I do have to exit ...tonight."

"That bad, eh?" I heard faint sounds of him sucking on his pipe. "Yes, I see."

"Just for five weeks," I added. "Then I take possession of my place in Horsham."

"Ah, well," Stewart said, still pondering. "I'm being transferred up to Aberdeen soon, so I'm thinking of selling ...but ...ah ...yes ...for five weeks, yes, that would work out. I can give you the small bedroom."

Thank God.

"Tonight, you say?"

"Yes. I'm packed. Brian's gone out and I really don't want another confrontation."

"Ah, the great escape!"

Maybe not as dramatic as Emma's from Tehran to Heathrow. Mine was merely Ifield to Three Bridges, but for me I thought, just as urgent.

"Do you need help?" Stewart asked. "We can get the gang together."

"Stewart, you're a lifesaver. Thank you!" But don't ask Emma, I thought.

He did ask Emma, and she was surprisingly affable about my brief stay with her unrequited love. And I was grateful for her help. As I followed a convoy of my friends' cars to Stewart's house, all of them packed with my meagre belongings, I thought about the letter I had left on the kitchen table. Brian would be hurt by my sudden departure, but it was for the best. It was, in fact, the only action he would finally comprehend. My absence. Forty-five minutes later I was installed in my temporary but safe new home.

As a "thank you" to my rescuers, a week later, I cooked dinner for Emma, and Stewart's other flat mates, my friends, Samantha and Jennie at #36. Stewart had been called to Aberdeen to do preliminary training. After our spaghetti bolognaise and salad, we all relaxed in the comfy living room, supping on a cheap-but-surprisingly-good Beaujolais, or as we called it, a noice bottle o' *Beau Jollies*.

"Stewart's asked me to move in with him!" Emma suddenly announced, flicking her hair out of her eyes and giving us her trademark told-you-so expression.

"What!" Samantha, Jennie and I exclaimed in unison.

We had all observed Stewart, and how he reacted to Emma's unsubtle expressions of undying love and bordering-on-stalking behaviour. In her presence, he would sometimes suck ever-more nervously on his pipe, his eyes darting from side to side as if looking for an escape route. Emma's announcement was indeed shocking.

"When?" Jennie asked.

"Not till April. After you've all moved out."

"Is that wise, Emma?" Samantha, ever the straight-to-the-point one ventured.

"So, Stewart's *not* selling his place then?" I asked. Just last week he had still been talking about putting it on the market.

"No, he's got a permanent contract with Dan," Emma continued, snuggling back into Stewart's favorite chair, as if imagining him wrapping his arms around her. "He's based up in Aberdeen now, but he's decided to keep the house here and he wants me to live here."

Now it made sense. His tenants, Samantha and Jennie—thinking that Stewart was going to sell—had agreed to move into my new three-bedroom maisonette with me. Stewart would now need at least one renter to cover his mortgage.

Triumphant, Emma beamed. "We'll be living together."

Oh God. Stewart probably chose her because she'd make a good care-taker, but she had interpreted his invitation as the two of them getting all domestic, and closer to the Big M. Had Stewart forgotten that possession might be nine-tenths of the law?

"You do realize that he won't be 'ere, don't you, Emma?" Samantha spoke as if a mother explaining to a simple child why she couldn't have her lollipop. "He'll be in Aberdeen."

"Well, yes. He'll come home sometimes, though. And I'll be living in *his house*."

It was no use. When it came to denial, frail as she was, Emma's iron will remained as impenetrable as the Berlin Wall. Then she added, "After all, *you* stole his lodgers didn't you, Natasha?"

"Yes, but that was when—"

"Poor Stewart," Emma sighed, eyeing us from under her long fringe as if we were all the wicked witches of the west.

"...he was going to sell ...so it was like a natural transition," I finished lamely.

"Just *teasing*." She grinned at me. "I'm grateful to you really. And after the Brian Hodges fiasco, who can blame you for getting female flat mates?"

At the beginning of April, Stewart said his goodbyes and transferred up to his new abode in Aberdeen, to begin flying 748s, two-engine "prop jobs." That week, Samantha, Jennie and I, now happily ensconced in my three-bedroom maisonette in Horsham, helped Emma haul her belongings across a budding spring lawn into Stewart's house.

"Talk about playing musical houses!" I commented, as I dumped her last cardboard box on Stewart's parquet hall flooring.

Though saddened by his absence, she was consoled by her new status, mistress of Stewart's home. Maybe we were all wrong and he really did love Emma, but I worried that the price for having his house lovingly cared for in his absence would be high—for one or both of them.

And hopefully there wouldn't be a need for another escape.

20

A REAL HARVEY WALLBANGER

March 1978

*S*mash! A groan came from the living room, "Oh, ffff ...u ...ddle!"
Abandoning the sauce pans I was fitting into the kitchen cupboard of my new home, I hurried down the short hallway to where my new boyfriend, Alex was unpacking my ornaments. Tall and blond-haired, he was bent over a half-emptied cardboard box, one hand clutching the long, elegant neck of my large collector's Galiano bottle, the other hand holding the broken glass bottom, trying to prevent the golden yellow liqueur from dripping through his fingers into the box.

"Hold on!" I urged, and ran to the kitchen, grabbed a glass bowl, then dashed back to the living room. Once I had positioned the receptacle under the dripping bottle, I told him. "Okay, you can let go."

As Alex removed the glass bottom, the liquid—containing glass chards—gushed into the bowl.

"I'm so sorry," he muttered knowing how much I valued my liqueur collection. "I dropped the box."

"Don't worry," I said, wondering if, and when, I would be able to get another one. I didn't care about the contents, but I did love the unusual, tall, elegant bottle. "We've saved most of it."

I saw him check his hand for glass splinters. "Are you okay?" I asked.

"Yes," he grinned. "Galiano is just *very* sticky."

We retreated to the kitchen with the bowl of yellow liquid. While Alex washed his hands, I foraged in my kitchen cupboards and brought out another larger glass bowl, and then I found a package of new blue jeye cloths lying on the counter and took one out. Alex dried his hands and moved over to the counter.

"What are you going to do with that?" He asked, peering at the pieces of glass in the bowl. "We can't drink it, now."

"Of course, we can! You're a steward. Don't you know the trick?"

He shrugged, appearing blank.

I stretched the jeye cloth over the second bowl. "Can you hold that taut?" I asked him.

He obliged as I took the Galiano in the smaller bowl and slowly poured the liqueur through the finely meshed blue cloth and into the other receptacle. The thin blue material glistened with glass splinters. I carefully lifted it off the bowl and put it in the rubbish bin.

Alex peered dubiously at the recovered bowl of liqueur. "Are you sure that's safe to drink?"

"Oh yes. Whenever there's a broken bottle on board, you don't think that we let spirits go to waste, do you?"

"No." He grinned. "Apparently not. Not if you work for Dan Air."

Alex worked for British Airways. We had met each other at yet another airline party. He had qualified to fly as a first officer on British Airways Tridents but, by the time he had finished training, there were a glut of pilots. In the meantime, and until a position became available, they had offered him a job as a steward.

"At least I'm still flying!" he had commented when he first told me the story.

"I'm impressed," I told him, grinning, as I tried to imagine one of our captains wearing a pinny and serving snacks to passengers. "That would never happen on Dan Air, not in a million years."

"It's not so bad." Alex said. "Of course, I'd rather be piloting the plane, but at least I have a job with the airline, and we still have fun in the cabin. When I *am* first officer and then captain, I'll have a better understanding of how cabin crew work."

"You're going to be such a rarity for a captain," I told him. "When do you think that will happen?"

"No, idea." He shrugged, not seeming to care about how long it would take, just confident that he would, one day, achieve his dream and pilot a 747.

By the third day in my new spacious maisonette, most of the cardboard boxes had disappeared and the living room, at least, looked like the semblance of a home. Samantha, one of my new flat mates, and I were enjoying a morning cup of coffee on the couch.

"What are you goin' to do with all that Galiano?" she enquired.

"Funny you should ask that. I was sitting here this morning, asking Self what can I do with a bowl of Galiano? And Self replied, throw a Harvey Wallbanger party!"

"Sounds a bit dangerous to me, chuck."

"Live a little, Samantha. Let's have a small housewarming on Friday. You and Patrick, Alex, me, Jennie and Brian, Graham, and Rufus."

"Isn't Brian still madly in love with you?" She enquired. "He won't like seeing you with Alex."

"He says he's truly over me now, and just wants to be friends."

"Let's 'ope so," she said gazing out of the window at the cherry blossoms in full bloom. "But that *is* a small party for you."

"I've got an early morning flight on Saturday. Five o'clock check-in."

"Well, I 'ope you know what yer doin'. But if Harvey Wallbangers don't warm up the 'ouse, nothin' will."

"By the way, do *you* know how to make a Harvey Wallbanger?" I asked.

She shook her head. "Eee, I can't remember, chuck. I just know it's vodka, Galiano and orange juice. Somethin' like that."

I shrugged. "How difficult can it be?"

Before my guests arrived on Friday, I retrieved the bowl of thick yellow, golden Galiano from the cupboard and inspected the liquid again for glass splinters. Maybe I should give it one more strain before I serve it to my friends, I thought. Having my guests go to the hospital with bleeding throats might not be a happy ending to a party.

Once the liquid was re-strained, I retrieved a bottle of vodka from my collection of spirits and opened the carton of orange juice from the fridge. I set them on the counter and tried to recall how much of what? Is the cocktail made with equal parts vodka and Galiano and a bit of orange juice or maybe it's orange juice, vodka and a bit of Galiano? No, I think it's the first one. Ah well, here goes nothing!

Alex was the first to arrive. "I'll pour drinks while you give your friends the house tour, if you like," he suggested. "Where's the stuff for the cocktails?"

"They're already made," I told him. "The jug's on the kitchen counter. Just add ice."

Once guests were armed with a drink, I took them on a tour of my first home. Despite the ghastly orange walls of the massive living room and the pea-green kitchen cupboards, my friends were kind enough to ooh-and-aah at my three-bedroomed maisonette. "Well, it's nice and ...big," one said, while another cooed, "Good for a starter, Natasha." "Well, it's got ...potential," Graham, a friend and neighbour said surveying the heinous colour scheme.

"I know. I need to do a lot of painting," I muttered, "but I like it."

"Well, that's all that counts then, isn't it?" Graham said and moved to sit down.

After we all congregated in the living room and I placed snacks on the coffee table, the party began. The first drink slid down very easily, the sweet yellow liquid warming us. The atmosphere in the room, I noticed, seemed livelier than even our larger get-togethers. Alex's friend Roger, another steward-pilot-to-be, had joined us. Samantha flirted with him with far less inhibition than her usually decorous self. Then she flirted with Alex. Graham tried to flirt with Jennie who was having none of it and only sipping on her drink while Rufus, Jennie's boyfriend, began confiding his deepest, darkest secrets to me. From the couch, Brian, regaled us with his jokes, curling up in a fetal position and giggling like a schoolgirl. Then Jennie and Roger competed for who had the funniest flying story to tell.

What was going on?

"These are amajing!" Roger slurred, clinking his glass on mine.

"Yes, they're good, aren't they?" Perhaps I had found the magic potion for good parties.

I offered refills. Everyone, except Jennie, eagerly handed out their glass to receive another drink. The Galiano would not go to waste after all, I thought happily. I sat on the floor observing my friends, having a good time, changing seats like musical chairs and flirting with whoever was sitting next to them. Even the bright orange of my living room walls now seemed less obnoxious.

After our third glass, like a hot air balloon coming in for a speedy landing, the gaiety in the room suddenly deflated. Samantha was the first to stop laughing. She suddenly clutched her belly and rushed out of the room and up the stairs.

Uh-oh.

Now everyone had stopped laughing. My friend's faces appeared distorted. My stomach didn't feel so good either. Brian staggered over to the door to my balcony and opened it. The blast of cold air rushing in was delightfully refreshing, but soon I heard the sound effects of him heave-hoeing over the balcony railing. *Oh, no.* My flat was on the third floor. I hoped my new neighbors below hadn't chosen that moment to stick their heads out and gaze up at the stars.

Samantha reentered the room, just as Alex rushed past her and up the stairs. Graham was now on his back on the floor, talking gibberish about ghosts in his bedroom.

Had some glass got into the Galiano after all? Or had I poisoned all my friends?

"I'm sho shorreee," I slurred to the room in general.

Jennie seemed to be the only one who wasn't acting strangely. "What the hell did you put in that drink, Natasha?"

"I told you. Harveeee W-a-a-aallbang'rs," I attempted with as much dignity as I could muster, which wasn't any.

"How did you make them?" Jennie persisted.

"Welllll, yoooooo know. Er… half Galian-o-o-o-o, half vodka and a teensy-weensy bit of ora-a-a-ange jooooce. Ishn't that right?"

"Oh, my gawd!" Jennie exclaimed, standing up. "No wonder everyone's doing a technicolor yawn."

"Who-o-o-ot did you shay?" I squinted at Jennie, but her pretty face kept changing shape.

"Harvey Wallbangers. You're supposed to stir the vodka and orange juice with ice in the glass, then just lace it with Galliano."

"Uh-oh." Even in my drunken state, I feared for my friend's lives. Had I given them alcoholic poisoning? "Ish everyone okay?" I tried to focus on the shadowy room and was sure I could see dead bodies strewn all over the floor.

"Go to bed, Natasha. I'll clean up." Jennie helped me up the stairs where I collapsed onto my newly acquired king bed. But not for long. As the room spun, I, too, had to make a dash for the one bathroom that was fortunately available.

A very rude and loud ringing sounded in my ear. When I turned to look at the clock, my head hurt. Then I realized my whole body hurt. When my eyes finally adjusted to the bright red digits, I saw that it was 3.30 am. Why in God's name had someone set the alarm for this uncivilized hour?

And then I remembered. *Oh no.* Naples. Five o'clock check in. Despite how ghastly I felt, I couldn't call in sick. I was the Italian speaker and there were only two of us in the whole airline. I would just have to do the flight.

An hour and a half later, shaking with suppressed nausea, and perhaps the DTs, I entered the crew room. Just what I didn't need this morning were 119 rambunctious Neapolitan passengers. I prayed that my crew would be sympathetic and let me go in the galley so I could still do the PAs but still hide from the Italians.

When I saw two names of the crew—and if I had been able— I would have leaped for joy and then groaned. The number one was my good friend and Yorkshire lass, Julia, the second was Mariabella, the only

Italian girl and second Italian speaker in the company. If I had known she was on the flight, I definitely would have gone sick. The third girl was Fiona Harvey who I didn't know well.

"Please, please let me go in the galley, today, Mariabella."

"But-a, Natasha-a, you know-a, these Italians-a they drive-a me crazy."

"*Si, lo so. Anch'io.* I know. Me, too. But I promise I will do the cabin next time we do an Italian flight. Just not today, *per favore.*"

Mariabella grimaced and surrendered. "You owe-a me-a one."

"*Si, veramente. Grazie mille.*" Thank you.

Even during the two and a half hours to Naples, my shakes didn't abate. With the dehydration that happens during flight, I felt closer to death than ever before. Somehow, I managed to make pots of tea and coffee, organize the catering, feed the flight deck and function like a coherent crew member.

When we landed at Naples and the last passenger had disappeared through the galley exit with a cheery *Buon Giornio, Signorina,* I went into the cabin and collapsed onto a front seat for a few minutes rest before more Italians boarded. Mariabella came and sat opposite me in a window seat, a novel in her hand.

"*Grazie a dio!*" she exclaimed, exhaling. Thank God.

"*Per que?*" I asked.

"*No passegeri a ritorno.*"

"No passengers! You mean, we're positioning back to Gatwick?"

"*Si.*" Mariabella beamed.

"Oh, there is a God!"

Just then Julia emerged from the shadows of the galley into the cabin. She sat down next to me. "Where's that Fiona?" she enquired, while getting her paperwork out of the brown envelope.

"She's-a down-a the back-a in-a the toilet."

Julia smiled secretly. "Hm-Hmm."

The slim fortyish captain came into the cabin, glanced at us, frowned, then peered at the rear of the plane. "Well, ladies the good news is we've got no passengers going back, as you know. The bad news is we've got to wait an hour. We lost our time slot so you girls can stay and relax down the front here. I need to check something down the back."

"Whatever you say, captain," Julia grinned up at him, mischief in her eyes.

Why did he want us to stay at the front? I wondered, as he carried on down the aisle.

"Strange-a man." Mariabella huffed and glanced out at the grey tarmac of *Napoli Aeroporto*.

While Julia continued to fill out her paperwork, and Mariabella opened her book, I sat back and closed my eyes. After the anarchy of Italian passengers, the relative hush was a balm for my still-shaky nervous system. The nightmare of the evening before was replaying in my mind. Had anyone died of alcoholic poisoning? I hadn't seen any corpses downstairs before I left the house that morning but ...

Then a thumping noise from the rear of the plane disturbed my already disturbing thoughts.

I opened my eyes. Mariabella looked up from her book and frowned.

Julia swiveled around and peered down the back.

She turned to me, her eyes large and her voice conspiratorial. "Oooh, I don't like the sound o' that." She smirked. "I better go and investigate."

"I'll come with you," I said, curious.

Mariabella returned to reading. I got up and followed Julia up the narrow aisle.

We were five rows before the Comet's rear vestibule when we heard a rhythmic thud-thud-thud against the port bulkhead. The banging was getting louder and faster. I didn't want to contemplate what was causing the noise. Ahead of us, I could only see the grey floor, the empty double jump seat flipped up against the aft bulkhead, the bar boxes sitting in their stowages. Where were Fiona Harvey and the captain? The thumping was coming from behind the bulkhead that faced our jump seat, out of our line of sight.

Julia turned to me and put her finger over her mouth in a "Sssshh" sign. I huddled closer behind her. Together we crept forwards and leaned over toward the starboard side. We were just two rows away now. The banging was accelerating. I was not sure I wanted to see them, and I was sure I didn't want them to see us.

Julia stopped and pointed downwards. I saw the tips of a man's shoes sticking out from trousers down around his ankles, a skinny, hairy, white leg visible. Soft, muffled moans came from both of them. The bulkhead bulged with each thud. Suddenly, he turned, and we caught a glimpse of the captain's white shirt, his hands gripping Fiona's buttocks and his head straining forward, his eyes closed, in what look liked ecstasy. One final moan and then silence.

Quickly, Julia wheeled around and looking horrified, pushed me back down the aisle. We hurried to the front of the aircraft and quickly resumed our positions. I sat in the middle seat, shed my shoes and rested my feet up on the opposite seat and half-closed my eyes. Julia picked up some paperwork and, breathing hard, pretended to be reading her flight report. Mariabella looked up from her book, a quizzical expression on her face.

"What's-a happening?" she asked.

Julia and I exchanged smirks. "Oooh, nuthin much," she muttered, not raising her head from her paperwork and trying to suppress a grin. "Fiona Harvey is just 'avin' it off with the captain down the back against the rear bulkhead."

"Mama Mia! You mean-a....?"

"That's right." I smiled. "Our Fiona Harvey is a real Harvey Wallbanger."

21

I CAN'T DO THIS ANY MORE

Summer 1978

"Ah, you speak Italian?" the man wearing a white collar and dark suit said, eying the green, white and red language badge on my uniform.

He had appeared at the top of the BAC 1-11 stairs and then stopped in front of me. Leaning in, he whispered, "Excuse me, I'm the airport reverend."

Well, bully for you. I had often noticed the chapel on the second floor of the main concourse, but I hadn't realized Gatwick had its very own vicar.

At four am that morning, I had dragged myself out of bed, donned the uniform, applied the face paint and driven on automatic pilot to Gatwick for my crack-of-dawn Milan flight. Maybe it was the exhaustion talking, but I had a bad feeling about this flight today. All I dreamed of these days was sleep. If we were lucky, and there were no delays, I could be home by early afternoon.

As I stood in the galley of the 1-11, for what felt like the thousandth time, a plastered grin on my face, greeting a mixture of Italian and English passengers as they ascended the front stairs with a Good Morning and *Buon Giornio*, I wondered, Why was the vicar here?

"There's an older lady, one of your passengers," he whispered, peering into the cabin. "Her husband died while they were on holiday here and she'll be flying back alone today. I wonder if you could take special care of her?"

"Of course," I agreed, my snarky attitude softening but not knowing how, on a one-and a-half-hour flight, in a cramped seat and with a snack of warm salad and sweaty ham, we would be able to compensate for her terrible loss.

Seeing my frown, he added, "She's on some heavy medication, so please watch her."

Oh, no. Did he expect her to die, too?

With a "God Bless" tossed over his shoulder, he scuttled back down the metal stairs.

The widow soon identified herself as, she stepped into the aircraft, patting her ample bosom and panting. "*Per favore, Signorina,*" she asked, gasping, "Can I-a 'ave-a glass-a water?"

"*Si, prego.*" I handed her the plastic cup, and she gulped it down in one swoop.

"My-a 'usband, 'e die. And I 'ave to take-a lotta pills-a." She patted her poor heart and sniffled, her leathery face sagging in grief. "*Grazie.*"

"*Si, mi dispiace.* I'm sorry," I told her, wanting to cry myself. For some reason, my emotional pain threshold was incredibly low these days. "*Sedete sei, per favore.* Please take your seat." I pointed to her assigned row on the left side of the cabin. "Number 11A."

"*Grazie, grazie, Signorina,*" she responded even more tragically as she hobbled, brushing her filled-to-bursting bags against other passengers already sitting. She squished herself into the aisle seat.

Just as the tourists were settling in, Trish, our number one, emerged out of the flight deck. "Natasha, I'll do a PA and explain, but will you please go to the rear and make sure passengers move forward?"

I groaned inwardly but nodded. The 1-11 was a small plane, and ballast for take-off with a less-than-full load was often an issue.

When I arrived at the rear, one obese, bespectacled man was just re-squeezing himself into a window seat, grumbling loud enough to be heard. "Bloody 'ell," he complained to his equally obese wife. "The only fuckin' reason we 'ave to move is because those fuckin' stewardesses are too bleedin' lazy to bring the bloody coffee down the back."

From some deep, dark place within me, years of unexpressed rage toward rude passengers rose up. I turned toward him. "Excuse me, *sir*," I said in the loudest voice I could muster so other passengers would hear, "I understand that you don't like sitting where you are. For your information, *sir*, the reason why you have to sit forward is so that the plane can take off. But if you really insist on sitting at the rear of the aircraft, we can unload *a-a-all* the passengers and *a-a-all* the luggage and rearrange the ballast just for you. Would you like us to do that, *sir*?"

By then, from three rows in front, heads had turned to stare at the man. Some were tut-tutting, and I heard one *How rude!* directed at him.

A wave of satisfaction washed over me as I saw that passengers were on my side. Rude Man, now realizing that he was the center of negative attention, shifted uncomfortably in his seat. "Oh, no love," he grinned, blushing. "That's all right. I was just kiddin'. Hey, maybe when we get to Milan, I can take you out for a drink?" He winked at me.

Oh God! I groaned and gave him my best not-even-if-you-were-the-last-man-on-God's-earth look. He sank down even further into his seat.

Feeling vindicated, I returned to the front of the plane. But having vented my initial anger, I wondered if he might complain. And if we didn't tell our version to the airline first, the passenger was always right. The Italian tour guide, I knew, was sitting in 2A. I would get the man's name from her and tell the senior Trish so she could mention the incident in her report.

"*Scusi, Signorina.*" I addressed the dark-haired woman as we taxied, who even though a tour guide, didn't appear to speak any English. In my limited Italian, I tried to explain by gesticulating that the man with the glasses at the back of the plane had been a problem and that I would like to get his name for our flight report.

"*Qui? Qui e?* Who? Who is it?" she wanted to know, straining her neck to look to the rear.

"*Non importa adesso.* It's not important now," I told her. "*Ma dopo il decollo.* After take-off," I added.

"*Si, si,*" she agreed, though frowning. "I'm sorry."

While I was grateful for her support, I didn't mean for *her* to feel responsible for the man's rude behavior.

For take-off, I sat with Lynn, the galley girl, on the forward jump seat. As soon as the *No Smoking* sign went off and working against the G-force of a steep ascent, we pulled ourselves up and went into action, preparing for the drinks service. That's when I glanced down the cabin, then looked again. *Oh no!* The tour guide was standing at the rear of the plane, angrily waving her arms, Italian-style, at a stunned, older man in glasses, who was cowering against the bulkhead, totally confused by her ranting. She was really giving him hell, but she was yelling *at the wrong man.* Now that the *Fasten Seat Belt* sign had been extinguished, the aisle was full of bodies aiming for the rear loos and there was no way I could get down there or even attract her attention to stop her reprimanding an innocent passenger.

The widow in 11A saw me staring down the aisle and thought I was looking at her. She beckoned me. "I am so sorry, *Signorina*," she said as I approached. "I don't-a want to be-a any trouble-a, but-a I need-a another glass-a of water."

"*Si, non c'e una problema.*" Not a problem, I told her and quickly returned to the galley.

She took the plastic cup gratefully and downed more pills. "I am-a so sorry to trouble you. If you like-a, I can-a 'elp-a you wash-a the dishes."

I smiled for the first time that day. "*Fa niente, Signora.*" It's nothing, I told her and touched her arm. "We throw the dishes away."

As the widow tossed back her third glass of water, the tour guide was making her way up the aisle. I contemplated making her aware of her mistake, but she also seemed frazzled. I returned to the galley to begin the drinks service.

The three nuns, who were sitting at the front of the plane distracted me with their shocking behavior. After each sister demanded to buy four half-bottles of Ballantines, I watched as they happily opened up their black robes and stashed their contraband in the stitched-in pockets made—not for carrying bibles apparently—but for duty-free whisky! And

I thought airline crews were naughty! Once the nuns had organized their stash, they all ordered three miniature whiskies and proceeded to drink them.

But the worst was yet to come.

Halfway through the inbound flight to Gatwick, I was pouring hot coffee into a passenger's cup when Lynn whispered in my ear. "Captain James has volunteered us for another flight after this one. We're doing a Zurich."

"Wha-a-at?" I groaned out loud. My hand involuntarily jerked with anger. The elegant Italian woman holding out her little plastic receptacle was lucky she didn't get scalded. How dare the captain just volunteer us like that! Didn't we deserve to be consulted?

"*Qualcosa non va?*" Is something wrong? my concerned passenger asked.

Just my whole bloody life, I was tempted to respond. "*No, Niente.*" Nothing, I assured her. "*Soltamente deviamo lavorare pui tarde ancora.* We have to work late again."

"*Ah, mi dispiace. Povera piccola. Si deve lavorare duro.* I'm sorry. You, poor thing. You work so hard."

For a moment the woman's sympathy took my breath away, and I wanted to rest my head on her shoulder and weep, but as I moved on to the next row, "*Grazie,*" was all I could muster.

On landing at Gatwick, our whole crew was rushed by bus over to the waiting Zurich-bound aircraft. As the transporter jostled us from side to side, I glowered at the captain sitting across from me, his gaze fixed on a point above my head. He was either oblivious to my murderous stare or was studiously ignoring my wrath.

After getting up at four am, we were all hungry, but before we even had time to grab a sandwich from our unhealthy hostie pack on this plane, German-, Italian- and French-speaking Swiss passengers were climbing the stairs. I managed a weary smile as I greeted them with a *Guten Morgen, Bonjour* and *Buon Giorno*.

When the outbound service was finally done and we were sitting in the galley scarfing down ham sandwiches, Trish came out of the flight deck with a grimace on her face. "Will this day never end?" she moaned.

"What's up?" Lynn asked.

"We have to wait at least two hours in Zurich for the inbound passengers to arrive. The bus bringing them from their ski destination has broken down in one of the tunnels."

"Well, perhaps we can sleep," I muttered, my eyelids already heavy with fatigue. I didn't know how I would get through the next six hours of this eternal duty.

"Just tell the bloody slave-driver of a captain not to volunteer us for cleaning another aircraft or loading baggage while we're waiting," Lynn snapped.

"Been there, done that!" I told her. "And checked in pax."

"What?" Lynn got up off the jump seat and tossed the rest of her sandwich into the black garbage bag. "We need a dam union in this airline!"

Maybe, I thought, I'm not the only one at the end of my tether.

Five hours later we were finally on our descent into Gatwick. As I returned to the galley with a tray of debris, I fantasized about climbing between fresh white sheets, but that's when Trish said, "I've got more bad news!"

"*Now* what?" I asked.

"Gatwick's fogbound. We have to fly into Bristol."

Passengers sitting in the first few rows probably heard our loud groans. So when I made the PA, telling them they would be taking a three-hour bus ride from Bristol to Gatwick, we empathized with their collective mumbling in the cabin.

By the time I finally got home at around 4.30 am, I calculated that we had done a twenty-three-hour duty. As I fell into bed and sleep, oblivion came fast.

"Natasha! Natasha!" Slowly coming back from a deep, dark place, I opened my eyes. Where am I? The familiar blue, pink and white floral wallpaper design stared back at me from my bedroom wall. Oh yes, I was at home.

"Eee, Natasha. Wake up, chuck." Samantha, my flat mate was standing in my doorway, wearing her uniform. I must be dreaming, I thought. Samantha worked for British Airtours and I often teased her about how often she departed not in uniform, but in civvies for positioning flights.

Then I realized she was real, and she *was* in uniform. "It's five o'clock, chuck," she said. "You've been asleep for ages."

"I didn't get home until early morning," I muttered.

"I know," Samantha responded. "But that were yesterday."

Had I really been asleep for two days? "Where are you going?" I muttered, trying to sit up. "Or are you coming?"

"Mauritius. Just got called out." Samantha hesitated. "Are you okay?"

I realized I was in pain all over my body. "I ...I'm not sure. I hurt. I think I might have the flu."

"Shall I make yer a cup o' tea before I go?"

"No, you go. Is Jenny home?"

"She's in Hong Kong. Remember? She'll be home on Friday."

"Okay," I said, not remembering anything, especially what day of the week it was. "Have a good flight."

After Samantha left, I turned over and fell back into my coma.

I wasn't sure how much later, but when I awoke again it was barely daylight. The red digits on my alarm clock said 4.54 pm. Had I slept another twenty-four hours? Before I could pull myself out of bed, the phone on my side table clanged in my ear. The noise was offensive. I fumbled for the receiver.

"Yes?" My voice sounded scary, like a low growl.

"Miss Rosewood. Dan Air crewing here," the young man said in a clipped tone as if I had already insulted him. "We would like you to do a Tenerife at 10:00 hours tomorrow morning."

"Tenerife?" I envisioned going through all the motions of an arduous twelve-hour duty. "No, I ...I can't," I moaned.

"What do you mean, you can't?" the voice sneered.

"I ...I'm sick."

"Oh, yes?" He sighed. "And when, Miss Rosewood, do you think you might be fit to fly again?"

"I don't know. I ...I'll let you know." A wave of absolute exhaustion washed over me. "Have to go...," I whispered and hung up. Then I turned over and fell back to sleep.

While my local GP talked excitedly about his imminent fishing weekend in Scotland, without a sniffle in sight, he diagnosed me with a cold. Then the following week, when I complained of kidney pains, he surmised that I was pregnant. "Not unless you believe in miracles," I scoffed. In my social recluse, sometimes comatose mode, I had hardly seen anyone, let alone a man for weeks—or was it months? Despite having doctor's notes for these various ailments, crewing, like Chinese water torture, continued to harass me daily. The conversation was always the same.

"Ms. Rosewood?"

"I'm still sick."

"When will you be fit to fly?"

"I don't know!"

Crewing staff were not noted for their compassion, but they were also somewhat jaded by the excuses stewardesses invented for getting out of flights— "my dog ate my uniform" or "my boyfriend wore it to a Vicars and Tarts party, and it got ruined."

My friends Alicia and Pauline were the only ones who had crewing wrapped around their little fingers. When they left for their holiday to Rio by the Sea-o, we looked forward to hearing about their two-week adventure on their return. But they did not come back. Days and then an extra week went by with no word or sign of them. Their parents, the airline and our circle of friends began to panic. Had they met with some dire fate? Rio, after all, had a high crime rate. Two weeks after they should have returned, and just before Interpol got involved, the two girls finally reappeared. Pauline sobbed to crewing that banditos had kidnapped them and dragged them up to their cave-like hideaway in the hills and they had finally made a daring escape. Sympathizing with their harrowing ordeal, crewing gave them another two weeks off for "stress leave." Then Pauline told me the real story. The two women had met some handsome doctors who had a large, gorgeous home in the hills behind the city. The girls had decided they wanted to partake of more Brazilian culture and pool-side parties before facing their short-haul jobs again.

Hide-and-seek between crewing and cabin crews was a never-ending game and with the exception of Pauline and Alicia—crewing had uncanny ways of finding us. Consequently, wherever we were when the phone rang—at our local pub, a friend's wedding reception or our great uncle's in a cottage in the Outer Hebrides–we would twitch. How *did* they know I was at my grandmother's on my day off? Were they psychic? Did they bug our phone lines? Or did the airline recruit spies?

If only there had been a way of knowing who was calling, it would have saved my sanity.

"Leave me alone!" I finally shouted at the voice on the other end in Crewing.

"Well, go and see the airline doctor then or ..." The threat was left hanging.

"Tomorrow." I muttered, exhaustion engulfing me again.

"I'll drive you," Emma offered. "I love Doc Leitch," she said of our airline doctor, who was also a 727 captain. I was grateful to Emma, not only for driving me to see a real doctor, but also because—even though she was busy flying yet again with Dan Air—she would drive thirty minutes twice a week to see me, make me a cup of tea or bring a cooked dinner. Maria, too, also seemed to understand and visit me between her long-haul trips. Instead of demanding that I get better or go for a walk, like my other concerned friends, she would just sit in silence and be with me.

Seeing my gaunt face, the airline doctor instantly recognized that I was suffering from nervous exhaustion and to my massive relief, insisted that I needed, at least, another month off.

When my time of complete rest—unharried by crewing calls—was over, I studied my reflection. The former grey, ghost-like specter that had looked back at me for so long had been replaced with someone with a pinker complexion and a little life in the dulled eyes. Though still emotionally fragile, I was looking almost human again. "Time for a change," I told the girl in the mirror. As Monty Python would say, "And now for something completely different."

"God, I hate Dan Air," Emma blurted, "and their bloody cheap plastic crew bags."

We were sitting in the lively Lamb's Inn in front of a roaring fire. Outside leaves were turning golden in the early September autumn. A huge hairy, wet dog was splayed across the rug in front of us and the buzz of other patrons talking filled the pub. To celebrate my slight improvement, Emma and I were indulging in a basket of fish and chips.

"Me, too," I said, staring into the fire. "I wish I'd known that seven other Dan Air girls had suffered from nervous exhaustion. Not that I would wish my experience on anyone, but it would have been so comforting to know it wasn't just me." And that I wasn't crazy like my psycho mother, I thought.

"Hardly surprising! With your languages, they were working you to death," Emma said, taking a sip of wine.

We both stared into the fire, mesmerized by the leaping flames.

After Emma's dice with death in Tehran earlier that year, and returning to Dan Air, I wondered if she had resigned herself to short haul forever.

"Well, I say fuck 'em." She plonked her glass on the table. "If I don't leave Dan Air soon, I'm going to drive into a tree."

"Emma!"

"Oh, don't worry. I'll make it look like an accident."

"Well, that's all right then," I teased, only half-joking, remembering that this was the second time she had made that threat.

"Instead of killing yourself, why don't we apply to the airlines again? You know, do the rounds—BA, British Caledonian...."

"After we've been tainted by Dan Air" she scoffed, "they probably won't touch us with a ten-foot barge pole. They like fresh meat, virginal air hostesses they can mold into yes-people, not jaded, seen-it-all hosties like us."

"You're right. But at least they know we're brilliant at handling emergencies and we make great landing drinks!"

We both laughed.

"We might have to feign naivete, humility and innocence?" I said. "Could you manage that?"

"Not a chance," Emma snorted. "It's all right for you. You've got your languages," she reminded me.

"Oh, I may not fess up to those anymore. And I've been a senior. Now there's a blight on my resume!"

"The airline industry must be the only one where you get penalized for being good and having experience." Emma stood to get another wine.

"Yes, I know," I agreed, "but I've always wanted to do long haul. In fact, that's all I ever wanted to do."

"Me, too!" she said, taking my empty glass. "Let's do it."

"I've got an interview with BA!" Emma's voice on the other end of the line sounded gobsmacked, as if she couldn't believe her luck.

"So have I!" I told her. "When's yours?"

"Next Thursday."

"You're joking! The 14th? That's when mine is, too."

"Is yours in Grosvenor Square somewhere?"

"Yes, that's it."

There was a pause. The obvious solution would be to travel up to London together. But I thought that our future employers might detect our combined anti-establishment attitudes—based in pure unadulterated jealousy—toward BA. With Emma's sarcasm, her disregard for authority and the thin aura of doom that pervaded her, maybe accompanying each other wasn't such a good idea.

"Let's go in together," she said. Sensing my hesitation, she added, "We could make it fun instead of torture?"

Emma could always sell me on any bad idea.

"Then when we fail their psycho tests, we can drive home together and commiserate at the pub."

While my intuition screamed at me, *Don't do it!* I heard myself say "Okay, I'll drive."

"We'll have fun," she added, perhaps knowing I still needed coercing.

Yes, we *would* have fun, I knew that much, but would that be a good or a bad thing?

We easily found the British Airways office in central London. Emma's appointment was an hour before mine, but we agreed that, if possible after our interviews, we would meet for lunch at the Victoria Cross, a pub on Kensington High Street, to celebrate or commiserate.

British Airways interviews were famous for their length and their intense Freudian-based interrogations thinly disguised with off-the-wall questions. We were even aware that when our first group interview was done, and we were shepherded into a small waiting room with other interviewees that the room was bugged so "they" could listen in on our chit-chat. Of course, I couldn't warn the other girls in the room, so I said what I believed to be all the right things. Maybe I was sucking up to the establishment after all, but if my ploy doubled my salary for working half the hours and it got me trips to Mauritius and Hong Kong, then even I could play the game.

One by one, we were called from the "bugged" room back into the office and sat facing four people. I guessed one was an ex-air stewardess, the man in the suit a human resources expert, the stocky woman a psychologist and perhaps, for good measure, the stony-faced older man a psychiatrist. I was sure that I had prefaced too many of my responses to their odd questions with "ums" and "ers." Judging by their bored, blank expressions, I knew that I had failed miserably, so I was stunned by their response.

"Miss Rosewood, would you be able to come back this afternoon for another interview at ..." the suited man checked his schedule, "er ...3:15?"

"Oh ...oh ...Yes, I'd love to. Thank you."

They all stared at me stony-faced, and finally sensing that their silence was my cue to leave, I exited the room.

When I walked into the Victoria Cross, Emma was already sitting propped up against the red velvet backing of a booth. She was sipping on a white wine ...and talking to a dark-haired man. Where did she find *him*?

"Hello?" I glanced from Emma to the man.

She blushed as though she'd been caught *in flagrante* but then decided she didn't really care and beamed at me. "Natasha, this is Derek. He's a friend of Stewart's."

Oh?

"We just bumped into each other down the street," Emma said.

"Oh," I repeated sounding cynical. "How did your interview go?" I asked.

"Oh, who knows?" she shrugged. "They ask such *pathetic* questions. I have no idea why, but they want me to go back this afternoon."

Uh-oh. Was Emma already sabotaging? She seemed more interested in the man than her future with BA.

"Me, too!" I told her.

"Oh, goodie." Emma beamed at me, genuinely happy for my success.

Over lunch, Derek kept us entertained with funny flying stories in his Scottish accent in Aberdeen where he was based. He was, indeed, a pilot friend of Stewart's, but his body language with Emma suggested a much more intimate connection. Maybe she hoped that word would get back to Stewart and he would be jealous? Why hadn't Emma told me about this man? But after the morning's KGB-type questioning with BA and all our laughter, I soon relaxed.

"Go o-o-o on!" Emma urged me. "Have another!"

This would be my second wine and I didn't want to show up at the afternoon interview tipsy. While the ability to drink was a pre-requisite for the flying life, I didn't think they needed proof of it at the interview. But feeling a little too happy and ignoring my inner voice, I let Derek buy me another Riesling. It did occur to me that I was getting caught up in Emma's downward trajectory of sabotage but instantly quashed the thought.

At the second interview, my good intentions of showing humility, naivete and innocence evaporated. I may have let it be known—but I can't be sure—that BA needed some inspiration in the fun department. The sour and shocked faces of my interviewers was a sign that I was speaking perhaps a little too freely. From somewhere outside myself, I heard what "bastards" Dan Air were, vociferous complaints about the too-long hours, and what fun emergencies could be when followed by strong landing drinks. On a downhill slide, I could not stop myself from talking about additional un-CAA-like deeds that we, the crew and the airline, had committed over the years. I realized I was the only one smiling. Seeing their eyes dilating in horror, pens resting on the desk in front of them, I thought, Ooops! I have blown it. The whole panel seemed to be twitching in their seats until, finally and not unexpectedly, I heard the tell-tale refrain, "Well, thank you Miss Rosewood. We'll be in touch."

With those words, I knew that was the beginning—and the end—of my BA flying career. As Emma and I drove home in silence, both subdued, I wondered what the outcome would have been if I had not agreed to that second glass of wine or had just gone to the interview alone.

We would never know.

"Well, who wants to work for those stuck-up people anyway?" Emma muttered as we neared Crawley. "And we never would have got in, you know. We've been tainted by Dan Air."

"We can't blame Dan Air," I reminded her.

And I couldn't blame Emma either, only myself.

Even though I wasn't sure how their Scottish uniform kilts would flatter my child-bearing hips but excited about the prospect of seeing Houston, Lima and Rio By the Sea-o, both Emma and I attended a British Caledonian interview, this time separately. We were still not accepted.

"Maybe we're doomed to short haul until the day we die?" Emma moaned.

"Perish the thought," I huffed, trying not to give up hope of my dream of long haul. "There are other airlines. We just have to keep looking."

"Yes," she said, "Do or die."

But neither of us, at that time, had the heart, or the energy, to risk even more rejection.

22

ARE WE THERE YET, MON?

Autumn 1978

The phone was ringing, but ...should I answer? The caller could be my airline bugging me again about when I would be returning to work ...or it could be a friend? If only my intuition was good enough to know who was on the other end. Curiosity won out.

"Natasha?" a cheerful female voice on the line enquired. Thank God. It was my friend Maria. "If I come by and pick you up," she said, "could you handle a pub lunch?"

I glanced through my windows at the trees lining the lane behind my Sussex home and took in the balmy stillness of the hot summer's day. Since going back to flying too soon, and then relapsing again with nervous exhaustion, it had been a while since I had ventured out. Why not?

One hour later Maria and I were seated on a not-so-comfortable wooden bench in front of The Plough Inn, a red umbrella with the name of some brewery on it sheltering us from the midday sun.

"So, what's up?" I asked my friend as we sipped on the blackish-red homemade wine.

Maria tilted her head. "How did you know something's up?"

"I'm psychic, remember? And you've got me out of my house for the first time in forever, so you must have a reason."

She smiled. My friend and I shared a sense of clairvoyance, although Maria seemed to have more experiences with dead people than I did— for which I was grateful. Palmistry was my thing.

"What you need is a damn good holiday," she said. "And a new romance."

"Holiday, yes. Romance, no." The only thing I wanted was rest, lots of rest.

"So-o-o ...you've heard me talk about my friend Sarah who I flew with in Bahrain?"

"For Gulf Air?" I nodded. Ever since I had known Maria, she had only operated long haul wearing British Caledonian's wee green tartan kilt, crisp white blouse, tailored jacket and tam-o'-shanter, but before we became friends, she had enjoyed other adventures in the Persian Gulf.

"Well, Sarah married a German called Georg and now they live in Barbados. They've invited me to come down for a visit. I wondered if you wanted to come?"

"Barbados!" I exclaimed. While I had travelled extensively, the exotic Caribbean island would be new territory. "Isn't it the most expensive destination in the world?"

Our lunch arrived, and as Maria slathered almost-liquid brie onto her bread, she shook her head. "Georg is the executive chef at the Barbados Hilton, and instead of paying a hundred pounds a night, he can get us a room for five!"

"Five!" That would be doable. I thought about how lovely it would be to have a real holiday to look forward to, far away from the demands of my slave-driving airline, away from rainy English weather in a place where sunshine could be guaranteed for two whole weeks. As Monty Python would say, *Luxury!* "When?" I asked.

"End of October." Maria responded, daintily dabbing her mouth with her serviette. "That's when BA lift their embargo on standbys."

"Okay. If we go, promise me one thing, Maria?"

"What's that?"

"No matchmaking."

"Well ...I know you're still not over Julian, but maybe you should remember what Mae West said. 'The best way to get over a man is to get under another one.'"

"I think that was Betty White, but Mae West *did* say, 'I'm single because I was born that way.' So *please* no matchmaking."

"Would I do such a thing?"

"Absolutely." We both laughed.

"Okay. Barbados, here we come!" I raised my glass and clinked Maria's. "I just hope we can get on the flight." Flying standby was always iffy.

Shaking her hands in the air Italian style, Maria declared, "*Eh, non ce una problema!*" No problem.

I wished I could have shared her optimism, but I had a premonition about that, too.

October 27 was a typically English autumn day. Rainy.

"I'll drop you off with the suitcases," Maria announced as we passed under the bridge with WELCOME TO HEATHROW splayed across its grey structure. "You can get in line, and I'll bring our hand luggage. *Va bene?* Okay." As my energy levels were still low, I was happy to have her take charge, but negotiating two heavily laden suitcases through a morass of passengers at the ever-busy Terminal 3 was going to be a challenge.

BA's staff travel area was at the far end of Departures. When I pulled the door open and saw inside, my heart sank. From the bottom of the three stairs all the way to the front of the large room, a mob of people were inching forward. Maybe they are going to other destinations, I thought, still hopeful. After five minutes a young female agent nervously clutching a microphone appeared behind the check-in desk and announced to the crowd, "There are only sixteen seats open on the Barbados flight, and I'm sorry," she said, now addressing those farther back, "but British Airways staff get priority."

A collective groan rumbled around the room.

She called out names as couples at the front moved forward to check in. "That's it for this flight," she informed the disappointed crowd. "But if you didn't get on this one," she added cheerily, "there's another Barbados next week."

Next week! Sod that for a game of marbles! I thought. We only have two weeks' leave.

"Oh, bollocks!" Maria's voice came from behind me. I swivelled around. Still panting, her cheeks rosy after running from the car park, she let our bags drop to the floor. "After all that!" she said, her shoulders drooping in defeat. But the disappointed mob had turned and were surging toward us now, wanting out through the door we were blocking. With heavy hearts, we dragged our heavy luggage back through the door and out of the terminal to the carpark.

Instead of sitting in a jumbo, sipping on a rum punch and winging our way to sunshine, we would now be driving in heavy traffic through south London in miserable, grey weather for a tortuous hour and a half back to Crawley. By the time Maria was negotiating the back-country lanes close to her home, my old friend, hopelessness had set in. "Maybe we should just go to the Costa Del Sol," I suggested mournfully. "Join all the other English girls with their flabby white thighs and eat fish and chips like good old British tourists."

"Not on your bloody life!" Maria retorted. "We're going to Barbados, and that's that! "When we get back to my place, I'll make some phone calls." Then in her Caribbean accent, she added, "Don't worry, mon. Be happy."

Two days later Maria and I settled into our seats at the rear of the British Caledonian Boeing 707 and sighed, relieved. She had snagged the last two seats on a flight to Caracas, Venezuela. From there, we were on standby with Viasa Airways to Barbados. Although this delay would shave almost three precious days from our two-week vacation, I was happy to be going somewhere. Finally, we were on our way!

"Vot are you knittink?" the bespectacled but handsome German sitting next to me asked as I tried not to stab him in the ribs with my needles. "Somessing for your boyfreindt?"

From her aisle seat, I felt Maria's encouraging nudge.

"No ...Yes, it's for my boyfriend," I lied. I hoped he couldn't see the pattern for a ten-year-old child's jumper lying in my lap.

"Zen you haff a lot of knittink to do. It looks very short."

I smiled and turned to Maria. "Do *you* want to sit in the middle?"

But the gentleman took the hint, sat back in his seat, folded his arms and closed his eyes.

If only the recipients of my gifts knew, I thought as I knitted, that each of my projects had been created out of flying mishaps. There was the Near-Death Scarf, the Bomb Scare Shawl, the Norwegian Nightmare Jumper and the Treacherous Tail-Plane Tank Top. This one would be the Three-Day Delay ...or longer if we got stuck in Caracas.

After the dinner service, a stewardess stopped at our row. "Hi Maria. Would you girls like some Nouky?"

The German stirred in his seat and sat up.

Maria saw my shocked expression. "Don't worry, Natasha. Noukaya is the South African wine we serve. We just call it Nouky."

Then she turned back to the stewardess. "Thank you," she said, and casting a glance at the German, she added, "Could you bring three glasses?"

When the Nouky arrived and the German, whose name was Wieland, gladly accepted some wine, I gave up on knitting. We discovered that he was a doctor on a sabbatical to research South American diseases, and he was single. Maria's pointed *he's-got-potential* glances continued, and though he was interesting, handsome and even funny, I only felt indifference.

After a couple of glasses, Maria sat back in her seat and relaxed. In a Monty Python accent, she declared, "Ee, ba gum, lass, this is luxury. We wouldn't 'ave got this treatment on BA, I can tell thee."

"You're right there, chuck," I nodded, easily lapsing into the vernacular. "I would 'ave thought it'd been gift week if we got a glass o' water!"

She laughed.

British Airways cabin crew were often the brunt of our jokes as they were paid twice as much as Dan Air and considerably more than British Caledonian staff but appeared to work much less. And maybe we were just jealous.

Ten and a half hours later Maria and I emerged into the Arrivals at Simon Bolivar International Airport, just 21 miles from downtown Caracas. Although we were soporific from the long flight, copious glasses of wine and the fact that it was past 3:00 in the morning UK time, the orange, yellow and purple zigzag pattern that adorned the floor, walls and ceiling of the terminal soon woke us up.

"Oof," I groaned, blinking at the shocking onslaught of colour. Airport terminals should be calming environments, with pastels and classical music playing, I thought. People were stressed enough getting on a plane and wrenching themselves away from loved ones.

"There it is!" Maria pointed to a Viasa kiosk at the far end of the terminal. Pushing my trolley loaded with our suitcases, I tried to keep up as she sprinted in that direction. Local men lounging against the walls on my left leered and hissed, "Taxi! Taxi!" Uneasy, I stared straight ahead, intent on not making eye contact and catching up to Maria.

Minutes later, after negotiating with the lady behind the counter, my friend approached, waving tickets and beaming, "We're on!"

Thank God! I didn't fancy being stuck anywhere for days again—especially with the unsavory men leering at us and overwhelmed by color shock.

"The bad news is we don't fly out until 8:00 a.m.," she added, taking my place behind the trolley, "so we're going to check the suitcases and then find somewhere to curl up for a few hours."

After we offloaded our luggage, the Viasa agent explained that we could go up to Departures and wait. She pointed to the other side of the terminal where stairs led to a mezzanine. I could just see the tops of orange chairs lined up there. Oh joy!

We were the only ones in this departure "lounge," so we stretched out across the hard, plastic chairs using our handbags for pillows. "God," I groaned as I lay down, "Barbados better be worth it."

But Maria was already asleep.

A child was crying. I stirred and opened my eyes. Where the hell was I? Blinding white lights and orange and purple zigzags dazzled me. On a chair opposite me a woman in a bright yellow silk sari edged with gold was comforting her crying two-year-old and studying me intently. Was I still dreaming? Oh, that's right. Caracas Airport. I sat up and smiled at the Indian woman. She smiled back.

Maria was already awake and chatting to the young, blonde, frizzy-haired girl on the other side of her.

"Welcome to the world," Maria said, smiling.

A twenty-something, very tall man appeared at the top of the stairs. From his longish, unkempt dark hair and rucksack, it was evident he was a traveller, not a tourist. He looked around the mostly empty room, and despite the many vacant seats, he chose to come over to our group. Mr. Rucksack told me he was a French psychology student on his way to Bogota to learn Spanish.

The woman on Maria's left was from Denmark and flying to Buenos Aires to go hiking in Patagonia. The Indian woman who was cradling her restless little girl was a doctor, going to join her husband in Sao Paulo. A Dutch couple who lived on a kibbutz in Israel told us they were travelling to Rio de Janeiro to work with the children in the *favellas* or slums. All of us had to wait for morning departures. Resigned to no sleep, we formed a large circle, and in a mixture of English, French, German, Spanish and Scandinavian, we exchanged life stories.

"What are *yo-o-o* looking for?" The Frenchman, Francois, suddenly fixed his gaze on me.

"Barbados and a rum punch?"

"Pfff." He shrugged, the French way. "Yo-ou know what I mean."

"Do I have to be looking for something?"

"No, but you are not at pe-e-ace with yourself." His intense stare was unnerving, but his accent melted my resistance.

"Oh, well. The usual, I suppose." I shrugged. "Love, money, health, happiness."

"But can you fe-e-eel zee miracle zat is your life?" he asked, dragging out the word "feel," and twisting the proverbial knife in my gut.

I hadn't been able to feel anything in a long time. "N-no." I blushed.

"If you stay open to ze miracles," he continued, his eyes softening, "you will feel again soon."

The Indian woman suddenly sat up straight. Wagging her head from side to side and sounding like a guru, she stated, "Yes, dat is r-r-right. Einstein said there ar-r-re only two ways to live your life--as though nutting is a miracle, or as though ever-r-ry little ting is a miracle."

I smiled back at her. "I think I'm getting a message here."

But how had Francois recognized my lostness? To be seen and understood by a perfect stranger was somehow oddly comforting.

I turned back to him. "Thank you." You will make a great psychologist."

"*Oui*." He smiled. "*Je sais*. I know."

Two hours after our United Nations group had parked themselves on the uncomfortable orange seats, the lively conversation suddenly stopped. We all looked at each other, realizing something magical was happening. We were complete strangers, coming together in this time and place from different corners of the world, from different cultures, religions, languages and even ages, but we were kindred spirits, all sharing our life stories and philosophies like old friends–and although we knew we would never see each other again, we recognized a unique snapshot of time well-spent, people well met. Humanity at its best.

A new hope stirred inside me. The diversity of people and cultures was so beautiful and interesting. This is what I've been missing, I thought. If only I could just get away from the slog of short haul flying and do long haul, travelling to far-flung parts of the earth. I could be meeting open-minded travellers instead of serving tourists going on their "hols" to the Costa Brava. How many times had I been envious listening to Maria talk about Lima and Lagos or been just a little jealous when my flat mate, Samantha regaled me with details of Hong Kong and Mauritius? Why shouldn't I do long haul? Why *not* me?

At 7.30 am, Francois accompanied us down the concourse to our gate. As we reluctantly parted, he peered into my eyes and said, "Remembair to expect *les miracles*."

Maria and I then exited down the finger and ducked into the shadowy interior of the old Viasa Airways DC9 for the final leg of our long, long journey. In one and a half hours, we would be landing in Barbados —with time changes—almost four days later than planned!

In-flight, and due to the curse of being a hostie always attuning to airplane noises and cabin routines, I couldn't sleep. So while Maria managed to snooze, I took out my knitting again.

"What are jyou doing?" the Venezualen stewardess asked, peering at my needles.

I looked up at her, puzzled. "Knitting?"

She frowned. "What is knitting?"

"Oh? Have you never seen this before?" I held up my handiwork.

"No." She shook her head.

"Well, you make a ton of knots, which then turns into this..." I showed her the picture pattern of the jumper for my nephew.

"Ha!" She shook her head again in wonder. "It's a miracle."

Is that what a miracle was? I wondered. Something that is beyond our current experience, but easily attainable. If I just opened my mind to new possibilities, would I find *my* miracle?

When the plane's doors opened in Barbados—almost four days later than planned—the warm wave of heat that greeted us melted away the edges of my fatigue. Tall palms waved in the breeze beyond the single-storey Bridgetown airport building, and a tinge of excitement— something I hadn't felt in a long time—rose up from some dark, dusty place within me.

Even before the taxi pulled into the Barbados Hilton driveway and I got a glimpse of the roofless lobby with its chirping birds darting in and out of the hanging vines and swooping around the indoor waterfall, I knew this epic journey had been worth the delay. While the valet took our cases up to our room, Maria and I couldn't wait to cross the lobby and glimpse the ocean.

Outside, a long rectangular pool was surrounded by tanned bodies draped over chaises longues, while some vacationers were sitting on the pool's edge, their legs dangling in the water. Others were swimming or learning how to use scuba gear. To the left of the pool, a short pathway angled off toward a small bar covered in pampas and then beyond that—ah yes—a fine white sandy beach dotted with tall coconut palms led down to the water. The faint sound of steel drums wafted on the breeze. Heaven!

"Com'on," Maria urged. "Let's go and see our room."

Waiting for us in room 310 was not just a breathtaking view of the turquoise ocean, but also a gift basket containing a bottle of wine, chocolates and exotic fruits. The card from Georg and Sarah read, "Welcome to the Barbados Hilton. Meet you at Happy Hour." As we unpacked, there was a light tap on the door, and a waiter entered and placed two pina coladas on our table. "Welcome to Barbados, ladies," he said in the lilting Bajan accent. After he left, Maria and I clinked glasses and exclaimed in unison, "We made it!"

After potent hot showers to cleanse ourselves of airplanes, airports and what felt like never-ending travel, Maria and I found our way to the Happy Hour location at the back of the hotel. Sarah, a petite, long-haired brunette, appeared accompanied by her husband, a tall, dark-haired German clad in a pristine white chef's garb. I warmed to them both on sight. Georg only had time to say a brief "hello" and hear our profuse "thank yous" for our room, the welcome basket and cocktails before excusing himself and rushing back to his kitchen.

Then while Maria and Sarah reminisced about their past Gulf Air adventures and long-lost flying buddies, I only half-listened, aware of the paradise that surrounded us. On this Caribbean evening, standing on a green lawn beside old British ramparts, leaning on weather-beaten cannons and sipping on a rum punch, I couldn't believe I was here. Above us a half-moon shone down from a starry sky and warm air enveloped us like a loving blanket. The whistling frogs croaked in an unrelenting rhythm that almost, though not quite, drowned out that wonderful, relaxing sound of waves crashing on the shore, which in the early evening shadows was a glistening black mass just fifty feet in front of us. Even though the fickle finger of Fate had cut our vacation short, I was already in love with Barbados.

In the days that followed, Maria and I quickly adopted a routine of going down to the beach every morning, pulling a chaise longue under a coconut tree midway between bar and ocean and settling in for a day of swimming, reading, tanning, sleeping and at a respectable hour, trying out various fruit-laden cocktails. The swaying palms and a subtle breeze softened the sun's intense rays while the background sounds of gentle waves splashing on the beach and the soft playing of steel drums soothed my soul. The hot Caribbean sun began to seep into my weary bones and melt away months of tension.

The sun's rays gave me renewed strength. I knew I was healing— physically at least. Emotionally, though, I still felt trapped inside a glass jar, separate from others. Would I ever be able to feel again, or would I always be just an outsider, a numb, neutral witness to people and life?

I reflected on my summer of hell. When had my descent into that black hole really begun? Five months ago ...or longer? Was it Dan Air's 23-hour duty in the summer that had finished me off and caused me to sleep for three days? When I had finally roused, my whole body had been in pain. Flying non-stop through the previous winter, thanks to my four European languages, and then the stress of buying my first house in March had probably contributed to the nervous exhaustion. Or did my demise begin with the heartbreak of losing Julian? Of course, the strain of my mother's psycho behaviour and her endless vitriolic threatening phone calls in the middle of the night was also, no doubt, a factor. Maybe all of the above. But would I ever feel normal again?

"What are you girls up to?" Maria and I looked up from our prone positions.

The sun was behind him, but I still recognized the profile of one of our new friends, Peter, his prematurely grey curly hair frizzier in the humidity.

"What we do best here," Maria responded, putting her book down and sitting up. "Absolutely nothing."

Peter was a salesman for a battery company, so we had quickly named him Eveready. Though this wasn't the brand of his employer, the name suited him as he always seemed ready to flirt with any woman who came along. But when neither Maria nor I had succumbed to his charms, he had given up and befriended both of us.

Peter perched on the end of her chair. "Do you want to go to the Garage later?"

"Why would we want to go to a garage?" I asked, lying down again.

"The Garage is a great club. You'll enjoy it." As he got up to chase two skinny blondes down the beach, he called, "Meet you girls at 9 in the lobby?"

Shortly after 9.30 that night, the three of us arrived in a taxi at what appeared, in the darkness, to be the middle of a thinly treed jungle. Then we saw a large hut, its corrugated iron roof shining in the moonlight, and the boom-boom of music emanating from inside the club making the flimsy walls shake.

"That's the Garage," Peter explained as we climbed out of the vehicle.

We followed him across the rough ground into the shack. Then Peter introduced us to the white man at the door. "And this is the owner, Roger."

"Fost drink's on the house," Roger said, his Bajan accent faint but unmistakable.

Passing from the jungle into The Garage was like entering the police box, Tardis in Dr. Who. The interior was a completely different world. The corrugated iron sheets only covered half of the hut structure, making the starry sky still visible above, and in front of us, waves crashed right up against a low wall where couples sat talking, ignoring the light ocean spray. Rising from the centre of the concrete floor was the massive trunk of a banyan tree, which sheltered a DJ sitting in a small lighted booth, his multi-coloured crocheted hat barely covering the top of his long dreadlocks. Scattered around the floor were a selection of antique cars that had been cut in half, with couples sitting in them talking and canoodling. Patrons were a mix of local and international, black and white, single and coupled, young and old. We hovered near the bar while Eveready ordered our complimentary rum punches. "Here you are, ladies."

"Roger sounds like he's been here a long time," I remarked. "He's got the accent."

Peter shouted over the music "He's a local and one of the few white Bajans on the island. And he's smart. This place is a goldmine."

"You want to dance, mon?" Except for his blue shirt, the tall, muscular Bajan standing in front of me was hard to see in the dark room. I could just make out the beads on his dreadlocks and, when he smiled, his white teeth.

"Love to," I said, as I handed my drink to Eveready and joined Dreadlocks on the floor.

As soon as we began moving, the music got even louder, and I lost myself in the rhythm. My partner beamed at me. "Oh, mon, you like to dance."

We smelled the rain before it came, sheets of water suddenly pouring down from the heavens. The music stopped and I was about to run for shelter when Dreadlocks touched my arm and said, "No, dawn't gaw. Keep dancin'."

"I Can See the Rain on My Window," began blasting from the DJ's booth, and perhaps to drown out the noise of the downpour banging on the corrugated iron roof, the music blared even louder. Some people had taken refuge in the cars, some had run to the bar for shelter, but others had come out onto the floor to deliberately get wet. As I wiped my soaking hair from my eyes and felt my cotton dress clinging to my legs, I giggled and kept dancing.

Ten minutes later just as suddenly as it had begun, the rain stopped, and as a fresh wave of warm humidity enveloped us, more people came out onto the floor. I wondered if I was emitting steam as, very soon, I realized my cotton dress was dry again and my long unruly hair had become even frizzier.

At last I was spent. "Thank you," I told Dreadlocks, "but I think I need a break."

"You is an island girl," he commented as he escorted me back to Peter and Maria at the bar. "You belong here."

Funny you should say that, I thought. On Barbados I did feel a sense of coming home.

Toward the end of the evening, we met three staff from the Oriana cruise liner which was currently docked near Bridgetown.

"I've had thoughts about joining a cruise line myself. What's it like?" I asked the large, bearded ship steward as he slung back his third rum punch. And I thought airline crews were alcoholics!

"Well...you're away from three to nine months, but if you're okay with that, it's great," he said, and ordered another drink from a passing waiter. "We can show you around the ship tonight if you like?" he offered.

When Maria, Eveready and I were given a tour of an almost empty *Oriana*, I was disappointed by the shabbiness of the boat and the claustrophobic size of the staff cabins.

"They're not very big, are they?" Maria commented.

"No," the steward replied. "And you have to share."

"Hmmm." I envisioned life on the ocean waves. "What if you don't like your cabin mate, or the rest of your crew?"

He shrugged. "Too bad."

"Maybe I'll stick to flying," I commented. "At least, if we don't like a crew member—which rarely happens—we only have to tolerate each other for hours or days, not months."

A few days later at the insistence of Georg and Sarah, Maria and I joined a bunch of international tourists for a day on the *Jolly Roger*, a local "pirate ship," which sailed along the Barbados coast. With the wind in our hair and while imbibing copious amounts of rum punch and snacking on Bajan delicacies, we danced, drank, sang, drank and—oblivious to any danger—leapt off the side of the ship into what could have been dangerously shallow waters. Even though some passengers, due to being paralytically drunk, were carted off in stretchers at the end of the trip, miraculously no one had fallen overboard.

"Will I see you again?" the French Canadian who had flirted with me the whole trip asked as—on our return to safe harbor—we teetered precariously down the gangplank.

"Probably not," I said, perhaps a little too honestly. Why pretend, I thought? I felt like a cold fish. And perhaps I was.

On the eighth day of our vacation, and with only two days remaining before we had to return to rainy old England, I lay in my usual position on the beach and watched as Sarah and Georg came down the sand toward me. They leaned into each other as they kicked their way through the white sand, laughing like teenagers.

"Maria's just getting drinks," I explained as they plonked themselves on her vacant lounger.

"We came to invite you both to dinner tonight," Sarah said as she reached up to tie her long brown hair into a top knot.

"Sounds lovely," I said, watching Georg as he helped her include an errant strand into her bun.

"Sarah, how did you know Georg was the one?" I asked, envious of their love.

"It's a feeling." She beamed at him. "You just know."

That's the problem, I thought. I can't feel.

As if reading my thoughts, Georg said, "You vill experience it one day, Natasha. You neffer know when it vill happen, und zat iss the miracle."

"This place suits you," Sarah remarked. "With that dark tan, you're beginning to look like a local."

I sighed, looking out at the ocean. "I don't want to go home."

"So why don't you both stay a few more days and fly home with me on BA on Monday?" After flying for just three years, Sarah had already confessed to being terrified of flying. Strange for an ex-stewardess.

"Well ..." Was this even possible? I wondered. "You're right. I do deserve a full two week's holiday."

Sarah nudged her husband. "Georg, can you arrange for Natasha and Maria to stay a few more days?"

He shrugged. "Ze hotel iss busy. It will be a miracle but, sure, I can ask."

"And I would need to check with BA," I added.

Georg pulled Sarah up from the chair. "Let us know tonight," she said over her shoulder as, holding hands, they ambled up the beach to their home.

Five minutes later I heard Maria's voice behind me. "Et voila!" she said, handing me our customary 4 o'clock pina coladas, a chunk of fresh pineapple secured with a tiny pink paper umbrella. As she sat down, she reminded me, "You do realize that this could be one of our last."

"Well ...I was going to talk to you about that."

"Oh, no. You're not going to do a Pauline and Alicia, are you?"

"Well, not quite. But if they can get away with staying an extra two weeks in Rio, and still get two additional weeks off for stress, why shouldn't we get a few extra days and our full holiday?"

Maria chewed on her pineapple garnish, thinking.

"I don't know about you, Maria, but I feel cheated losing three days just to get here ...or was it four?"

Finally, Maria shook her head and took another sip. "No, Natasha. I can't. I have to get back."

I understood. She worked for an airline that was good to her. She had loyalties, whereas Dan Air had almost killed me with their harassment and slave-driver management. I felt no such loyalty or—I was surprised to discover—guilt. They owed me one or two or three of something.

"Georg is going to ask at the hotel. I'll call BA for their Monday flight. It's just Dan Air that needs to be informed ..."

Maria grimaced. "You want me to call them, don't you?"

"Somebody has to, or crewing will show up here and drag me home."

"Natasha, I'm not a good liar."

"I know."

"What would I say?"

"That I'd fallen into a vat of rum punch and drowned?" I ventured.

Maria laughed. "No, I know." She sat up. "You got drunk, fell off the *Jolly Roger* and into a bed of sea urchins. Now you look like a porcupine, and you won't allow the local Bajan men to pee on you to get the needles out, so you have to wait for them to die and break off."

"Or ...or...," I said, warming to the topic. "I was kidnapped by pirates and they've demanded a ransom. Dan Air would never pay!"

Maria and I both fell back on our chairs laughing. Then we became quiet.

"Or I could just tell them you got food poisoning," she offered.

"That works, too ...Then ...you'll do it?"

"Maybe I'll get Alicia or Pauline to call in for you. They're much better at fibbing to crewing than I am." She paused, thinking. "Will you be okay on your own?"

"Oh, yes." Some alone time would give me time to think, the locals were friendly, and I felt safe in Barbados.

"Well ...all right," she agreed reluctantly. "But you know, you'll owe me one!"

"Thank you, Maria," I answered, grateful for my full holiday. "And don't worry, you're already in my will and ...oh, by the way, Sarah and Georg have invited us to dinner tonight."

After day one of my prolonged holiday, and already missing Maria, I opted to go to the beach bar for lunch. As I approached, I heard English accents, people laughing and saw a group of men and women who, judging by their very white skin, were new arrivals.

"Are you airline crew?" I asked one of the women as I perched on a bar stool next to her.

The rosy-cheeked brunette turned to look at me. "Yes, we're BA. Are we that obvious?"

"Well, I am, too, but not BA," I told her, now faced with my nemesis airline. "I'm on holiday."

"Lucky you," the blonde next to her slurred, already having downed her rum punch.

"Are you here alone?" Brunette asked me.

I told her the story of our incredible journey and how I had extended my stay.

"My name's Sarah," Blondie offered, "and this is Mary," she said, pointing to Brunette.

"And I'm Simon," a tall, skinny man piped up from the other end of the bar.

"Natasha," I told them.

"Which airline are you with?" Simon asked.

"Dan Air," I muttered, inwardly cringing.

"Oh, Dan Dare!" Simon cooed. "We love you! You're so friendly and you always look like you're having *so* much fun!"

"It's because we're always drunk ...and stunned after having survived yet another emergency!"

There was a shocked pause, and when they saw my smile, they all burst out laughing. But I wasn't really joking.

"Natasha, why don't you join us tonight? We're meeting in room 101 for drinks. Then we can decide, or you can tell us where it's good to go. You must know the island?"

My previous nasty impressions of snotty BA crews evaporated. They were all so nice and *ordinary*. "Thank you," I said. "But I don't want to intrude."

"Hell, we don't know one another either. And anyway ...you're one of us," Mary added, smiling.

Later that night, after Simon had abandoned us for his bed and the two girls and I had teetered from the Hilton down the pot-holed road in our high heels, we sat in what appeared to be a dilapidated shack at the open-air Flying Fish Restaurant. With waves lapping almost at our feet and over a meal of a delicious fresh local catch and chips, we exchanged flying stories. I realized that BA crews had as many challenges as Dan Dare crews did. They were just different. As BA was a larger airline with larger aircraft, they had larger cabin crews who rarely flew together more than once so they—unlike us—never got to develop a bond. And due to the more hierarchical structure of their airline, their flight deck crew, they informed me, stayed in separate hotels down route from the girls. As a result, they didn't enjoy the same camaraderie or fun that Dan Air enjoyed. However, they did fly to many more exotic destinations and were paid twice as much.

"I really want to do long haul," I confessed.

"Then why don't you apply to BA?" Mary asked.

"Oh, I did and even got as far as the second interview." I omitted the rest of the story about showing up slightly inebriated and lecturing my interviewers on needing a sense of humour.

"Don't give up," Sarah urged. "I know a girl who got in after her fifth interview."

"Really?" I was liking these people more and more. "Maybe I *will* reapply."

As we placed our Bajan dollars on the table, Sarah said, "I'm really sorry, Natasha, but I'm too tired to go to the place you mentioned. The Garage, was it? Could we just go to the hotel's club downstairs?"

"The Flambeau? Of course!" I had forgotten my new friends had done a twelve-hour duty that day. "That's supposed to be a great spot, too."

At the Flambeau Club an hour later the three of us watched from a padded seat on the edge of the dance floor as purple and white lights cast ghostly shadows on the gyrating bodies dancing to the disco music. One man after another asked Mary and Sarah to dance, leaving me conspicuously alone.

Suddenly a giant Bajan waiter loomed in front of me. "Do you want another drink?" he shouted over the noise.

"Yes, please." I smiled, happy to get some attention. "Pina colada," I yelled back.

He nodded and disappeared into the crowd.

The waiter soon reappeared and with a flourish placed the cocktail in front of me. I wrote my room number and signed his receipt then looked down. This cocktail was orange! Whatever it was, on principle, I didn't want an orange drink. I picked up the glass and headed over to the bar. To my dismay, a sea of heads was between me and the bartender, and any hope of getting my drink changed.

I was debating whether to give up and just drink the orange concoction when a dark-haired man in front of me suddenly turned around and spoke. "I was jost going to ask jyou to dance?" he said and grinned shyly.

I don't know whether it was his smile, his voice or his whole being, but in that instant, something momentous happened. As if a giant beam of light had been cranked on and I was bathed in its glorious warmth, I felt each cell in my being coming back to life. I felt elated. I felt. Oh my God. I could feel again!

Stunned, I responded, "Er ...I was just going to change my drink."

"Let me do it for jyou. What do jyou want?" His soft South American accent was mesmerizing.

"Pina colada," I breathed. Before I could say another word, he had taken my glass and thrust his way back into the melee. A few minutes later he reappeared holding the familiar yellow cocktail.

"Shall we sit down?" He pointed to where I had been sitting.

In my own personal bliss-filled bubble, I wafted to my table where we sat. Now I was grateful that the two girls were still dancing. Jose and I exchanged geographic locations, what we did for a living, why we were in Barbados and more. But all I could think about was this amazing feeling of coming back to life. I couldn't take the stupid grin from my face. In a happy daze, I let him lead me onto the dance floor, but either drunk from alcohol or love, I teetered precariously on my high heels, so for safety's sake, he escorted me back to our table.

Suddenly we were talking about UFO sightings and aliens and people who missed time after seeing strange lights. Having lived in a small town in the north of England close to a space station, I'd had my own scary experiences as well as hearing about other mass sightings in the area. UFOs were my favourite topic.

At some point we both stopped talking and stared at each other, beaming. Then we glanced around the room. The music had stopped! The club was empty of people. Waiters were stacking chairs on tables.

We stared at each other, with what? Shock, recognition, love? Somewhere in the back of my mind, I heard a physical "click."

"I think we better leave." He grinned and took me by the elbow. Outside the club, standing before the lift in the bright light of the foyer, we hesitated. I didn't want this night to end, and neither it seemed, did he.

"Can jyou waterski?" he asked.

"Yes," I responded, choosing not to tell him I had only done it once, just a few days earlier, and with a hangover to boot. After my sixth attempt, the man in the boat had yelled at me, "You got to let de boat do de work for you." That's when I finally got up on the skis and gracefully completed four figure eights on the ocean while spectators watched and cheered from the beach.

"If the water is good tomorrow, do jyou want to go waterskiing?"

"Yes, I'd love to."

He beamed and then we entered the lift together. Once inside, he said, "I'll meet jyou on the beach. About eleven?"

The lift doors opened at my floor.

"Goodnight." He leaned in and kissed me softly on both cheeks.

"Goodnight," I breathed, resisting the urge to throw myself into his arms and never let go.

That night as I sat in the dark on the edge of my twin bed and stared at the moonlit ocean for ...I don't know how long, all I kept thinking was: It's a miracle! I can feel!

When I woke the next morning, everything was different.

Down on the beach, the ocean seemed bluer, the sun brighter, the sand whiter, as if someone had flicked a colour switch and I had come fully and completely back to life. I removed my beach wrap as a gentle breeze caressed my shoulders.

"Can I help jyou with that?" It was Jose's voice behind me.

I turned and saw him striding toward me. The sight of him, in shorts and his open shirt flapping in the breeze made my heart leap, but it was his boyish grin that took my breath away.

"Good morning," I said huskily.

"I jhave some bad news." He stood surveying the ocean.

I held my breath. *What?*

"We won't be able to go water-skiing. Thee water ees too rough."

Oh, that!

He affixed his brown eyes on me.

I melted. "That's okay," I said, attempting to disguise my relief. Taking a few ungraceful tumbles in front of my new love would probably not have been the impression I wanted to create.

He sat beside me on my beach lounger and lit a cigarette while I stared at the ocean, aware of his closeness and feeling joy.

"Jyou know," he said, staring meaningfully at me. "I tried to postpone my flight for a couple of days ..."

My heart leapt. "You did?" More time with him would be heaven.

"Jyes ...but they don't jhave anything, so I jhave to leave jhere at 1.30 today."

Oh, no. So soon.

We sat side by side on the chaise longue, almost touching, asking each other questions about our jobs, our travels, the languages we spoke. When he talked of having emigrated from Venezuela to Boston, there was a sadness in his energy, something that forbade me to ask. He joked, I teased. Then we sat in silence, not needing to speak. I exhaled. Being with him felt like coming home.

He peered at his watch. "Oh no! It's twelve o'clock already. Let's go for a drink before I jhave to leave jyou." He stood up and offered me his hand. When I laid my palm in his, an electric energy passed between us, familiar, warm and comforting.

Seated at the bar, the midday sun shone down on us. As I sipped on a pina colada and he drank his G & T, I silently began counting down the precious minutes we had together.

"'ello, darlin'." Eveready stood in front of us, eyeing my companion.

Jose frowned, annoyed at the intrusion.

"Hello." I smiled up at Eveready. "Peter, this is Jose." The men shook hands and nodded, assessing each other as if preparing to step into a boxing ring.

"What are you up to?" I asked.

"I've rented a scooter and I'm going to tour the island this afternoon," he said. "Why don't you come ...if you're not doing anything?" He cast a glance at Jose.

Jose tensed. While I didn't want to make my new love jealous, I also didn't want to be alone after he left. Although we had spent less than four hours together, his departure was going to leave a big hole in my day, and my life.

"Jose has to leave soon, so yes, I'll come... That'll be fun."

Jose gave Eveready a hooded glare.

"Meet you in the lobby at one?" Peter said, and then turned and carried on down to the beach.

Jose downed his drink and smiled at me ruefully. "I jhave to go," he said. "I want to give jyou my number, but my cards are in my room upstairs. Do jyou mind coming up with me?"

"Of course," I said, devastated that our time together was almost over.

As we rode up in the lift, he asked "What is jyour room number?"

"Oh? Er ...310." Why did he want to know?

Inside his room, I perched on the end of his unmade bed, his half-packed suitcase lying on the other side. He handed me a business card. "I'm in the process of moving, so for the time being, I will jost give jyou my business number."

"Oh, okay." A little voice at the back of my head tried to mutter something, but I silenced it immediately.

"If jyou ever come to Boston, jyou will call me, yes?"

"Yes, I'd love to." Boston wasn't exactly one of Dan Air's destinations, but I could get a cheap flight to visit. "Do you ever come to England on business?"

"Well, actually," he smiled again, "I am supposed to come next jyear, in March."

Hope soared. "Well, maybe," I said standing up, and reluctantly moving over toward the door, "I'll see you then." March was *so-o-o* far away, but maybe this wasn't an ending but a wonderful new beginning. There was hope now, for me, for life. At least, I could *feel* again.

With the door ajar, and my palm on the handle, before I left, I turned to take a last look, imprinting his face in my memory. How I wanted him to take me in his arms and just hold me. I waited. Instead he leaned in and brushed his lips against one cheek, and then the other.

"*Hasta lluego,*" he whispered in my ear.

"Goodbye." I turned and walked woodenly away.

As the elevator took me back down to ground level, elation, disappointment, and joy tumbled around inside, all vying for attention. I was grateful that Peter would be keeping me preoccupied that afternoon, taking the edge off the void I was already feeling by Jose's absence. When I arrived at the waterfall in the open-air lobby, Eveready, true to his nickname, was chatting up two young women. As I approached, they moved away.

At around 8:00 that evening, when Peter and I returned to the hotel, a now-black ocean was twinkling like a star-studded heaven under a bright moon. The tour of the island had been fun, and we had survived the pot-holed roads, local Bajans ambling in front of us oblivious to traffic, and Peter's sometimes precarious driving. Now I just wanted to go my room and be alone with my thoughts of Jose. But Peter wanted a nightcap.

Not wanting to be ungracious, I joined him at the beach bar. To the sound of waves lapping on the sand and frogs whistling loudly in the warm night air, we discussed the challenges of relationships.

"I would never tell a man I loved him," I said, still smarting from my breakup with my ex, Julian.

"Don't you think he'd want to know?" Peter asked, surprising me with his tenderness.

I shrugged, aware of my own penchant for sabotaging "the good ones." My aversion to happiness was probably an emotional hangover from my verbally abusive upbringing. Maybe I didn't deserve to be loved? Was I merely imagining that Jose was just as taken with me as I was with him? "Well, not be *the first* to say it, anyway," I added.

While we were talking, one question kept bouncing around my brain. Why had Jose wanted my room number? Would there be a message waiting for me?

As if reading my thoughts, Peter asked. "Who was that man at the bar?"

"Oh, I met him last night at the Flambeau," I said, trying to sound casual.

"He *really* likes you."

"Oh, do you think so?" I beamed, but I was still puzzled why Jose had not been more affectionate. "How do you know?"

"The way he looked at you."

Men can normally tell, I thought. Had Jose also felt the same as I did, as if struck by a thunderbolt? It didn't make sense, but I was already aching for him.

After Peter and I had finally said our goodnights, the hotel lift would not move fast enough. When the doors opened, I ran along the open balcony to my room. I unlocked the door, and as I closed it behind me, I stood in the shadowy vestibule peering at the floor. No card, no letter had been slipped underneath. Nothing. I had fooled myself. He doesn't feel the same, I thought. This is all in your head, Natasha. Devastated, I turned and faced the lighted room.

Then I gasped.

There, straight ahead of me, on the coffee table, haloed under the bright glow of the bedroom light was a large basket bursting with an array of vivid pink, yellow and red tropical flowers.

I ran toward it. Tucked inside the cellophane was a small white card. As I took it out, I saw that Jose had made a crossword out of the word

Venezuelan and the initials *UFO*, our favorite topic. At the bottom of Venezuelan, he had linked the words, *See you again.*

"Yes, you will!" I cried out loud. "Yes, you will!"

"Hey Natasha!" On my last day in the Caribbean paradise, I was lying on my beach chair lost in thoughts of Jose. Now Sarah was standing over me, her long dark hair lifting in wisps in the breeze. "Are you ready to leave tomorrow?" she asked. "Please don't change again. I'm terrified of flying alone."

"'I've been meaning to ask you. You flew for ...what ...three years, but ...now ...you're afraid of flying! Why?"

Sarah perched on the end of my chaise longue and looked out at the very blue ocean. "I think it's a crap shoot. I've done so much flying and got away with it. One of these days, I think that I'm just going to run out of luck and be in a crash."

But did luck have anything to do with any event? This whole holiday had felt fated. If Maria hadn't known Sarah in Bahrain, if Georg hadn't miraculously found rooms available at the peak of the season, if we hadn't been delayed in getting here, if I hadn't opted to stay an extra three days to get my full holiday, and if the BA crew I had hooked up with had agreed to go to The Garage instead of the Flambeau, and then if the waiter hadn't brought me the wrong drink, would I have met Jose? We could so easily have missed each other. The miracle was that we *did* meet. Whatever it was—fate, luck or divine intervention—meeting Jose had given me new hope.

The next day as Sarah and I winged our way back over the Atlantic Ocean to an almost-guaranteed cold, wet and windy welcome at Heathrow and then a coach-ride to Gatwick, I thought about Dan Air, the short haul airline which for four years I had given my life to–and almost my soul. When I had first joined them, my colleagues and I had been told that, after a year, we would be flying long haul on 707s to the US and Canada. The thought of being able to visit my brothers in Vancouver and Calgary was exciting then. But because they had promoted me early to senior stewardess ...on short haul, I knew they were never going to give me the long-haul experience I had dreamed of. Dan Air's slave labour conditions weren't ever going to improve. Maybe because of my failed interviews with BA and British Caledonian two years ago, I had parked my dream for a while, but it was still there. I made the decision. It was time to make the break.

"What about Laker?" Sarah suggested when I told her of my intention. "They fly to the US, and they also come into Barbados. Then you'd be able to visit us."

"The US *and* Barbados!" I could see more of Jose! I thought. And revisit my island friends. "Oh mon, I'd love dat."

When Maria came to collect me from outside Concorde House at Gatwick, she stopped and just stared at me, gobsmacked.

"Oh!" she exclaimed, taken aback at something in my appearance as if I was a stranger.

"What?" I asked, puzzled. *"What?"*

"You've met the one, haven't you?"

"Yes!" I beamed, unable to contain my joy. "Yes, I have. I've met the one."

About the Author

Natasha Rosewood, who was born in England, has always been fascinated with people, travel, languages, storytelling and metaphysics. At 22, with three European languages under her belt, Natasha began a career as a flight attendant, while at the same time studying palmistry and reading willing victims. In 1983, after eight years of flying international routes, including a contract in Libya—and having acquired conversational proficiency in three more languages—Natasha emigrated to BC, Canada where she evolved into a master metaphysician and prolific writer of books and films. Her first three published books— ***Aaagh! I Think I'm Psychic (And You Can Be Too), Aaagh! I Thought You Were Dead (And Other Psychic Adventures)*** and ***Mostly True Ghostly Stories***—continue to elicit the highest accolades for her writing, teaching skills and humor. Her intention is to heal and empower using quantum healing techniques and inspirational stories to reconnect humanity with its greatest potential and sense of humor!

Books by Natasha J. Rosewood

All books are available on Amazon in Print, Kindle, additional e-stores and soon to be in Audible format. Please refer to natasharosewood.com for a list of bookstores or visit Amazon.com.

Aaagh! I Think I'm Psychic (And You Can Be Too) is a sometimes humorous, sometimes heartbreaking account of Natasha's reluctant psychic awakening. Her story is accompanied by metaphysical endnotes to help the reader recognize and develop his or her own inherent intuitive ability, and to offer a deeper understanding of the psychic forces that were at play when Natasha magnetized these events to her. Prepare for a sense of déja vu. Aaagh!

Aaagh! I Thought You Were Dead (And Other Psychic Adventures)
…"Do you see dead people?" a potential psychic client once asked me. "Oh, yes. All the time," I responded. "And so can you …if you are open." But seeing spirits is only a small element of Natasha Rosewood's life as a psychic development coach, spiritual healer and writer. Join Natasha in Aaagh! I Thought You Were Dead (And Other Psychic Adventures) as she shares just some of the fun and fascinating-true life experiences from her personal and professional life as a psychic. Her fast- paced, light-hearted storytelling entertains as it

empowers us all to explore our greatest mind potential. The "Dear Natasha" responses that follow each out-of-this-world tale answer the questions that many of us would all love to ask a psychic.

Mostly True GHOSTLY Stories

GHOSTLY is a collection of ten spooky, fictionalized tales inspired by the real-life experiences of ex-flight attendant, psychic and author, Natasha J. Rosewood.

Whether set in a haunted youth hostel in France, a ghost town in Death Valley, California, over the Alps at 35,000 feet or in the alien-invaded English countryside, every story will have you teetering on the edge of the abyss between reality and illusion.

Printed in Great Britain
by Amazon

40294516R00188